The ADR Practice Guide
Commercial Dispute Resolution

The ADR Practice Guide

Commercial Dispute Resolution

Second edition

Karl Mackie

Of Gray's Inn, Barrister
Chief Executive, CEDR
Special Professor in ADR
University of Birmingham

David Miles

Solicitor
Partner, Glovers

William Marsh

Solicitor
Director of ADR Services, CEDR

Tony Allen

Solicitor
Assistant Director ADR Services, CEDR
Consultant with Bunkers, Solicitors

Tottel
publishing

Tottel Publishing, Maxwelton House, 41-43 Boltro Road, Haywards Heath, West Sussex, RH16 1BJ

© Tottel Publishing Ltd 2005

Reprinted 2005

First edition 1995

A CIP Catalogue record for this book is available from the British Library.

ISBN 0 406 91057 X

Typeset by B & J Whitcombe, Nr Diss, Norfolk, IP22 2LP
Printed in Great Britain by Cromwell Press, Trowbridge, Wiltshire.

Foreword

The Second Edition of *The ADR Practice Guide* is welcome, timely and valuable.

It is welcome, because ADR grows in scope and vigour almost by the hour. The acorn of a decade ago is maturing into a forest tree.

It is timely, because the procedure of the courts is undergoing its most radical transformation for well over a century. Conventional litigation processes and ADR are not enemies, but partners. Neither can ignore developments in the other.

It is valuable, because it makes available to readers the vast experience and expertise of CEDR, built up over the years.

I feel sure that this Second Edition will build on the success of the First. The authors are to be congratulated on this comprehensible and easily-assimilable treasury of guidance.

Lord Bingham of Cornhill

October 2000

Preface

We cannot help remarking that the publication of the second edition of this book coincides with the tenth anniversary of the founding of CEDR – the Centre for Dispute Resolution – and reflecting on the changes which its decade of life and growth have seen. A socio-legal historian called upon in decades to come to write an account of the changes within the legal system in England and Wales at the turn of the second millennium will have a huge task. A bewildering range of factors – financial and legal, technological and philosophical – have been brought to bear on the processes of resolving disputes between citizens, commercial entities and public institutions. An immense amount of thinking and ingenuity has been invested in transforming institutions, attitudes and systems which were perceived to be unsatisfactory, and the extent of the resultant revolution is yet to be measured.

Looking at the legal world as it was in 1990 at the beginning of CEDR's life, the civil justice system was on the cusp of change. In 1991 Sir Jack Jacob QC observed:

> 'All the portents presage a prolonged cycle of radical and frequent changes being made or developing the practice and procedure of the Supreme Court. There is a climate of change pervading the whole of the civil judicial process, penetrating almost every area in which it operates, so that there is no longer any surprise at the rapidity or the nature or the extent of the changes that are being made or are likely to be made in the machinery of civil justice.'

His prophetic words had hardly been borne out by the time he wrote them in July 1990. It is true that the Courts and Legal Services Bill was making its way towards becoming law, redistributing court business, enlarging rights of audience, creating the Legal Services Ombudsman and confirming a power in all courts to order pre-trial exchange of factual witness statements. There was no hint then of the Woolf Reforms, nor of the introduction of a largely unified civil court system under the Civil Procedure Rules (the CPR), nor implementation of the European Convention on Human Rights. The second edition of the *Guide to Commercial Court Practice* issued in March 1990 made no mention of ADR. Nor was there much sign of the sudden globalisation of legal practices and commercial institutions such as banks and insurance companies, with huge law firms merging across the UK and then into Europe and the US, with reciprocal expansion coming the other way. In another part of the system, the Legal Aid scheme was still more or less intact. There was the first potential authorisation of conditional fee agreements (not to be implemented until 1995) but otherwise no sign of the revolution in financing litigation which appears to be upon us in 2000.

ADR was an acronym of which few had any understanding at that time. The last decade has been one of slow growth followed by rapid, almost exponential, growth. CEDR has accredited over 1,000 mediators from over 30 countries, and delivered ADR training courses to over 2,000 professionals. It has handled over 4,000 mediation enquiries, and conducted well over 1,000 mediations. It is becoming increasingly involved in custom-built dispute resolution design for commercial and governmental institutions in the UK and abroad. It has an acknowledged place at the table in discussions with government and judiciary over matters within its remit. It has grown into one of the largest ADR institutions in the world. All one can say is that from the standpoint of CEDR's earliest days, its present shape is a world away from what looked feasible then. CEDR is not alone, of course: other ADR providers have grown, emerged and flourished, particularly since the introduction of the CPR.

Whether or not it is true that the early growth of ADR in this jurisdiction was hampered by lawyer self-interest, to a great extent the CPR have removed any choice about ADR from the legal professionals. Embedded as it is in the heart of active case management and the overriding objective, it has become part of the mainstream of civil litigation in this jurisdiction. What is more important is the fact that the litigation culture has changed, buttressed by costs sanctions for those reluctant to believe it. The way lawyers are supposed to litigate now is entirely congruent with the aims and methods of ADR processes, and all the signs are that the judiciary will require intelligent and committed use of ADR.

The debate has undoubtedly moved on. The issues for ADR at the start of the third millennium involve the debate between facilitation and evaluation; how to regulate a new profession of mediator; whether the courts should make use of ADR more or less mandatory? Should, for instance, the probable consequence of failing to engage in ADR before any trial be that the loser will be presumed to be open to indemnity costs or the paying or forfeiting of interest at penal rates? Will the courts impose a special fee to discourage court-door settlements which ADR could have brokered perhaps months before?

One of the inherent benefits of ADR has always been the concept of voluntary engagement in the process. It is ironic that the development of a consensual, informal process has had to be fostered by a degree of compulsion, or at least pressure, generated by the formal legal system. Yet the arguments for its systematic use and development remain best understood and adopted from the voluntary standpoint to see what clients really want, and how ADR might be built into the thinking of law firms, barristers chambers and, most significantly of all, the parties who are their clients.

The 1990s have also seen a change in the business focus for ADR. Whereas the civil justice system firmly belonged to lawyers in 1990, there are clear signs that change and development are being customer-driven. The initiative for using ADR is being taken by the funders of the litigation system. The last few years have seen an enormous growth in the use of 'beauty parades' to select external lawyers for client work, and in the general insurance market there has been a major rethink by insurers as to the composition of their panels and the requirements placed upon panel solicitors. Banks are doing the same. Both state and commercial funders of litigation are now requiring their lawyers to report regularly on whether ADR has been used in each case, and if not, why not, expecting proper and sophisticated reasons. In-house lawyers, with whom CEDR has worked closely throughout its life, have taken on a greater role in reviewing and managing of bought-in legal services and are making very proper demands of both external lawyers and ADR service providers for delivery of best value.

A very similar change of approach occurred in the development of ADR in the US. Faced with unacceptable delays in the courts, corporate clients themselves demanded use of ADR to deliver what they wanted in terms of speedy and economic outcomes to problems. Lawyers found that if they did not approach the conduct of litigation and the use of ADR in the way required by their clients, they lost their work. The fact that clients are apparently taking the same path in the UK, especially given the current level of judicial encouragement of ADR, is perhaps the latest example of the maxim that lawyers who ignore their clients' interests do so at their peril.

This book is offered as a practical guide to lawyers and clients alike who want to understand the place of Alternative Dispute Resolution in the scheme of civil justice and civil claims. We have revised it extensively in the light of the Woolf reforms and the developments in ADR usage and practice. However, it has been of comfort to find that much of what we put into the first edition as to the nature and purpose of ADR still holds good five years on. It leads us to suppose that the basic aims and broad shape of ADR process and practice continue to be well adapted for use in the UK and that they will continue to be so.

We have reorganised the chapters in this edition of the book, and divided it into three parts, dealing in turn with the conceptual, the legal, and the practical frameworks of ADR. This is in the hope that readers will find it easier to delve into the most relevant section for their interest in the topic. In the practical section, we have tried to gather together our joint practical wisdom in several series of bullet-points to maximise its availability and approachability for use in the real world of ADR.

Karl Mackie
David Miles
William Marsh
Tony Allen

August 2000

Contents

Contents

Contents

Contents

Part A

The conceptual framework of ADR

CONTENTS

Chapter 1

ADR in civil and commercial disputes

1.1 THE ROOTS OF ADR

There are many positive reasons for adopting Alternative Dispute Resolution ('ADR') processes as a means of trying to resolve civil disputes. However, it is probably true that initial enthusiasm for ADR stemmed primarily from a negative source – dissatisfaction with the delays, costs and inadequacies of the litigation process, particularly in the US where ADR first developed. UK lawyers for many years tended to dismiss ADR as a phenomenon specific to the US. Companies there were seen as more litigious. They were faced by claimants whose cases were funded by lawyers paid through substantial contingency fees. Trials were in courts where liability and damages were often determined by a jury, and there was no prospect of recovering legal costs from an opponent in the event of victory. Much the same features distinguish the US from the UK even today.

However, by the late 1980s and early 1990s, a more considered recognition grew that ADR was playing an increasingly useful part in the industrialised common law world in overcoming some of the disadvantages of a highly expensive and often rigid adversarial system. The pace of business life picked up sharply through this period, driven by new technology, increasing domestic and global competition, and more active and critical consumers. The legal system lagged behind these developments, and ADR was one of the key responses which sought to meet such business concerns in the new environment.

The late 1990s saw the civil justice system in England and Wales itself go through an enormous revolution on a scale not seen since the great reforms of the 1870s. This again was in response to the perceived need for fundamental change, highlighted with unanswerable persuasiveness by Lord Woolf's monumental report *Access to Justice* and then implemented in a remarkably short time by the Civil Procedure Rules 1999 ('the CPR') and the Access to Justice Act 1999. These changes represent not merely a consolidation and a rationalisation of a messy system, but truly a change in the culture of litigation itself. As the Lord Chancellor, Lord Irvine of Lairg, says in his Foreword to the CPR,

'We should see litigation as the last and not the first resort in the attempt to settle a dispute . . .'

and he confirms the intention of the CPR by noting that:

'. . . the changes introduced in April [1999] are as much changes in culture as they are changes to the Rules themselves.'

This is certainly what Lord Woolf advised was necessary in his Interim and Final reports, and all the signs are that this is being achieved.

Those who have been active in ADR development in the UK during the 1990s contributed to the debate over the Woolf Reforms. It is gratifying to see how much the thinking that makes ADR attractive to its users underlies this change of culture from an unduly adversarial to a more co-operative approach to dispute resolution. ADR is specifically recognised for the first time at the heart of the civil justice procedure, as a tool of active case management, the means by which the courts are to attain the overriding objective set out in CPR Part 1. This is set out in full at section **4.3.1**.

ADR came of age in England and Wales when the CPR came into force on 26 April 1999. No longer is it a sign of weakness to propose ADR, but a sign of sophistication entirely consistent with the spirit of the Woolf reforms as embodied in the CPR. There has been a major increase in the use of ADR and more and more lawyers and business people are learning the skills required to mediate or represent clients at mediation.

But it is still salutary to remember the essential advantages of ADR as they always were and still remain, namely to extend the range of options on offer to businesses or litigants who find themselves in deadlocked negotiations with others, whether before, during or outside litigation. ADR offers many of the beneficial features of the litigation system without some of its inherent disadvantages. It offers structured formal third party intervention but without either a requirement to fit into the rigid routines of traditional litigation or the high risks of a legally binding judgment from a judge imposed upon the disputants. Thus the 'Alternative' description is given to this approach. However, the label is frequently criticised as misleading, and with some justification. ADR techniques may have begun outside the system as an alternative to litigation or arbitration, but they can and frequently do accompany such processes. Indeed ADR is often most powerful against the backcloth of existing litigation or arbitration. In that sense, as Senior Master Robert Turner memorably remarked once, formal trial litigation itself becomes the true alternative dispute resolution process.

ADR can also be used for situations where litigation is not really a viable alternative. This might be where a family business wants to develop more consensus on the future shape of the business but is struggling to do so by direct discussions between those concerned. A joint venture between multinational companies needs to be re-negotiated to meet changing participation and changing commercial pressures, and where there is not really a 'dispute' as such to litigate. As ADR theory has developed, stress has been laid on choosing techniques to match the needs of the dispute and the joint interests of the parties. Thus 'Appropriate' dispute resolution is often canvassed as an alternative component of the ADR acronym. 'Amicable' has also been proposed, particularly in the construction industry, to stress the non-adversarial objectives and processes of ADR. This fails to reflect that many thoroughly 'non-amicable' disputes are amenable to ADR. It is certainly true that ADR leads to accelerated dispute resolution in most cases.

In this book we seek to provide an introduction to and assessment of the major techniques and practices of ADR in commercial disputes, with particular reference to the law and practice of England and Wales, but not forgetting that ADR is particularly amenable to dealing with cross-border and cross-jurisdictional disputes. Indeed, there are signs that London may become a forum of choice for international ADR just as much as it has been the forum of choice over many years for the litigation and arbitration of international commercial disputes. The intention of this book is to enable parties and professional advisers to recognise where various techniques and processes are appropriate and when and how they can be used.

The problems with litigation, certainly until the CPR were implemented, are well-known and need not be dwelt upon further here. Injunctive procedures or other means of rapid relief available in special cases, such as freezing orders and search orders (formerly *Mareva* and *Anton Piller* orders respectively) can swiftly be obtained. Otherwise litigation has usually involved parties in delay, cost, distraction from day-to-day management, disproportionate worry and uncertainty and loss of control of the claim once conduct has been 'handed over to the lawyers'. Such problems tend to exist in whatever jurisdiction litigation is conducted, albeit to varying degrees. Most businesses can readily quote horror stories about efforts to achieve satisfactory 'justice' in a business dispute, particularly across frontiers. It is this common international phenomenon that has encouraged ADR to spread across the globe. Despite the attempt to dismiss ADR as an essentially American creature meeting very particular American needs, most countries have evolved elements of ADR in order to escape some of the difficulties of litigation, without labelling them as ADR as such. Examples are administrative tribunals, Ombudsman systems, family and labour conciliation agencies and laying duties on judges to conciliate. However, the promotion of the use of alternative methods of resolving the general class of civil and commercial actions, and the promotion of ADR as a more systematic business and professional discipline were a novel development wherever this occurred.

The legal profession has often been held responsible for the problems of the litigation system by both non-lawyers and reforming lawyers alike. Indeed the thrust of the Woolf reforms has been to take control of the litigation process away in large measure from the lawyers and give it, perhaps with a degree of optimism (certainly as lawyers saw it), to the court. Cynical commentators claimed that lawyers controlled the system to generate revenue for themselves in the same way that other businesses seek to generate income from the ventures they control. More often (and perhaps more justly), blame was attributed to the 'system', about which the average litigant or litigator could do little. Whether the CPR and the Woolf reforms will be seen to have altered the system to give greater satisfaction is still being closely considered as we write. But wherever the blame truly lies, the result is negative for the client.

Furthermore, the strength of ADR does not depend upon apportioning that blame. It seems reasonably universal that systems of 'justice' tend to be expensive and slow. Such systems require the judge to find the truth of the matter – by adversarial or inquisitorial means, based on the evidence laid before the court. Since the parties have a great deal at stake in the decision reached, there is a natural tendency to produce the best arguments and evidence (and therefore the best advocates), while doing the utmost to undermine the opposing side's evidence and arguments. It has never taken much by way of imagination or pressure of interests, business or otherwise, for parties to extend this dynamic by adding an element of gamesmanship through use of procedural ploys or manoeuvres to wear down, undermine or even bankrupt the other side. In turn, such ploys confirm and strengthen hostility and intensify the emotion and the stakes in the dispute and its outcome. The extent to which the Woolf reforms can be used to punish and outlaw such conduct is emerging. The first signs are promising.

Quite apart from any procedural drawbacks to the litigation process, there are substantive or jurisprudential questions which also need to be considered in estimating the value of the litigated result in the common law system. The judge's duty is not to make a determination on grounds of truth or justice in the abstract, nor on what makes commercial sense or improved business relationships, nor in personal injury cases on sympathy for claimants or willingness to raid the deep pocket of an insurer. Outcomes are determined by the evidence and arguments put before the court, in accordance with technical legal principles. Furthermore, the question of whether business or personal circumstances have changed or may well change for the parties before the court is usually irrelevant. The essential judicial task is to decide 'according to law', which is almost always an exercise in examining the past and allocating blame. Was there a contract? What were its terms? Was a contractual term broken? By whom? Was the defendant in breach of duty or negligent? What damage flowed from breach?

The litigation process in England and Wales can be said to work tolerably well, with the hope of even greater efficiency under the CPR, mainly because of the good sense of the judges and its users. But the system is not in itself guided by a creative search to establish problem-solving remedies or commercial solutions for difficult issues. Many disputes are not clear-cut, yet judges must reach a determination 'on the balance of probabilities', often determined on a rather narrow view taken of aspects of a case or the legal principles involved. It is not surprising that many litigants feel aggrieved when they 'lose'. This sense of grievance is potentially multiplied in terms of cost, delay, uncertainty of outcome and potential for manoeuvre created by the appeals process.

What about arbitration? Designed initially as a process whereby 'commercial' people determined their own disputes, it boasted considerable advantages. Parties can agree simplified procedures, and an arbitrator can be appointed who possesses specific knowledge in a given technical area. Arbitration might thus be regarded as 'the' alternative to litigation, in which the parties achieve a legally binding adjudication in accordance with law, but without the full trappings of litigation, and without its publicity or its judges, who may have no particular qualifications in the subject-matter of the dispute.

Sadly, many commentators, including many members of the arbitration community, feel that arbitration has been 'hijacked by lawyers', and that its promise has not been fulfilled. Arbitrations can be just as procedurally complex and lengthy as court trials, leading to an award which can be just as uncertain as that of a judge. There is the additional disadvantage of having to pay for the arbitrator, whereas a trial judge does not attract an hourly rate, even with the increased court fees. There are also arguments about whether arbitrators have proved to be sufficiently robust when dealing with lawyers trained in the adversarial and over-complex procedures of the courts. If post-CPR judges demonstrate their mettle as invited so to do by the reforms, arbitration may be the last haven for the adversarial approach, despite the reforms introduced by the Arbitration Act 1996 which has improved matters considerably. Whatever the merits of this debate and its historical twists and turns, it must be said that arbitration remains intrinsically susceptible to these problems because it carries the essential character of litigation – a procedure designed to find for or against parties on the basis of evidence and legal argument.

It is important to note, however, that arbitration does still represent a viable alternative to full litigation procedure, principally in freeing the parties to determine their own procedure, elect their own judge, proceed in privacy and avoid appeals to the courts in many circumstances.

It can thus have significant advantages for certain parties. However, its location at the adjudicative end of the dispute resolution spectrum stretching from negotiation through to litigation, puts it close to litigation both in form and content. Its separate historical development in the US has led it often to be described there as a form of ADR. In the UK and elsewhere, arbitration is usually excluded from the range of ADR techniques. We follow that convention in this book and do not discuss arbitration any further in detail.

1.2 WHAT IS ADR?

As a field which has evolved for differing motives and with different emphases, there are many ways of defining ADR. The most common classification is to describe ADR as a structured dispute resolution process with third party intervention which does not impose a legally binding outcome on the parties. Mediation is the archetypal ADR process falling within this classification. While a useful rule of thumb, it is not a perfect definition. Some techniques outside standard arbitration and litigation can be useful in resolving disputes although they may be binding in certain forms – for example, an Ombudsman may give decisions which can be binding on a commercial party but not a consumer. A Disputes Panel or adjudicator in the construction industry can make an adjudication which is said to be legally binding if neither party chooses to challenge it within a specified period of time. A labour arbitration may be treated by the parties as 'binding in honour only'. Are these ADR procedures?

Like many areas of social practice, definitions are not watertight and conclusive. What is more important is to recognise the intent behind the development of ADR. This is to avoid the inflexibility of traditional procedures and institutions for resolving disputes, and to focus instead on analysing how the parties might achieve a similar or better result than might have been achieved by arbitration or litigation, with the minimum of direct and indirect cost. Embracing the concept of 'Appropriate' or 'Additional' (in the sense of complementary) Dispute Resolution helps to dispel the feeling that ADR is somehow an 'alternative' culture and not quite 'mainstream'. Indeed, ADR should be a *primary* option for parties faced with a dispute, a view clearly endorsed by the spirit behind the CPR, the pre-action protocols, and new judicial willingness to make penal costs and interest orders dependent upon pre-action and post-action unreasonableness in the conduct of litigation. One of the most telling recent developments in Australia is the move to describe *litigation* as ADR or Alternative Dispute Resolution, rebranding all extra-litigation dispute resolution processes (which would include what we call ADR in this country) as *PDR*, or *Primary Dispute Resolution*.

These various A-words are also used to emphasise another vital aspect of ADR. Alternative Dispute Resolution may be used in the true sense of an alternative to litigation or arbitration. But it is probably used far more frequently now alongside litigation or arbitration to complement and improve the quality of settlement negotiations. Most civil litigation ends in out-of-court settlement, but very often late in the day, and quite often at the court door, under great pressure of time and in less than ideal negotiating conditions. Classically it takes place just before a trial is due to start, or even during the course of that trial. At that point the vast bulk of the legal costs have been expended, and the people most bewildered at the sudden forestalling of the daunting process of trial and evidence-giving are the parties themselves. The lawyers are often content to move on to their next case. ADR as accelerated dispute resolution can create a much earlier settlement event, thus saving the parties time, costs and the wastage of concern in anticipating the trial, by creating a much more leisurely settlement process and better or at least different outcomes than trial can normally achieve. We shall consider below how this claim can be justified, and the circumstances necessary to achieve these results.

First we examine the spectrum of dispute resolution processes in a little more detail, whether alternative or mainstream.

1.3 THE DISPUTE RESOLUTION SPECTRUM

The way we have chosen to classify ADR processes is by looking at the degree to which the parties themselves have control over both the process and the outcome.

1.3.1 Unilateral action

At one end of the spectrum is the unilateral decision of a party to escape or avoid the conflict, for example a consumer not making or following up a complaint, a company writing off a bad debt, or a motorist deciding not to claim for a minor injury. Unilateral action can of course also be taken, not to avoid a dispute, but to influence events in one's own favour. This includes the use of publicity or economic leverage, or direct action which might be potentially lawful, such as self-defence, or the abatement of an alleged nuisance, or unlawful, such as physical retaliation. An extreme version of this would be to issue proceedings as a threat or a gag, or as a way of mobilising the state's powers to crush an opponent financially or otherwise. In all such unilateral action, the protagonist has complete control of both process and outcome.

1.3.2 Negotiation

Negotiation is the next most powerful method for a party in terms of their control of the process, subject only to the constraints imposed by the other party (or their constituents). This is the business method that is used more than any other to resolve disputes, and with good reason – it is the most flexible, informal, party-directed, closest to the parties' own circumstances and control, and can be geared to each party's own concerns. Parties choose location, timing, agenda, subject-matter and participants. It need not be limited to the initial topic in dispute: either party can introduce other issues as trade-offs for an acceptable agreement.

The growth of interest in ADR has in turn been fuelled by a wider interest in the 'science' of negotiation, particularly because new theories of negotiation have emphasised the more extensive possibilities for joint gains and interest-based outcomes. It will be useful to examine negotiation in more detail in order to understand why third party methods may become necessary to resolve deadlocked negotiations or even to make negotiations which are not deadlocked more efficient or productive (see Chapter 2). A common first reaction from many lawyers or clients, on hearing about the interest-based or business-directed aims of ADR is to assert that this is what they have always done in their own negotiations. They say 'I've been mediating all my life', or even 'I don't need ADR to add to my existing negotiating skills'.

1.3.3 Mediation and conciliation

These are the third-party ADR techniques closest to negotiation. 'Conciliation' is a term sometimes used as a synonym for mediation, and we discuss the distinction drawn between the two concepts below. Essentially 'mediation' is a process of negotiation, but structured and influenced by the intervention of a neutral third party who seeks to assist the parties to reach a settlement that is acceptable to them. The mediator does not make an award, nor, in the purest form of mediation, is there any evaluation of each party's claims. However, the dynamic of third party involvement is potentially much more subtle than this bald description suggests. The chapters on mediation articulate the various roles of the mediator in greater detail.

For present purposes we can distinguish between *facilitative* mediation, where the mediator facilitates the parties' own efforts to formulate a settlement; and *evaluative* mediation, where the mediator additionally assists the parties by introducing a third party view over the merits of the case or of particular issues between the parties. Such evaluation can be informally requested or built formally into the process from the outset. Proximity of a court or arbitration hearing can at times encourage use of this style of approach. Indeed, in a number of legal systems a duty to mediate is imposed upon the judge who is to hear the case, who may tend to do so by giving the parties an indication of which way the judicial mind is moving.

In some forms of ADR, evaluative mediation may involve the third party giving to the parties a recommendation, usually in writing, on how they should settle the case. Where this flows out of a less legalistic context (as in UK industrial relations mediation) recommendations may be based upon what the mediator regards as reasonable terms of settlement. In a more legalistic context, such recommendations will usually reflect the mediator's view of the merits. In the most formal of contexts (for example under some forms of construction contract or in court-annexed mediation in some US states), these recommendations may be used in further proceedings. If a party fails to obtain an improved award from the court above what was recommended but not accepted, the recommendation may actually bind the parties, or may affect responsibility for litigation costs.

A distinction is sometimes drawn between 'conciliation' and 'mediation' over whether the one process leads to written recommendations or third party settlement proposals, whereas the other does not. There is no international consistency over which term is to be applied to which type of process, and we do not find it a useful distinction to draw in this book. We will henceforth only refer to mediation as encompassing both possibilities and distinguish, where necessary, between facilitative and evaluative modes of mediation. However, while we do not dwell on these distinctions in terminology, it is important to remember the substantive distinction in terms of process possibilities, and also the need to check in unfamiliar contexts exactly which definitions parties or their advisers have in mind.

Nevertheless, whichever approach is taken in mediation, control over the decision as to the final outcome rests firmly with the parties and not with the mediator, however evaluative the mediator is invited to be. The parties also usually control whether to ask the mediator to move from facilitative to evaluative mode.

1.3.4 Evaluative processes

Mention of recommendations or opinion moves us on to third party processes where the parties have less control over the outcome than in facilitative mediation. Rather than involving a third party directly in the negotiation process parties may seek some form of neutral and independent evaluation, perhaps an expert opinion on the case or one of the issues, or a third party review of the case in terms of likely litigation outcome. This is sometimes described as 'early neutral evaluation' – a preliminary assessment of facts, evidence or legal merits designed to assist parties to avoid further unnecessary stages in litigation, or at the very least to serve as a basis for further and fuller negotiations. Processes such as 'judicial appraisal' also come within this definition.

Again, the categorisation is not watertight, since clearly a process such as evaluative mediation spans the divide between these approaches. It does, however, provide a useful starting point from which to assess what each process really offers.

1.3.5 Adjudicative processes

Finally we enter the adjudicative range of the spectrum, where the processes culminate in some form of decision or judgment being delivered. Within this range are many variations. For example, parties can contract for a third party to provide an 'expert determination' of all the issues between them; or to decide certain facts, leaving the parties to negotiate the financial implications of those findings. Or they can invite an 'adjudication' which does not have the exact features of arbitration (usually to avoid the binding finality of an award). The parties may agree to a 'non-binding' arbitration, or to an adjudication which will only become effective as an arbitral award if one party does not seek to challenge or appeal it within a certain specified time.

Also within this range of adjudicative processes lie the various Ombudsman or grievance resolution schemes, which have evolved as cost-effective and readily identifiable systems of redress in many consumer sectors. Typically the industry, government or public body involved adopts the approach as a collective solution to a gathering cloud of individual consumer grievances that threaten the reputation of the body involved or are adding pressure for statutory regulation of its affairs. The detailed mechanisms of Ombudsman schemes vary, but often they combine the processes of neutral fact-finding, mediation and adjudication in various tiers through which consumers may pursue their complaints.

Finally, 'arbitration' and 'litigation' also lie within the range of adjudicative processes. At this end of the spectrum, party control of the process is very limited – indeed, engagement in litigation for the defendant is virtually compulsory if interests are to be protected – though perhaps more control is available in arbitration. Even in litigation, however, there may be elements of process choice: for example, choice of forum or whether to proceed in a lower track than the value of a claim might permit.

1.3.6 Hybrid processes

It is important to note that because most ADR procedures are creatures of contract and of practical utility to suit the parties, there is not the same rigidity of procedure as is imposed by litigation or even arbitration. There is no mediation equivalent to the civil procedure manuals of the courts, nor should there be, since much of its potency is derived from its inherent flexibility and freedom from rules. Also, the categories mentioned above are merely the more common ADR choices. Since the whole thrust of ADR is to adopt the process most suited to the particular problem, it follows that numerous hybrid versions of the basic procedures exist. For example, there is the 'mini-trial', which is a more formal version of evaluative mediation; and 'med-arb', a mediation process at the outset which switches to arbitration mode to resolve any issues outstanding from the mediation. Party control of ADR choices opens up these and many other possibilities.

1.4 WHY ADR WORKS

Despite the fact that the most common ADR techniques do not *guarantee* resolution of the dispute, most such techniques do in practice lead to a binding settlement. Further, ADR works where previous negotiations have failed. Indeed, it is usually not resorted to until negotiations reach deadlock. How does ADR achieve these results? It is important to understand the dynamic underlying ADR to understand why and when it is appropriate, and why it works.

1.4.1 Creating a focus on settlement

ADR procedures usually involve the parties' coming together, normally both lawyers and clients, with a view to exploring and achieving a settlement. This factor alone probably contributes considerably to the success of mediation in particular, and explains why it is the leading ADR process. When direct negotiations seem to be unproductive, with parties locked into entrenched positions or into a serial litigation dance, it can be hard to create even the right context or environment for a negotiated outcome. ADR procedures offer a *formal setting* to bring advisers and clients together for a serious attempt at resolving the problems between them.

In many cases, this may be the first occasion in months or even years that the parties have jointly addressed the question of settlement. Thus ADR intensifies the *objective* of settlement.

Further, if negotiations have broken down, or been conducted at arms length between advisers (for instance by formal Part 36 offers and counter-offers) the ADR event may be the first or even only occasion before trial when the parties have a serious and credible forum in which to discuss issues and concerns *as a joint effort*. Certainly since the Woolf reforms, there are signs that a number of parties and lawyers are conferring credibility on ADR processes by integrating them into the range of dispute resolution techniques in mainstream practice.

1.4.2   The role of the neutral

It is very difficult to provide a simple analysis of the effect of a third party neutral on ADR negotiating processes. We look at the role of the prime instance of such a third party – the mediator – in Chapter 10. Suffice it to say here that the presence of a third party adds to the sense of forum, of objective debate and seriousness of intent. Quite apart from the competences and qualities of the neutral, the very presence of a third party generates a feeling of a 'hearing' or 'a day in court' at which all disputing parties are present, something which is statistically rare even in the litigation process. This in turn imposes a form of discipline or structure on the proceedings, with the neutral being able both to permit and control the flow of argument and emotion which will inevitably characterise such occasions.

1.4.3   The qualities of the neutral

Parties are often most sensitive to this aspect of ADR, neglecting the other elements which contribute to the underlying dynamics. But the quality and competence of the neutral inevitably add an important element to the success of ADR. The effective neutral uses the other factors to achieve maximum impact in the process. Thorough understanding of the ADR process is vital, alongside the ability to generate trust and respect with all parties, to facilitate communications, to defuse emotions, and to deploy sound negotiating strategy and tactics as a neutral to assist the parties towards resolution.

1.4.4 The structure of the process

Broad ADR procedures have evolved over time to optimise the opportunities to achieve resolution. In *mediation*, for instance, the structure of a joint meeting, followed by private meetings with each party and further joint meetings if appropriate, creates scope for making real progress on the case. Firstly, the parties have a chance to 'hear' each other. Then they have the opportunity to communicate more fully, frankly and privately with and through the third party neutral. In a *mini-trial*, there is a formal setting, in which senior executives can take a more detached view of their subordinate managers' and lawyers' previous actions.

1.5 ADR IN THE MAINSTREAM

As awareness has developed of how ADR can complement arbitration and litigation, and can indeed settle intractable cases, removing them from log-jammed court lists, ADR has during recent years been brought increasingly into the mainstream of official dispute resolution. Even before the Woolf reforms were implemented, a number of lawyers and users were systematically deploying it because of its perceived advantages. There has also been increasing inclusion of pre-agreed ADR mechanisms in commercial contracts and organisational policy guidelines as a first process of choice for resolving contractual difficulties. Most importantly now, ADR is being integrated into court practice.

1.5.1 Integration into court practice

The trend towards 'court-annexed', 'court-directed' or 'court-referred' ADR has taken a number of forms. In the UK, the earliest developments are to be found in Practice Directions in the Commercial Court and then in the High Court generally, requiring pre-trial consideration of ADR by legal advisers. In the CPR, specific provision is made by Part 26.4 for a stay of proceedings to be considered at the stage of allocation of a claim to the proper track, so that settlement by negotiations or ADR may be tried. Cases are now referred to ADR at this stage, and also at case management conferences or even pre-trial review. Furthermore, the various published Practice Guides, Practice Directions and Protocols in the specialist jurisdictions, such as the Commercial Court, the Technology and Construction Court, the Mercantile Courts and the Chancery Division itself, all provide for consideration of ADR at case management and pre-trial review stages. The pilot scheme pioneered by the Central London County Court has now become a permanent fixture there, and other regional county courts are setting up similar schemes with the encouragement of the Lord Chancellor's Department. Most innovatively, there is a mediation scheme attached to the Court of Appeal for dealing with settlement of appeals already lodged. This has produced good results in a range of cases. In the employment field, ACAS also has a statutory duty to seek to conciliate within the greatly enlarged jurisdiction of the Employment Tribunal. Court-approved mediation in the area of family law (which is outside the scope of this book) has now been endorsed by statute within that highly delicate area of human relations.

1.5.2 International variants

Globally, interesting variations are evident, with most variety being found across the many US State Courts and in Australia. The following are some of these variations.

Early neutral evaluation

Case appraisal at an early stage of proceedings by a judge, senior lawyer or expert, expressing an authoritative view derived from such a person's status or experience. This is designed to help the parties settle and may be combined with attempts at mediation, arbitration or continued litigation case management. The Commercial Court in London has been offering this formally to parties for some time now.

Case settlement conferences

A court requirement placed on trial lawyers (sometimes with clients) to meet formally in order to review the case and attempt to negotiate settlement. There has been an increased use of such occasions in the UK, particularly in personal injury claims.

Court-directed mediation

A mediator is appointed by or at the instigation of the court to help the parties explore and achieve settlement.

Advisory arbitration

A court-appointed arbitrator makes an award which becomes binding if one party does not appeal it. There may be costs awards against a party who appeals from the arbitration but fails to improve on the arbitrator's award.

Settlement weeks

Certain weeks are designated as periods in which parties with cases filed can seek to mediate a settlement. The court writes to litigants to give notice of the procedure.

Multi-door courthouse

The court may encourage litigants to have an initial meeting with an information officer who can guide the litigant towards the most appropriate process – mediation, arbitration, small claims, case appraisal, case management or full trial – all of which are made easily available by or through the court itself.

Judge conciliators

In certain parts of Europe and Asia, judges themselves are given the duty to try to settle cases where possible as part of standard litigation procedure.

1.5.3 Summary

All these manifestations of officially encouraged ADR generate their own theoretical and practical issues, but none (except where specifically noted above) has emerged so strongly here as to merit further detailed discussion in a practitioner's guide dealing primarily with the UK and European context. Such issues are best left for debate in relation to the details of a particular scheme. Their existence and growth does confirm the irresistible trend internationally for ADR to be confirmed as an integral part of dispute resolution activity and a useful tool by which lawyers and other advisers can extend the services they offer to clients. Furthermore, clients themselves can hope to achieve better, quicker and more focused outcomes when problems or claims emerge.

CONTENTS

Chapter 2

From negotiation to ADR

2.1 ADR AND NEGOTIATION

Interest in ADR as a structured form of third party assistance to settlement has contributed to a growth in understanding of negotiation skills and practice. Why do direct negotiations often fail where third party mediation can succeed? What does mediation or ADR add to direct negotiations to make them more effective? Does ADR understanding improve negotiating performance?

Lawyers often latch onto the emphasis in ADR on achieving commercial settlements, in order to claim they have been practising ADR throughout their professional life, their objective having always been, as they see it, to achieve a good settlement for their client. However, this underestimates the differences between direct negotiations and third party assisted negotiations, even though good ADR builds on good negotiating practices.

To understand ADR's contribution, we therefore need to review how negotiation works and particularly how negotiations (and sometimes ADR) can fail. Indeed, the starting point of ADR may be dispute diagnosis. If we know why direct discussions are not making progress, we can develop ideas of what cure to bring to an ailing negotiation. Equally, understanding of what ADR adds and why it works may in turn help professionals to rethink their core negotiating strategies, so that they can improve results from direct negotiations.

2.1.1 Disputes, negotiations, consensus-building

Before reviewing negotiating practice and ADR's curative role, we should not forget the broader context of disputes. Some disputes can be said to follow a breakdown of existing commercial relations or an existing negotiation relationship – for example, an argument over payment for goods or services that the purchaser claims were defective. Other disputes arise where the parties have not had a previous relationship, say a claim for breach of intellectual property rights or breach of a tortious duty of care. There may be attempts at negotiation in the latter type of case or an immediate initiation of legal proceedings. In either case, litigation is only one of the options open to the aggrieved party. They may attempt to exert pressure on the other side through the use of economic pressures (non-payment, boycotting purchases of other products by the offending company) or business contacts (an individual or business association that is a contact common to them both). Finally they may accept a business loss and walk away from the situation rather than choose the time, trouble and expense of legal proceedings.

ADR has been used most in disputes which have entered or are likely to enter legal proceedings, having developed further as part of lawyers' litigation practice than it has in business management practices. However, the other sectors should not be ignored, as ADR can and does make a significant contribution in business disputes which have not entered litigation. Indeed, these areas can represent major potential for practice development amongst ADR practitioners, whether as neutrals or partisan advisers.

Finally, there are settings where negotiations may not be part of the standard practice or culture, albeit that behaviour by one party may cause grievance to others. Typical of these would be the development of consumer action groups protesting against world labour exploitation, or the environmental side-effects of business operations, or the inequity of a business practice in an industry in terms of its impact on small business suppliers or consumers. Another common example would be the impact on interest groups of decisions taken by public authorities or regulators, where there may even have been 'consultation' before a decision but where 'negotiation' seems an inappropriate term for a 'consult–decide– defend' sequence of public decision-making.

These approaches to decision-making, which frequently generate grievances rather than disputes or overt negotiations, have also begun to be influenced by ADR theory and practice. Consensual decision-making, involving all interest groups in the relevant community, may be more effective for long-term stability than unilateral decisions which lead to campaigns by disaffected interest groups attacking the source of the grievance and lobbying public bodies to amend what they regard as 'bad laws'.

The application of ADR to these fields tends to introduce negotiation practice or at least problem-solving committee approaches to decision-making practice. The environmental and public policy areas have become a growing field of ADR practice in the US in particular, although usually under the label 'consensus building' rather than ADR (since there may be no clear initial dispute). The most advanced legal recognition of this has occurred in the US where statute now enables regulatory agencies to draft regulations by negotiating processes and not only by traditional consultation methods. (To add to the terminological complexity, this branch of consensus-building is often described as 'reg–neg', regulatory negotiation.)

Normally, therefore, ADR intervention either builds on existing negotiations or generates a forum in which negotiations take place. For that reason it is important for ADR specialists to understand negotiating practices.

2.1.2 Bargaining in the shadow of the court

The issuing of legal proceedings has a significant impact on all negotiations, and in turn ADR, for three reasons.

Firstly, it sets *deadlines* for processing and ending the dispute. This may increase the pressure on parties to enter negotiations and certainly to conclude them before the risk of an adverse judgment or of incurring significant cost, if the case is allowed to proceed towards trial. There will often be a pressure on both parties to negotiate just before the stages of procedure which heighten costs or risks. The clearest of these stages is immediately pre-trial when most civil actions settle even without ADR.

Secondly, it may alter the *agenda* of the negotiations, adding arguments over likely trial outcomes, costs of preparation, principles of law applicable, and perhaps publicity issues, to what may have been a dispute framed in other ways by the business parties. Indeed the fact that one party enters litigation at all may provide a justification to another party for breaking off negotiations or raising the stakes by issuing a counter-claim or making a formal offer to settle which carries costs consequences.

Finally, litigation usually introduces for most business parties a new *principal–agent relationship*. Negotiations become to some extent taken over by litigation specialists who bring to the case their own judgments and professional agendas of how to manage settlement opportunities or discussions in the phases leading up to trial. While professional theory suggests that the client takes all decisions about a claim, even after proceedings have begun, in practice many business users of litigation will defer to the advice of the professionals unless they are repeat players such as insurance companies, used to dealing with a stream of litigation.

Litigation therefore is double-edged in its impact. It can speed up settlements or it can prolong the dispute. Overall, however, most forms of civil litigation at some stage induce settlement by negotiation between parties or their legal advisors.

2.1.3 ADR as 'alternative'

We see, therefore, that the concept of ADR in the context of an overview of disputes is a more complex issue than normally considered. Equally its potential is richer if used effectively. We can summarise ADR's links to negotiating practice as drawing on four strands:

1 ADR is often not an 'alternative' to court trial at all, but an alternative to traditional settlement practice within those proceedings. For ADR to be justified, it must prove faster, cheaper or more 'effective' in its outcomes than those that can be achieved by the parties and their advisers working within a litigation system without ADR.

2 For disputes which have not entered litigation, ADR must provide an effective alternative to negotiations which would otherwise break down, or to disputes which would otherwise enter litigation without the adoption of ADR.

3 In some situations where negotiating practice is not a standard response, ADR approaches may assist in the development of negotiating structures and processes to help parties generate consensus on an issue.

4 In its most refined form, ADR may be promoted where it can be suggested that in some sense parties might achieve a 'better' or more efficient outcome through its use, even if they might anyway achieve some form of negotiated settlement without it.

In all these contexts, negotiation practice is a central question.

To assist us to understand why ADR works where negotiations

fail in the above senses, we outline below three core negotiating strategies and the problems they raise. The strategies are a little caricatured to emphasise their features, but are still broadly accurate. We can then consider how to design and implement ADR to meet some of these problems.

2.2 NEGOTIATIONS: WHY THEY WORK, WHY THEY FAIL

2.2.1 Positional negotiating

The classic negotiating strategy, taught to managers and lawyers alike, can be described as 'positional' negotiating. The assumption behind this in its elementary version is that negotiations are a competitive game in which you need to distrust or at least be wary of the other side. The aim is to outsmart them by following well-known tactics which strengthen your likelihood of coming away with a greater slice of the 'pie'. 'Positions' need to be carved out in advance or adhered to during negotiations, in order to strengthen your hand.

The aim in positional negotiation is to maximise your outcome. Of course the other side will have their own positional framework worked out too, unless they are naive negotiators. In negotiations the key is to be able to test how far up your claim ladder they will go, or even whether there is in the first place a possible overlap of negotiating positions – their bottom line is above your top line.

If there is an overlap in the bargaining range, the negotiators effectively compete to assert the strengths of their case and to undermine the other side's in order to come out higher in the range towards their ideal. If it appears that there is a mismatch of expectations, deadlock may ensue and the parties are forced back to litigation or other means of bringing the other party back towards a realistic position.

The following are typical tactics associated with positional negotiations.

- *Preparation of the bargaining range chart*

Good preparation of your own positions, as well as a good idea of the likely stance of the other party, helps you as negotiator establish your own aspirations and provides a means of assessing the other side's likely expectations.

2.2.1 *From negotiation to ADR*

● *Aiming high*

There is evidence that negotiators who start with high aspirations tend to do better. So think through your best case and work from that. Strongly positional negotiators find ways of starting from extreme positions.

● *Planning and pacing of concessions*

In positional negotiating, you know that movement from your high opening position is likely. But how much movement? When? How often? And how will this be presented? Positional negotiating theory has a number of maxims to help negotiators strengthen their outcomes. 'Move small, move slow', 'never give without getting', 'try only to make concessions of high value to them but low value to you'.

● *Concealing information*

In a situation where negotiators are looking for means to exploit their advantages, giving the other side fuller information may expose your weak points. Therefore positional negotiators often withhold information which may make their side vulnerable to exploitation. A statement by an injured claimant's solicitor that 'my client does not want to have the stress of a trial' will only assist the insurance company defendant.

● *Making threats or bluffing*

Threats and bluff are often associated with positional negotiating because of its competitive nature and the need to find means to dislodge other negotiators from the firm positions they have taken (as recommended in classic negotiating training).

● *Haggling*

When a deal becomes more visible after the initial opening phases of positional negotiation, the challenge in the final phase of sewing up the deal is how to score the last few points within the negotiating range by haggling. 'Never give without getting' and 'move small, move slow' become intense features of the process as each side tries to raise or lower the final offer or demand.

26

● *Agreement somewhere near the middle of the bargaining range*

The ritual dance of concession-giving in positional negotiating means that parties often work inwards from opening positions and end up (in an evenly matched contest) somewhere near the middle between the real opening positions adopted. Both may come away feeling they have had a tough contest and extracted less than their ideal but perhaps above their worst-case 'bottom line' position.

2.2.2   Principled negotiating

The classic world of positional bargaining was turned upside down by the work of the Harvard Negotiating Project, crystallised in the international best-seller on negotiation *Getting to Yes* by Roger Fisher and William Ury (2nd edn), published by Random House. Their theory of principled negotiating (sometimes referred to by other writers as problem-solving negotiating) suggests that one can avoid the gamesmanship and competitiveness inherent in positional bargaining. The key is to look for the settlement that will satisfy both sides' interests by keeping a clear sight on one's best alternative to a negotiated agreement (BATNA) and on options for mutual gain. While the goal of positional negotiating is victory, the goal of principled negotiating is a wise outcome reached efficiently. Whereas negotiations become more difficult if both parties are trained in positional bargaining, negotiations become easier if both sides approach a negotiation with a principled negotiating style. There are four key principles which underlie this approach.

1   Separating the people from the problem

It is easy in competitive negotiations to mix up aggression over the issues with attacks on the people on the other side. Principled negotiating stresses the need to be 'hard on the problem, soft on the people', in other words to be firm in searching for ways of meeting one's interests while simultaneously working towards good relations with the other party. Good relations make it easier to solve problems.

2   Focusing on interests, not positions

This is one of the essential differences between principled bargaining and positional bargaining. In the latter, the negotiator sets demands based on apparent interests: for example, 'we need to claim £½m for this loss'. As a result negotiations become a process of digging in and justifying this position, with the other side countering it with rejection or a lower offer, making it difficult to move from these stated needs. In principled negotiation, the key question is 'Why – what are the interests that underlie such a demand?' By focusing on these instead, the way is opened to problem-solving, to more fluid discussions and opportunities to generate other options such as staggered payments, new contract arrangements, offers of free publicity or whatever else might be appropriate to meet the real needs of a party. The classic example quoted on this by Fisher and Ury is of the mother discovering two sisters arguing over an orange. When she asks each of them why they want the orange, one says she needs the peel to bake a cake at school, the other wants to eat the flesh. Both needs can be met when interests are discovered. With a purely positional approach, the assumption is that each should have half – in fact not fully meeting the interests of either. Structured settlements in personal injury litigation are a good example of the evolution of a legal outcome that can better meet the interests of both parties than traditional one-off lump sum damages.

3 Inventing options for mutual gain

By focusing on interests, it becomes easier to explore a range of ways of meeting the real needs of each party. However, the need to problem-solve, brainstorm, look for ways of 'expanding the pie' is also an explicit requirement of principled negotiating. Out of this can come 'Win–Win' opportunities, rather than the 'Win–Lose' or 'Lose–Lose' outcomes typical of positional bargaining. Negotiators are encouraged to search for a variety of options before deciding which option best meets the interests of the parties.

4 Insist on objective criteria

Part of the principled aspect of this approach to negotiating is a search for rational standards by which settlement terms can be judged, rather than the subjective demands made by negotiators. Is there an objective criterion against which to match an offer: for example, the price paid by other customers, the market rent, or the level set by legal precedents. Objective criteria can be applied to *process* as well as *substantive factors*, as in the traditional ploy to prevent arguments between children cutting a cake – 'you slice, he chooses'.

2.2.3   Pragmatic negotiating

Principled negotiating theory has provided a very powerful counter-weight to the classic instruction manuals of the positional negotiator, and has helped reshape practice in many negotiation settings. However, many experienced negotiators believe the real world of negotiating remains more complex and requires often a mix of positional and principled approaches. Even in those settings where it is possible to 'expand the pie' and search for 'Win–Win' options, at some stage it is necessary to slice any pie and allocate rewards. 'Claiming' then takes precedence over 'creating'.

Similarly, being open about one's interests and preferences may in some situations leave one vulnerable to exploitation by a competitive negotiator. The negotiator's dilemma is therefore inherent in the tension of balancing the openness needed for effective problem-solving in any situation with the avoidance of misuse by the other side of information they have been given. Even a matter as basic as telling the other side how much you are really willing to settle for will tend to preclude them from offering you more.

Skilful negotiating therefore requires a sense of balance in the approach adopted and an ability to lean towards one direction or another in any negotiation or stage of negotiation. Typically, principled negotiating practice is easier to adopt when the negotiations are with parties with whom there is a longer-term relationship or greater trust. Positional negotiating may come to the fore in one-off deals such as in claims for damages from a party unlikely to be encountered again, such as in the sale of a house or in a motor accident. Similarly, certain types of negotiator are more inclined to adopt competitive, positional practice and it can be risky or simply too difficult to try to change their approach towards a preferred practice of principled negotiating.

It is important, however, to stress caution to hardened positional negotiators who are inclined to dismiss principled approaches. Principled negotiating can be applied to one-off deals or with parties one distrusts, and can yield better, perhaps unexpected, results in many cases. Would-be mediators should in particular work hard at learning this approach, as it underlies good mediation practice.

2.3 DESIGNING ADR TO OVERCOME BARRIERS TO SETTLEMENT

Having reviewed the negotiating and dispute contexts in which ADR can play a part we are now in a better position to understand how and why ADR can add value to current negotiating practice. ADR interventions, whatever their exact design, always change in some way the dynamics of a negotiation or dispute. Bringing in a neutral third party itself adds a new figure to the equation, at least temporarily shifting the attention of the parties from their conflict and the personalities in it towards the contributions of the neutral and the third party procedure. Good ADR design is about using intelligent analysis or intuition to determine exactly when, how and why such neutral intervention should be applied, whether formulated in initial ADR contract clauses or as a one-off intervention in an existing conflict.

ADR design is not an exact science nor does it offer a universally applicable fixed procedural remedy such as litigation. Rather it is often as much a question of people judgment and process analysis as of issue analysis. Hence the justified prevalence amongst ADR techniques of the flexible approach of mediation, which leaves individual mediators free to choose from a range of tactics and techniques to assist settlement in any particular case. However, mediators also must assess within a mediation why previous negotiations have failed and therefore decide which approaches will best help the parties reach a settlement that they can accept. We need, therefore, to consider the underlying causes of settlement failures or inefficient negotiations, and the implications of these for the design of ADR techniques or approaches.

2.3.1 Problems inherent in implementation of negotiating strategies

1 Positional negotiating

Of the three core approaches described in the last section, the one with perhaps the greatest inherent chance of breakdown is competitive or positional negotiating (borne out in an empirical study of US litigators by Gerald Williams). The essence of the game is to hold out for maximum gain whatever the cost to the other side. Delay, insistence on positions, minimal concession-giving, refusal to acknowledge weaknesses or uncertainties in their case – all may work to their advantage in a certain percentage of cases. However, in others, particularly where matched with competitive negotiators on the other side, this approach will grind negotiations to a halt, as neither side will budge.

In litigation proceedings, this gamesmanship will take parties 'up to the wire' as they engage in bluff to force the other party to duck out before the next phase of risks and costs imposed by the adjudication system. Indeed, one might argue that the strict theory behind adversarial litigation procedure is premised on competitive negotiating – the object is to win by presenting one's best case rather than for the adjudicator to investigate the truth or justice of the dispute, as more typically occurs in an inquisitorial approach. This is to some extent a caricature of each system, but it does reflect inherent tendencies found in them.

At the extreme, competitive negotiators will be unable even to open up negotiations. A mere request to negotiate may be perceived by them as a sign of weakness. The result may be that no real negotiations take place until immediately before the threat of an imposed decision by the adjudicator, generating a settlement on the steps of the court which perhaps may force one side suddenly to offer a large concession. The problems of this approach are self-evident. Costs, delays and lack of trust are driven up to high levels, in a way that tends to epitomise lose–lose approaches. Ultimately the parties will martyr themselves (either literally or at least to professional fees) rather than give way. If it is the lawyers who are responsible for this sort of negotiating approach, there is a serious risk that it will disaffect the client.

At its broadest level, the encouragement to use ADR represents a challenge to the ethos of adversarial negotiating practice among litigators and businesses. Even within the traditional culture, positional negotiators have some sense of a need to consider the costs of total intransigence.

Designing an ADR approach for this circumstance means finding ways to assist the parties to explore the bargaining range without loss of face. A contract clause requiring an ADR stage early in any dispute will help parties overcome any feeling that the suggestion of negotiations may undermine their claims. The absence of such a clause often makes it much more difficult for such negotiators to agree to ADR in the early stages of a case. ADR intervention becomes a delicate matter of indicating to all parties that an ADR procedure is a neutral effort to save all parties costs rather than an indication of any side's unwillingness to fight on.

Mediators faced by parties locked in a competitive strategy are usually able to take some, but by no means all, of the games-manship out of the negotiation. To begin with they can channel communications and offers or counter-offers in a less competitive or confrontational way than the parties may have done. As shuttle diplomats, they can extend and defuse the 'haggling' stage, making it easier for parties to review offers without the antagonism or face-saving requirements generated in direct, face-to-face negotiations. For example, parties will often reveal to a mediator that they are willing to move their position if the other side will move, or they may tell a mediator what they say they will *really* settle for, if the other side will also indicate their position. Usually such offers will be given initially to the mediator in confidence so that the potential for useful further bargaining can be assessed – in other words, have the parties come close enough in their offers? Stating such an offer publicly to the other side would appear to compromise their overt claims.

Most commercial mediations may go through a stage like this where a financial settlement is involved. Mediators therefore need to know how to work with positional bargainers and to know how to detect whether there might be further movement possible that has not yet been revealed to the mediator. Competitive negotiators may use gamesmanship in mediation as well as elsewhere. Good mediators, however, should also explore the potential for principled negotiation, and for more creative options than positional negotiators would normally have reviewed.

2   Principled negotiating

Impasse between principled negotiators is likely to reflect inability to agree on the standards to apply as criteria for settlement terms, or failure to find adequate means of solving a problem in a way that meets their interests. In these circumstances, mediation is again the most likely ADR route to breaking a deadlock, although in some cases a technical expert in a facilitative role may also help the parties towards a deal. Amongst the tactics a neutral could adopt would be:

- to help the parties re-evaluate their commitment to standards for decision-making;

- to help the parties identify and collect information on the case relevant to sensible decision-making;

- to assist them with further efforts at brainstorming solutions; or

- to rework earlier options canvassed in negotiations to see if a new formula might be prompted to emerge to overcome the deadlock.

3   Pragmatic negotiating

In the real world, mediators are rarely dealing with one of the pure models of positional or principled negotiating. Mediators will find they are working in most cases partly in the mode of problem-solvers, helping the parties search for options or appropriate standards to justify settlement terms, but also partly working with positions and attempts to secure the best slice of cake that the parties perceive to be available.

In each negotiating strategy, mediators also provide an independent review of the case, which may not be an expert or formal evaluation but rather a broad-brush or common sense appraisal, with each party, of the strengths and weaknesses of their case. Mediators not only work through the issues relating to possible terms of settlement, but also consider with each party how they see their BATNA (Best Alternative to a Negotiated Agreement) as well as their WATNA (Worst Alternative to a Negotiated Agreement) as an aid to encouraging realism.

4   Unskilled negotiators and strategy mismatch

Negotiations can break down not only because of difficulties inherent in negotiating style but merely because negotiators lack basic skills or training in effective negotiating. Many professionals and managers learn their negotiating tactics by trial and error or by sitting beside the senior partner in a negotiating team. This may not equip them effectively for certain types of negotiations or for more complex or multi-party cases. Thus one can meet ineffective competitive negotiators who threaten and bluster, but are unable to cope with subtler shades of bargaining; or with principled negotiators who have learned the value of 'reasonableness' but who interpret it to mean only the way they see the case.

A particular form of this occurs where there is a mismatch of strategies adopted by the parties to the negotiation. Neither side may be sufficiently flexible or perceptive to understand why they seem to be failing to communicate. This difficulty may be further exacerbated by difference of style and effectiveness between a party and its professional advisers. Mediation intervention can again work if the mediator creates a safer environment through which each side can explore their case more thoroughly and communicate more effectively. To achieve this a mediator needs to bring communication skills and mental flexibility to the negotiation.

2.3.2 Problems inherent in the structure of negotiations

1 Principal–agent tensions

Negotiations are not always conducted directly by the principals. They may have effectively handed the negotiating over to their professional advisers or may have left negotiations to someone lower down the corporate hierarchy. In some negotiations, this can create a further likelihood of impasse or delayed settlement. The middle manager may not want a realistic settlement, as it may expose his own failings on a project. The litigation lawyer may be following a blinkered legal agenda and be less used to taking a purely commercial approach. Incentives can also be different – there may be little direct financial incentive for opposing lawyers to settle a case early when they are charging on an hourly rate.

Mediation can assist in these cases by ensuring that those with decision-making authority are required to be present during a mediation and hence involved directly in focusing on settlement options and the real costs of any alternatives. Also, a good mediator may in the course of a mediation identify the need to involve a more senior manager in discussions, or to review commercial settlement options as well as strict legal principles.

Similarly, a mini-trial format explicitly employs a mediation approach of greater formality which calls on more senior managers to review a case and negotiate a settlement.

2 Litigation and the bargaining context

The timing and nature of settlement discussions may be profoundly affected by the way the court system works in a particular jurisdiction. Do judges have a duty to conciliate or not? Is disclosure of documents a formal part of its procedure? How is information collected and assessed? What is the extent of delays in the courts, and so forth. Such variations are likely to impact on the timing of settlement discussions and on pressures to settle. The development of court-annexed ADR schemes is a result of the

34

recognition that, when left to their own devices, parties may not work up sufficient enthusiasm for ADR without court prompting. This mirrors the view taken by Lord Woolf that case management needed to be transferred to the judges because of shortcomings in the way litigation had generally been conducted between parties and their lawyers.

3 Resistance to negotiations

Related to the above, the balance of power between parties may induce one party to delay settlement, for example to avoid immediate cash payments. ADR clauses, summary judgment procedures, more efficient litigation systems, interim payment requirements and other procedural features may also be necessary to generate movement towards negotiation or ADR.

Also, as discussed in the last chapter, there are occasions such as consumer and environment disputes or public policy-making procedures, where there has been no previous culture or practice of negotiated consensus. In these settings ADR specialists may perform a lobbying role, encouraging parties to adopt consensus-building approaches. Mediation or facilitation in this area can require more complex and protracted judgments over tactics and process. Questions will arise (among other issues) over –

- how to identify interest groups to be represented in negotiations;
- managing spokespersons and their constituency relations;
- the role of expert evidence and procedures for reaching consensus;
- the provision of neutral funding resources to assist groups without special funding;
- identifying effectively neutral 'host' organisations who can sponsor the process.

2.3.3 Problems inherent in the psychology of conflict

It is well established in common sense and in the psychological research on conflict that once parties begin to slide into conflict they act, perceive and think about their situation in ways that make it harder to settle the dispute. Ethnic, national and religious

2.3.3 From negotiation to ADR

conflicts exemplify this phenomenon over centuries. Lawyers too, faced at a first interview by an angry client, may find it awkward to engage such clients in immediate discussions on the weaknesses of their case or on the advantage of settlement discussions, with or without ADR.

The impact of conflict on parties is to reduce their interest in communicating openly with the other side. Communications that do take place are interpreted in ways that devalue offers made or actions taken to fit the hostile perception and judgments brought into the situation. A maxim of positional negotiation that reflects this is the phrase 'Always make them work hard for a concession'. In other words, concessions easily won are immediately devalued by the recipient. Thinking grows more rigid about the situation and team members who suggest concessions or the need to re-evaluate the situation can become outcasts and be regarded as betraying the true interests of the group. The concept of *reactive devaluation* dominates the assessment of each side's communications – 'if the other side say that, I shall assume that it is wrong!'

Bringing such disputes to lawyers or litigation does not necessarily incorporate a more reasoned approach into the situation. The litigation itself, and the lawyers involved, may be used as an extension of the parties' search for weapons to defeat the other side rather than to resolve a dispute wisely – hence some of the criticism of lawyers' role in divorce proceedings.

Mediators have a particularly challenging task in resolving such problems. A primary need is for mediators to conduct themselves in a way that ensures that all sides continue to see them as truly neutral rather than partisan. In this way they can cautiously open up lines of communication, or can help a party move beyond recriminations into thoughts for the future, or can serve as a lightning rod on which each side can finally vent their long-held grievances and hostility with regard to the other party. Mediation thus provides emotionally a form of 'day in court' for such cases and can help release the pressure. Mediations in more complex versions of these cases will very often lead the parties towards new institutions, policies, practices, dispute resolution procedures or other approaches which help establish new structures for the future that can begin to turn party energies towards a more constructive future.

At a simpler level, a concession offered through a mediator may appear to have been given more reluctantly and formally (and hence appear more worth winning) than if a party offered it directly.

36

2.3.4 Judgments of risk

In addition to the psychology of conflict, the psychology of judgments made under risk or uncertainty is relevant to negotiation or mediation. Apparently, faced with a loss, more people will prefer to take a risk and gamble to recover their losses even if the predicted loss will be even higher, instead of cutting their losses. One form of this is the attitude to 'wasted costs' or the phenomenon of 'throwing good money after bad'. If I have spent £50,000 so far on litigation, I may prefer to spend another £100,000 to pursue the chance of succeeding at trial rather than waste the first £50,000 by withdrawing from the action. This is so even though the fact that I have spent £50,000 has no real impact on the probability of success. Combined with a sense of anger at the other side, this is a powerful cocktail to encourage continuation of the conflict rather than a realistic resolution.

The converse phenomenon is that a party faced with a choice between a certain outcome now and a doubtful but better one in the future will very often prefer to accept what is available, even in the teeth of advice to the contrary from an adviser. The party's agenda will rarely be the same as the lawyer's and, with complications over conditional fee funding, there is even a potential for conflict between lawyer and client. So a party may feel that their private interest or target has been met, and simply want to be disentangled from the claims process and its attendant risks and strains forthwith. Mediators have to be alive in such cases to the confusion over ownership of the dispute which such internal pressures can create.

Mediators may help parties and their advisers think through the risks more carefully. Alternatively, a party may be willing to accept a non-binding view or reality-test from a credible third party as a way of finding a more tangible justification for cutting their losses earlier.

2.3.5 Genuine and good faith disagreements

Finally, barriers to settlement may arise from a genuine clash of judgments on the facts of a case or on the principles which should determine terms of settlement or the outcome, or other legal rights which apply. The psychology of conflict, however, suggests that all parties will justify their positions in such terms. Parties and their lawyers inevitably find ways to justify their reasoning as they grow involved in the clash of positions.

Mediation may help strip away some of the other barriers to settlement that are not at the core of the dispute, such as poor negotiating skills, communications, team member problems. However, most mediators also have to deal with good faith disagreements. To some extent these can again be tackled by the mediator by reviewing the case with each side, exploring strengths and weaknesses, and probing for settlement opportunities. Mediators can informally challenge existing stances and help the parties to re-assess their case.

However, where there is a defined and critical issue that divides the parties, other ADR options may have to be considered. For instance, the mediator may have to allow witnesses to be called and to question them so that the parties can reach a considered view on their credibility. Alternatively, the mediator may have to give a formal evaluation of the merits of the issues dividing the parties (if qualified to do so) or call in an expert to give such a neutral appraisal. If it is clear from the start that there is a core disagreement along these lines, a mini-trial or neutral evaluation format may need to be adopted in preference, or supplementary, to mediation.

2.4   ADR ORGANISATIONS AND DISPUTE SYSTEMS DESIGN

In overcoming the various barriers to negotiated settlements it may be necessary to work to more than one design. While parties themselves or an appointed neutral may be quite capable of doing this, there are many disputes where an ADR organisation's input may be more powerful. For instance, there may be an informal 'mediation' required even to get all parties to consider going to an ADR process, followed by a further phase of refining and agreeing the details of procedure or the neutral(s) to be appointed. Involving the individual neutral from the beginning of this whole process has the advantage of allowing the parties to develop a relationship with, and trust in, the neutral, and (where relevant) the ADR provider through which the mediator was appointed.

However, it has the major disadvantage that, in the sensitive early stages, a mediator's preference for certain aspects of procedure may sow seeds of distrust regarding the mediator's neutrality or effectiveness. Also, early discussions on the design of the process may reveal the need for a different kind of neutral (in terms of skill, credibility or expertise) than first considered. Finally it is common experience amongst ADR organisations that parties locked in antagonistic conflicts find it initially difficult to agree on anything, least of all the name of a neutral. The fact that one side puts forward a name confirms the other side's presumption of bias!

The essential thrust in ADR design is to take gradual steps towards procedural agreements while retaining maximum flexibility. Attempts to impose too rigid a set of rules or dispute terms of reference in difficult cases can often merely serve to provide grounds for further argument between parties already deadlocked on key substantive issues. Furthermore, too great an enthusiasm for design may end up with parties reinventing a litigation system.

It follows, then, that there is a substantial and critical process of diagnosis required of the dispute resolution professional at many stages during the life-cycle of a dispute. Only by identifying the barriers to settlement in a case can serious attempts then be made to overcome or circumvent them. In the absence of such a diagnosis the dispute must inevitably become harder to resolve.

It also follows that each different diagnosis will imply the need for a different remedy or, in procedural terms, that the different processes of negotiation, ADR, arbitration and litigation can all prove effective if applied at the right time. The key to the successful understanding and use of ADR techniques is to recognise what they contribute to a dispute, and then to be able to apply the right technique at the right time. Many of the problems of litigation arise not just from its inherent procedural flaws, but from the fact that it is treated as a universal procedural remedy and applied to cases for which it is sometimes highly appropriate and sometimes highly inappropriate. Or, to quote the old adage, 'if all you have is a hammer, everything will look like a nail'.

The diagnostic process is illustrated in the diagram at the end of this chapter, showing some of the main barriers to settlement and suggesting ADR techniques which might be appropriate to handle them.

For many dispute professionals, the availability of such a wide range of dispute resolution techniques will be entirely new. Thus any previous diagnosis they have conducted will have been limited to making the choice between starting or continuing proceedings, and attempting direct settlement discussions. The extension of choice provided by ADR puts an onus on dispute professionals to approach all disputes with much closer diagnostic scrutiny, and a much more creative range of procedural options.

2.4 *From negotiation to ADR*

Understanding these options and how best to implement them are increasingly important for professionals who work in the context of negotiation and dispute management.

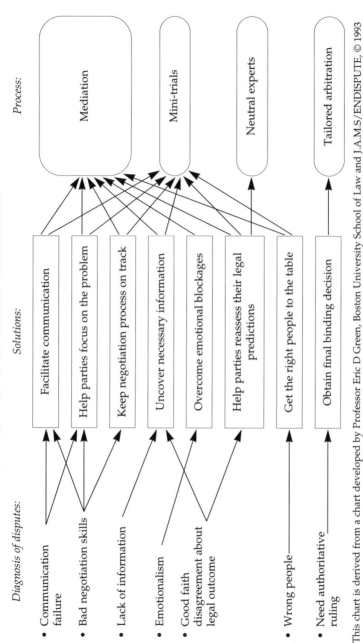

UNDERSTANDING THE BARRIERS TO SETTLEMENT

Diagnosis of disputes: *Solutions:*   *Process:*

- Communication failure
- Bad negotiation skills
- Lack of information
- Emotionalism
- Good faith disagreement about legal outcome
- Wrong people
- Need authoritative ruling

Facilitate communication

Help parties focus on the problem

Keep negotiation process on track

Uncover necessary information

Overcome emotional blockages

Help parties reassess their legal predictions

Get the right people to the table

Obtain final binding decision

Mediation

Mini-trials

Neutral experts

Tailored arbitration

This chart is derived from a chart developed by Professor Eric D Green, Boston University School of Law and J.A.M.S/ENDISPUTE, © 1993

CONTENTS

Chapter 3

An overview of the dispute resolution landscape

3.1 FINDING THE MOST APPROPRIATE PROCESS

As we have seen in the first two chapters, there are a number of ways to classify ADR methods, both in terms of the extent of party control and also in terms of its relationship to negotiating technique. We have touched upon some of the forms of process that have developed to meet the needs which these various approaches illustrate, and given some early ideas as to how to select procedures appropriate to cases. The diagram at the end of Chapter 2 is a useful guide, but only a very rough tool.

This chapter looks in more detail at the ways in which specific ADR processes operate, summarising the main practice points associated with these techniques, and identifying some variations. There is an important array of options, and it is important for professionals to ensure that they select the dispute resolution forum that will be the best one to overcome barriers to settlement in their particular case. Mediation will only be looked at in outline in this chapter, as it has become by far the most significant ADR process both in the UK and world-wide, and will be examined in considerable detail in Chapters 7 to 12. Mini-trial, or executive tribunal is examined in detail in Chapter 13, and adjudication and expert determination in Chapter 14.

ADR processes are classified in broad terms only, and then again can vary in detail and emphasis according to the cultural or professional background of the neutral. Many ADR specialists hold to the view that ADR processes should remain flexible to avoid the descent into rules and rigidity that have undermined the reputation and effectiveness of traditional litigation or arbitration. It has to be observed that even the reforms introduced by the CPR feel somewhat rule-driven. The drive has been to understand, learn and mobilise the new rules. Oddly, it is just where the rules stop and wide discretions are left to judges that some of the most trenchant criticism of the CPR begins to take shape, in making it seem harder for litigated outcomes to be predictable. Predictability based on the doctrine of precedent and on transparent statute law and court procedures is the essence of the legal system. The message may be that where there is a wide choice for action, it may be better to retain control over its exercise rather than confer that wide discretion on an outside arbiter. Control over one's own destiny is one of the core attractions of a number of ADR processes. The fact that some are chosen deliberately to divest control and confer it to some extent on another neutral perhaps highlights the ambivalence that parties in dispute often feel about finding the right way out.

Many ADR techniques have only been systematised in the last 20 years or so, and their variations, strengths, terminology and procedures are still evolving with experience. There is nevertheless a surprising unanimity of practice that has grown up around the globe. As a result, ADR has become an especially useful technique for dealing with cross-border disputes where there is at least a minimum level of ADR awareness and training. Advisers operating in an international context should, however, check that terms and processes are being used to mean the same thing, as variants do occur.

We shall adopt a slightly different classification of dispute resolution processes for this chapter, based on the three primary distinguishing features of the dispute resolution landscape which give to each ADR method its characteristic central driving force.

These are –

- *Negotiation;*
- *Mediation;*
- *Adjudication.*

3.2 NEGOTIATION PROCESSES AND VARIANTS

While strictly not an ADR technique itself, there being no third party intervention, negotiation underlies much ADR practice, as we have seen in Chapter 2, and negotiated outcomes are seen as the objective of the main ADR techniques. Indeed, mediation is often referred to as 'assisted negotiation'. We shall revert to that in the next section.

Interest in commercial ADR has emerged from and fed back into a growing literature on negotiating science in the last 30 years. The development of 'principled bargaining', allied with a sense of the interdependence of business, consumer and public relationships, have stimulated a search for third-party ADR mechanisms to reduce the adversarial tendencies of many commercial or litigation negotiating practices. As a by-product, many professionals who have trained in ADR methods report that the principles they have learned often improve their direct negotiating practice.

3.2.1 Facilitation of discussions

Some third party interventions occur at a much lower level than formal mediation or adjudication, in essence to attempt to facilitate or broker the start of negotiations at all. Interventions by ADR providers or even the mere suggestion of mediation by one party frequently stimulates parties to open or re-open discussions and reach their own directly negotiated settlements. Such techniques might be described as 'facilitation', 'using good offices' (in a diplomatic setting) or 'conciliation', though there tends to be little systematic theory or language in this sector of dispute resolution.

3.2.2 Evaluation for guidance

Parties may seek the view of a third party on aspects of their case which helps them to address their differences. This kind of approach may contribute to the parties' negotiating material but does not seek directly to influence the path or even the process of negotiations (as in mediation), nor to offer any binding judgment. The following are techniques of this kind:

1 Neutral fact-finding

This involves an investigation and report of what the facts of a case must have been in the view of an independent third party.

2 Expert appraisal

Where there is an issue of quality or professional assessment, an expert assessment can give a stronger foundation or objective criteria for subsequent negotiations.

3   Early neutral evaluation

This is a technique used in certain US state courts, and offered (though rarely taken up) by the English Commercial Court and the Technology and Construction Court, where senior lawyers or judges evaluate the likely outcomes of a case: this is expected to lead to more realistic negotiations between the parties.

4   Executive amicable settlement procedure

Many commercial dispute clauses attempt to deal with the 'wrong people' problem in negotiation by moving the required negotiation stage to senior executive or director level before external dispute resolution. Not only is there then a broader corporate view taken of the problem, but in theory senior executives will be less personally involved in the personal antagonisms or career or budget sensitivities that may have afflicted middle managers dealing directly with the dispute.

3.2.3   Preventative dispute resolution techniques

Many of the ADR third party processes can be said to help settle disputes earlier and more informally and thereby prevent dispute 'escalation'. However, thought should also be given to the many 'better management' approaches which can either reduce conflict or handle it more constructively to prevent a formal 'dispute' emerging. Amongst such systems could be included:

- Training in *principled negotiation* (positional negotiating training may increase the rate of conflicts over time!).

- *Team working*, education and consultancy (how to collaborate better, solve problems in group working, etc).

- Application of *quality management systems* to customer or supplier relations ('Total Quality Management' or ISO 9000).

- *Partnering* (a term used in the construction industry to refer to team-working arrangements between the various parties to a construction project, with early joint education, regular meetings, funds for contingencies and other mutual support systems).

- *Reg–Neg* (a term used in the US to refer to an approach used by administrative agencies of negotiating new regulations with interest groups rather than the traditional public administration approach of 'consult–publish–defend– amend').

A number of these efforts at improving direct negotiations also involve third parties as educators or consultants. More formal third party approaches to the same end might include:

- *Dispute resolution adviser* (a process involving the presence of a disputes assessor and facilitator with a standing role on a major construction contract).

- *Advisory mediation* (a term used by the UK industrial relations agency ACAS to refer to the appointment of a facilitator-mediator to work with an employer and employees to devise agreed negotiating or employment procedures that will enhance relations between the parties).

3.2.4 Negotiating skills and third party intervention

Advisers or neutrals working at the level of more formal third party resolution approaches should at least be aware of the range of techniques to facilitate better direct negotiations, even if not themselves skilled in them. In their role as, say, mediators, not only must they have a thorough sense of how negotiations succeed or fail. They may also wish to draw on some of these techniques during mediation (for example, expert appraisal) in order to overcome obstacles or to propose methods of future working relations between the parties.

3.2.5 Managers as dispute resolvers

Equally managers should be better informed of the dispute landscape to enhance their own range of techniques. In particular managers and advisers should have an ability to recognise when to initiate third party intervention before conflicts escalate. Mediation and other approaches are often only employed as a last resort, or once arbitration and litigation also become options.

In fact many public and private sector negotiations will have dragged on or festered for months or years before this stage. Alert managers should be able to trigger constructive intervention before this level of aggravation and inefficiency is reached.

3.3 MEDIATION PROCESSES AND VARIANTS

Mediation is the central and most frequently adopted ADR technique around the globe. Its uses stretch from the highest level of international diplomacy to the humblest of inter-personal problems. We deal in full detail with it in later chapters, and confine ourselves here to a summary of its essential shape, with the major procedural variants found in practice.

3.3.1 Normal mediation procedure

Mediation involves the appointment or intervention of a neutral third party who seeks to help the parties in dispute to reach a negotiated agreement. The mediator becomes actively involved in the negotiation process but has no power to adjudicate or impose an award. Typically, mediations in civil disputes are conducted on a confidential basis and 'without prejudice' to other legal rights or remedies of the parties in the event that they do not reach an agreement to settle their differences.

A typical non-family civil dispute mediation goes through four basic phases.

1 Preparation

This includes drawing up a mediation agreement, appointment of mediator and delivery of written submissions and document bundles to the mediator and other parties, plus any pre-mediation contact by the mediator with the parties, either by telephone or sometimes in a pre-mediation meeting.

2 Opening joint session

Introduction by the mediator and brief presentations by each party of their case at a round-table meeting.

3 Private meetings or 'caucuses'

'Shuttle diplomacy' by a mediator who seeks in confidential sessions with each party to clarify privately the nature of their case and their settlement interests, and to help the parties to design their own acceptable settlement.

4 Conclusion

Joint meeting to agree or sign written terms of settlement, which are usually a legally binding contract or consent order; or to terminate the mediation process. This may occur at a range of levels. Negotiations may have completely broken down; agreement may be reached on further information needed before negotiation can start again; agreement may have been reached on some issues leaving a narrower range to be litigated or discussed later.

3.3.2 Main variants in mediation procedure

1 Joint and private meetings

Mediators often differ in how much they rely on joint meetings or on private meetings and on how flexible they are in mixing the two. In UK family mediation, for instance, private meetings are rare. In public policy or environmental mediation, meetings are sometimes held in public. Confidentiality is the norm in commercial mediation. This refers both to confidentiality as between all parties in the mediation and third parties outside the mediation: and confidentiality of communication between mediator and a party in a private session unless the mediator is authorised by that party to disclose information to the other party or parties.

2 Facilitative/evaluative mediation

There is a spectrum of styles of approach among mediators, in theory at least. At one end is the facilitative approach, where the mediator avoids giving opinions and judgments, and merely assists parties to clarify their communications, interests and priorities. At the other end is said to be the evaluative approach, where the mediator expresses opinions on the merits of issues in dispute in order to generate movement towards settlement. There is a tendency to characterise the facilitative approach as 'soft' and the evaluative as 'hard'. The truth is much more complex. Facilitative mediations will very often entail robust reality-testing by the mediator, which is all the more telling because of the mediator's neutral status. The giving of an appraisal or an opinion over settlement range (sometimes provided for in a mediation agreement at the parties' and mediator's option) may need very 'soft' presentation by a supposed evaluative mediator.

3.3.2 *An overview of the dispute resolution landscape*

There is also a tendency to characterise the two approaches as the only two possibilities for mediators. In reality there are endless 'shades of grey' among mediators, not least derived from differing personalities and styles. Furthermore, wherever a mediator works on this spectrum in the course of a mediation, decisions over the outcome will always remain the parties' ultimate responsibility.

As we shall see in our later discussion of mediation practice, the above distinction is often too simplistic to catch the richness of mediation practice. However, it can be a useful framework for parties in terms of choosing an appropriate mediator (known to be facilitative or evaluative in style) or deciding what they need from mediation to overcome obstacles to settlement between them and the other party (or between them and their own advisers).

3 Conciliation

This term has traditionally been used to refer to a process similar to mediation but distinguished from it by virtue of the fact that in one of the processes the third party is more activist in putting forward terms of settlement or an opinion on the case. For example, the UK's statutory industrial relations agency, ACAS, distinguishes conciliation from mediation, where third parties issue a written recommendation. Unfortunately there is no international unanimity on which term is regarded as the more activist. Increasingly the term *mediation* has been adopted as the generic term for third party facilitation in commercial disputes whether or not the third party is activist. We therefore do not use the term conciliation again in this book.

4 Mini-trial or executive tribunal

This is a more formal type of mediation practice and associated clearly with an evaluative approach. Formal, but abbreviated, presentations of their best legal case are made by each party to a panel of senior directors from each company with (usually) a neutral chairman to manage proceedings. After the presentations the executives adjourn and attempt to negotiate a settlement on the basis of what they have heard. The neutral adviser is there to facilitate negotiations or to mediate, if the parties' negotiations stall. The neutral adviser may give a view on the likely outcome if the case went to trial or arbitration in order to facilitate settlement. The executive tribunal is a powerful approach for major corporate disputes and is therefore reviewed more extensively in Chapter 13. It is not used as frequently as mediation, however.

5   Consensus-building

This expression is often used as a substitute for mediation (or facilitation) in environmental or public policy dispute resolution approaches – for example over planning the location of a new chemicals factory in a community or setting new environmental standards.

It refers usually to a more protracted process where a third party consultant seeks to identify the various interest groups connected with a development, and to facilitate consultation, discussions or negotiation between them. The aim is thereby to achieve a 'wiser' and more consensual outcome than in the normal public policy approach of either lack of adequate consultation or consultation without full participative decision-making. It helps to combat the NIMBY phenomenon ('not in my back yard') on the one hand and on the other hand the defective political process of decision-making that can be summed up as 'Consult–Announce Decision–Defend Decision–Amend Decision'. This is when those consulted realise that the decision does not meet their interests and battle politically or through the courts to amend it. Consensus-building approaches have been most widely used in the US and Australia and fall within variations on assisted negotiation as well as mediation.

6   Med-arb

Sometimes parties wish, for reasons of cost or time, to avoid the possibility that a mediation may not achieve final determination of a dispute if the parties fail to agree. They therefore contract to give the mediator power to 'convert' to an arbitrator role and make a legally binding award, in the event that mediated negotiations do not lead to settlement of all issues.

A variation on this promoted by the American Arbitration Association is MEDALOA, mediation followed by 'last-offer arbitration' (see below for a description of this form of arbitration).

This technique, called med-arb, is not widely used but interest in it is growing, for example in the US construction industry, and some jurisdictions have legislated to deal with the potential legal problems for arbitrations conducted under these circumstances.

The main theoretical arguments against med-arb are two-fold.

3.3.2 *An overview of the dispute resolution landscape*

First, the process appears to run counter to traditional rules of natural justice that a party should hear the evidence and arguments put forward against it and have a chance of reply. Private meetings in the course of a mediation undermine this principle unless the mediator is allowed to reveal everything said in private. Alternatively it has to be accepted that the mediator has put out of mind any unilateral information in handing down an arbitral award, a very difficult thing for the mediator to do.

Med-arb also theoretically undermines the power of the mediation process because each party may feel reluctant to be as open with the mediator on their offers or vulnerabilities, if there is a chance that the mediator will become an arbitrator of their case.

Despite these major theoretical drawbacks, there appears to be growing support internationally for med-arb practice. Parties are said to value the more robust commercial approach involved, and there are many cases where little really sensitive information is revealed in private sessions. However, as yet it is not commonly used in the UK and parties should be warned of the theoretical disadvantages. Perhaps if they do use it, they should afford themselves a contractual opportunity to opt out of the arbitration phase which would otherwise follow the mediation phase, although this still undermines the robustness of the process.

3.4 ADJUDICATIVE PROCESSES AND VARIANTS

In determining which appropriate dispute resolution method to adopt, consideration must of course be given to the option where a third party hands down a judgment. Some of these techniques are associated with the discipline of ADR, although the traditional alternatives of litigation or arbitration are commonly held to be outside ADR. Indeed, the desire for adjudicated outcomes has been regarded as in part the reason for ADR's development in the US, where it has been more common to regard arbitration as one of the new 'alternatives'.

It is also important to stress the difference between adjudication as a conceptual category of techniques involving imposed decisions (as used in this section) and adjudication as a specific ADR process (dealt with in Chapter 14).

Adjudications by definition imply non-negotiated outcomes, involving decisions handed down by a third party, on a Win–Lose basis. However, some of these assumptions may be modified by party control of parts of the procedure, or by way of substantive legal principles (for example, as the concept of contributory negligence reduces the damages awarded to a claimant).

3.5 MAIN VARIANTS IN ADJUDICATION

3.5.1 Litigation and court trial

In common law systems, the civil litigation system has increasingly become a settlement system. Typically over 90% of claims issued do not proceed to trial, and even more cases fail to proceed to judgment. However, ADR has been perceived as a valuable complement to this system, not just because it helps prevent some cases going to trial, but because it is said to speed up the process of settlement and thereby reduce the cost and management time allotted to litigation. Finally, the litigation system is geared to a specific range of legal principles, legal remedies and historical analysis of cases. ADR techniques offer potentially more flexible, creative and future-orientated outcomes.

It will of course frequently be necessary to decide that litigation is the appropriate route to take either in general or as an initial step to:

- establish a legal precedent;
- make a public statement on the importance of an industry practice;
- achieve summary judgment;
- enforce judgments/awards/agreements;
- compel and examine documents/witnesses;
- obtain rapid injunctive relief;
- force another party into settlement discussions or into judgment.

Also relevant to the choice of litigation as a primary approach would be questions which can vary substantially according to the case and jurisdiction involved:

- speed of getting to trial;
- costs involved;
- likely recovery of costs;

3.5.1 *An overview of the dispute resolution landscape*

- likely recovery on judgment;
- quality of judgment;
- management time and energy used;
- publicity value/damage.

Four other major aspects of litigation practice should be noted in considering dispute resolution options:

1   common law jurisdictions (and civil law perhaps to a lesser extent) are increasingly seeking ways to improve the efficiency, speed and price of access to the courts. This will have some impact on the use of alternatives;

2   as part of these attempts at reform, courts and legal systems are increasingly adopting active case management systems, amply demonstrated by the reforms embodied in the Civil Procedure Rules 1999 in England and Wales;

3   also as part of these reforms, courts are increasingly attempting to integrate ADR methods into court procedures by way of 'court-annexed ADR' or 'multi-door courthouse' concepts. Thus lawyers and parties may be advised to consider ADR, or informed of the options, or directed to use it subject to rights of opt-out or costs sanctions;

4   in several civil law countries and other jurisdictions (for example Japan) judges have a duty to seek to bring the parties to a pre-trial settlement. The nature and thoroughness of this 'conciliation' duty varies but will often involve the judge giving the parties a preliminary view of the case rather than employing facilitative mediation.

3.5.2   Arbitration

Arbitration has been the traditional private alternative to court, with parties contracting to be bound by a third party private award that is normally legally enforceable as a court judgment.

As a dispute resolution approach, the advantages claimed for arbitration are that it is private, and that parties can tailor procedures and time-scales to their needs rather than be bound by fixed court systems. Finally, the parties can choose their decision-maker, who may have specialist background knowledge to bring to bear on the case. Over the years, however, arbitration's reputation has suffered, mainly because it has become increasingly costly and proceedings have become as protracted as court time-tables. Also parties are not always as free to choose their arbitrator as they would wish, and often become upset on 'losing' their case 'unjustifiably' due to what they consider a poor-quality arbitrator, as compared with judicial standards.

A vigorous debate has taken place in the arbitration world on how to address such issues. The reforms in the Arbitration Act 1996 have made appreciable improvements. We look at some special types of arbitration in the next section, but otherwise leave arbitration as being outside the scope of this book.

3.5.3 Tailored arbitration

A number of variations of arbitration are worth noting in terms of the landscape of dispute resolution.

1 Documents only arbitration

A simplified arbitration based solely on documentary, and not oral, evidence or argument, used in a number of consumer arbitration schemes.

2 'Amiable Compositeur' or 'ex aequo et bono'

An additional arbitration approach found in civil law systems where awards can be guided by equitable or 'fairness' considerations and not according to strict legal rules, used more often in consumer cases, but not recognised in common law systems.

3 'Hi-lo' arbitration

A process where parties agree a limited range of figures within which they will accept an award, ie with a minimum and maximum. The arbitrator may or may not be informed of the agreed range. Not widely used as an approach.

4 Final-offer/last offer/pendulum/baseball arbitration

A process where parties agree that their last offers will be placed before an arbitrator who can only choose one side's offer or the other side's claim figure. Mainly used in industrial relations contexts with the rationale that it will help parties decide to put forward only reasonable figures.

3.5.4 Expert determination

In some instances the parties may be divided only by a technical question, for example the valuation of a company. In such cases a common approach is a contractual agreement to appoint an expert to adjudicate. As a valuation, this approach has been treated by the courts as having different legal characteristics and remedies from an arbitral award, although the distinction between the two is not always clear. This is dealt with fully in Chapter 14.

3.5.5 Adjudication

This expression is often used in a technical sense in construction contracts. It is intended as a procedure that will bind parties to a decision soon after a dispute notice is given. Parties usually have an option to reject the decision and initiate litigation or arbitration proceedings within a certain time period or after substantial completion of the construction contract. Adjudication in this sense is dealt with more fully in Chapter 14.

3.5.6 Dispute review board

This is a 'standing' adjudication panel system used in major construction contracts. The board is generally appointed at the outset of the project and stays in close touch with it, adjudicating disputes as they arise. A well-known example of this was the dispute review board appointed to resolve problems arising out of the Channel Tunnel and the Hong Kong airport construction projects.

3.5.7 Ombudsman

The ombudsman system has evolved as a successful approach to delivering prompt responses to citizen or consumer complaints, so as to protect public sector or industry reputations. An ombudsman office is established as an independent agency to review and adjudicate on complaints. Usually fact-finding and adjudication are involved, and sometimes also efforts at mediation during the inquiry stage.

3.6   DISPUTE RESOLUTION SYSTEMS: OLD OR NEW?

The range of available dispute resolution processes continues to grow as both society and the commercial world evolve, together with rethinking of the field of dispute resolution of which ADR is a creative part. For companies, public sector organisations or sectors faced with recurring disputes, the landscape of dispute resolution offers the opportunity to apply some systems management thinking to their problems. Can a dispute procedure be devised which delivers greater benefits, such as reduction of cost or delay, improved relations, minimum management diversion or other criteria?

Use of one of the major landscape features – negotiation, mediation or adjudication – may suffice, but there is also the option of adopting a *multi-step procedure,* for instance *negotiation → mediation → adjudication* (litigation or arbitration) or a *multiple choice system,* for instance the *multi-door courthouse,* with adequate means of guidance to the parties. These approaches can be embodied in contractual terms.

It is certainly not beyond the wit of those in dispute and those engaged in ADR to devise yet more useful adaptations to the existing landscape features to meet individual needs. The principles have already been discussed at the conclusion of Chapter 2. For example, ADR is increasingly becoming the tool of choice for dealing with cases that might be regarded as 'untriable', perhaps because of the sheer complexity of issues, involvement of huge numbers of parties or multi-jurisdictional problems. While settlement of the whole dispute is the ultimate hope, there is much that ADR technique and its deployment in the hands of a skilled facilitator can achieve along that road in what might be called 'mega-litigation'. Design of how to make the issues in such a case manageable and how to deal with classes of party in a consistent but personally sensitive way, are crucially helpful. There is a critical balance between trying to tackle the outcome globally and breaking it into comprehensible components.

Such processes will usually spread over weeks and months, rather than the more typical finite mediation process confined to a day or two. A true project management approach is required, with the facilitator (or quite often two facilitators) working in close conjunction with each party's team. Future editions of this book will undoubtedly need to reflect learning from engagement by ADR providers in a wide range of such processes which is beginning to develop.

We now turn in Part B to consider the legal framework of ADR. In Part C we examine the practical framework for ADR with particular reference to mediation. Then in Part D we examine some specialised processes and areas of interest, together with a fresh look at practice development issues for those still not fully engaged with ADR processes in daily practice.

Part B

The legal framework of ADR

CONTENTS

Chapter 4

ADR and the courts

4.1 THE WOOLF REPORT: *ACCESS TO JUSTICE*

As Lord Woolf observed in the opening chapters of his 1995 Interim Report *Access to Justice*, problems of expense, slowness and complexity were still besetting the civil justice system, despite numerous attempts to reform it. He took the view that the basic principles for an accessible civil justice system were that it should be:

- *just* in the results delivered;
- *fair* and seen to be so, by ensuring equal opportunity to assert or defend rights, giving adequate opportunity for each to state or answer a case, and treating like cases alike;
- *proportionate*, in relation to the issues involved, in both procedure and cost;
- *speedy* so far as reasonable;
- *understandable* to users;
- *responsive* to the needs of users;
- *certain* in outcome as far as possible;
- *effective* through adequate resources and organisation.

His aim was to change the whole approach to civil litigation from a wasteful adversarial mind-set to one of co-operative problem-solving by encouraging settlement rather than trial of disputes. There could be no more appropriate role for ADR than in a legal system with such aims. Lord Woolf reflected this by including a chapter on ADR (Chapter 18) in his Interim Report. He advocated court encouragement of the use of ADR rather than compulsion. He was also clear that in deciding on the future conduct of a case, a judge should be able to take into account a litigant's unreasonable *refusal to attempt* ADR. In the 1996 Final Report, he went further and recommended that courts should also take into account unreasonable behaviour *in the course of* ADR. By that time he was expressing less certainty about not providing for compulsory referral to ADR. The debate which he initiated on these two topics remains unfinished, as we shall see. He also specifically recommended that solicitors for clinical negligence claimants and those seeking judicial review should consider ADR; that the topic of ADR should be considered at case management conferences; and the courts and the Lord Chancellor's Department should raise the profile of ADR.

The first general manifestation of this new philosophy of litigation, with implications for the whole of the civil court system, emerged in the January 1995 Practice Direction from the Lord Chief Justice and the Vice-Chancellor. Introducing the first of a wide range of procedural reforms and improvements, Lord Chief Justice Bingham said:

'. . . the aim is to try and change the whole culture, the ethos applying to the field of civil litigation.'

There can be no doubt that these first steps, followed by the recommendations in Lord Woolf's Final Report and culminating in the Civil Procedure Rules 1999 and the Access to Justice Act 1999 have changed the face of civil litigation and the culture in which it operates radically and irrevocably. The result has been to bring ADR firmly into the mainstream of dispute resolution in England and Wales, with signs that it is developing in similar ways in Scotland and Northern Ireland.

4.2 THE PRE-CPR PRACTICE DIRECTIONS

Even before the CPR, the courts in England & Wales had begun to devise a more express duty for lawyers to advise fully on ADR. First the Commercial Court issued its *Practice Note: Commercial Court; Alternative Dispute Resolution* [1994] 1 All ER 34 requiring lawyers to bring ADR to their client's attention. The Practice Note required legal advisers in all cases to:

'(a) consider with their clients and the other parties concerned the possibility of attempting to resolve the particular dispute or particular issues by mediation, conciliation or otherwise; and

(b) ensure that parties are fully informed as to the most cost-effective means of resolving the particular dispute.'

Whilst this stopped short of making ADR a mandatory step in the court process, it did make it mandatory for lawyers to consider ADR with both client and other parties. The Commercial Court's subsequent track record shows that it has taken this duty very seriously, and has probably been the forum in which gentle but firm persuasion on parties to try ADR has been applied most effectively. From the start, the court's judges have required a high level of understanding among commercial practitioners about ADR and its practical application to commercial cases. Take-up in this sector has consequently been at an increasingly high level, as satisfaction levels have increased with experience. The judges have developed various types of order as their contribution to this development. These are discussed in more detail in section **4.3.7** below.

The Commercial Court's approach was subsumed in general terms across the High Court by the *Practice Note (Civil Litigation: Case Management)* [1995] 1 All ER 385 issued by the Lord Chief Justice and Vice-Chancellor (touched upon above), introducing for the first time a generally available case management role for judges. A slightly different approach was adopted. Legal advisers conducting cases were required to lodge a checklist at least two months before trial. This included questions as to whether the advisers had discussed the possibility of using ADR, both with their client and with the other side, and whether they considered that some form of ADR might assist in resolving or narrowing the issues.

In response to Lord Woolf's particular concerns about clinical negligence claims, Queen's Bench *Practice Direction 49* was issued on 16 November 1996, dealing with cases in the specialist Clinical Negligence list in the Queen's Bench Division. This required the parties to state at the first summons for directions 'whether ADR has been considered and if not why not and if ADR has been rejected why this is so'. This lacked the specific requirement for mutuality of approach characterised by the Commercial Court. The ADR enquiry by the court was arguably a little too early in the process of exchange of expert opinion. ADR was still not made mandatory.

The extent to which glib or opaque answers were given to these questions has remained a matter for the masters and district judges to investigate and determine. But the effect of these directions has been to open up the possibility that the courts might call advisers to account for and justify the answers given, perhaps in relation to post-trial applications for costs.

4.3 THE CIVIL PROCEDURE RULES 1999 (THE CPR)

The Civil Procedure Rules 1999 came into effect on 26 April 1999. They represent the most extensive overhaul of the civil justice system since the Judicature Acts 1873–75, reinforcing the messages already given by Lord Woolf MR and Lord Bingham LCJ.

The significance of the CPR goes far beyond a mere rationalisation of High Court and county court procedures into one coherent and reasonably readable set of procedural rules for the large majority of actions, convenient though this may be. It is the change of culture in litigation to a higher level of inter-party co-operation, which was clearly demanded and intended by Lord Woolf, that has turned out to have been substantially achieved. Such a change happens to be entirely congruent with the culture in which ADR will flourish. Instead of arid confrontation, procedural warfare and aggressive positioning, co-operative problem-solving is welcomed. Those who choose not to change their ways face costs sanctions. It is perhaps this fundamental culture change that is the greatest surprise and the greatest achievement of the civil justice reforms. The results of the revolution in funding (which we also discuss in outline below) are not yet so clear.

We set out below some of the specific ways in which the CPR have sought to achieve this culture change, commenting on the inter-relationship between the CPR and ADR processes.

4.3.1 The overriding objective and active case management

For the first time in this (and probably any) jurisdiction, the court has set itself an overriding objective, to be found at the very head of the Civil Procedure Rules 1999 in Part 1. It is a guide for all court users – lawyers, judges and parties – to the essential purpose of the civil litigation process, against which to test any issue that may arise. The overriding objective is such a novelty, and so fundamental to the effect of the CPR and the place of ADR within the new scheme of things, that we set out the key provisions in full:

'CPR 1.1(1) These Rules are a new procedural code with the over-riding objective of *enabling the court to deal with cases justly.*

(2) Dealing with a case justly includes, so far as practicable:

(a) ensuring that the parties are on an equal footing;

(b) saving expense;

(c) dealing with cases in ways which are proportionate to the amount of money involved, the importance of the case, the complexity of the issues and to the parties' financial position;

(d) ensuring that it is dealt with expeditiously and fairly;

(e) allotting to it an appropriate share of the court's re-sources.'

The court is placed under an obligation to further the overriding objective by *actively managing cases,* a phrase which is defined in the CPR to include:

'CPR 1.4(2) (a) encouraging the parties to co-operate with each other in the conduct of the proceedings [**tellingly, this is a new illustration which heads the list in the final version of the CPR but which did not appear in the first draft**];

(b) identifying the issues at an early stage;

(c) deciding promptly which issues need full investi-gation and trial and accordingly disposing summarily of the others;

(d) deciding the order in which issues are to be resolved;

(e) *encouraging the parties to use an alternative dispute resol-ution procedure if the court considers that to be appropriate and facilitating the use of such procedure;*

(f) helping the parties to settle the whole or part of a case;

(g) fixing timetables or otherwise controlling the progress of the case;

(h) considering whether the likely benefits of taking a particular step will justify the cost of taking it;

(i) dealing with as many aspects of the case as it can on the same occasion;

(j) dealing with the case without the parties needing to attend court;

(k) making appropriate use of technology; and

4.3.1 *ADR and the courts*

> (l) giving directions to ensure that the trial of a case proceeds quickly and efficiently.'

This is the practical way in which the CPR have sought to achieve the basic principles for an accessible civil justice system enunciated by Lord Woolf in *Access to Justice* and set out in section **4.1** above.

It is a highly significant demonstration of the culture change which the Woolf reforms aimed to achieve that the delineation of active case management in CPR Part 1.4(2), set out above, is so congruent with the aims and objectives of ADR. Indeed, the management obligations laid on the court might themselves (with minor modifications) describe what a mediator seeks to do. The specific mention of ADR at para 1.4(2)(e) is the first official recognition of ADR in the court rules themselves in England and Wales, and is perhaps the best indication of its having arrived in the mainstream of civil justice here.

4.3.2 Pre-action conduct and the protocols

Furthermore, the CPR have introduced three further related concepts which are already revolutionising thinking among litigators over strategy, timing and tactics.

1 Pre-action conduct

Under Part 44.5, the court is entitled to take into account in determining what costs orders to make in any case the reasonableness of pre-action conduct as well as what it has always examined, namely post-action conduct of each party. This most fundamental change enshrined in the CPR was prefigured by Lord Woolf's remark in Chapter 7 of his Final Report. He said that his recommendations were intended, among other objectives to:

> '. . . make the court's powers to make orders for costs a more effective incentive for responsible behaviour and a more compelling deterrent against unreasonable behaviour.'

If proceedings are, in a court's opinion, unjustifiably issued, even an apparently 'successful' party may be penalised in costs. Until the CPR, judges were extremely reluctant to look in any meaningful way at pre-action conduct.

2   The pre-action protocols

The CPR now append pre-action protocols which give guidance as to what is best practice before proceedings are issued. The protocols, drafted by sector practitioners rather than either the Executive or Judiciary, in effect define in broad terms what constitutes reasonable conduct, providing a yardstick against which the judge can later, if necessary, assess a party's approach. Those at present promulgated deal specifically with personal injury, clinical negligence claims, construction and engineering disputes, and defamation. Others will almost certainly follow. However, the Practice Direction to the current protocols makes it quite clear that actions of all other kinds should be conducted in the spirit which informs these protocols. Failure to do so can be expected to provoke the sanctions provided for by Part 44.5.

The two newer protocols – for construction and engineering disputes and defamation – are both more specific about considering ADR than their predecessors. The former provides for a pre-action meeting at which the parties should consider whether some form of ADR would be more suitable than litigation. The court may be told who did not attend such a meeting and the grounds for their refusal. The latter specifically provides that both claimant and defendant will be expected by the court to provide evidence that alternative means of resolving their dispute were considered, mentioning by name expert determination, mediation and arbitration, 'or any other form of ADR'.

There was debate among practitioners discussing the personal injury and clinical negligence protocol as to whether ADR should be mentioned specifically. It will be interesting to see if the approach of the second generation of protocols might influence the wording of the first generation protocols on redrafting and later generations from the outset.

3   Pre-action offers to settle

Offers to settle can now be made before issue of proceedings by any party. These can have the adverse costs and interest consequences more fully set out under section **4.3.5** below, where we deal with Part 36 offers and payments into court. While so-called *Calderbank* letters were used to try to achieve a similar effect, their true effectiveness was much more doubtful than the much clearer regime under the CPR.

For all these reasons, there is now serious pressure on parties to consider settlement through ADR or otherwise before proceedings are issued.

4.3.3 Stays for ADR and settlement at allocation stage: the multi-track and fast-track

The one moment when the CPR specifically raise the possibility of ADR is at the allocation stage, when the court decides, assisted by the comments of the parties, into which track the claim should be allocated. The process is triggered by filing and serving a defence to the claim, at which point the parties must file an allocation questionnaire, the claimant paying an allocation fee in almost every case or face being struck out. Part 26.4 provides that:

'(1) A party may when filing the completed allocation questionnaire make a written request for the proceedings to be stayed while the parties try to settle the case by alternative dispute resolution or other means.

(2) Where –

(a) all parties request a stay under paragraph (1); or

(b) the court, of its own initiative, considers that such a stay would be appropriate,

the court will direct that the proceedings be stayed for one month.

(3) The court may extend the stay until such date or for such period as it considers appropriate.'

It may seem carping to criticise such a provision, as many cases are indeed referred to mediation by court intervention. However, experience from the courts suggests that this is happening not so much at allocation stage as at case management conferences and pre-trial reviews. The Allocation Questionnaire sent out by the court asks at Question A:

'Do you wish there to be a one month stay to attempt to settle the case?'

The form's guidance notes talk about the parties being 'able to negotiate a settlement' but there is no specific mention of ADR as there is in CPR Part 26.4.

As we shall see later, it is important that, by the time of mediation, each party should have sufficient information available to be able to advise and consider settlement safely and responsibly. The allocation stage is relatively soon after issue of proceedings, at which point any case unsettled by then ought either to be considered for mediation, or if not then ready, left to a later stage. In fast-track cases, currently dealing with claims up to £15,000 in value, there may not be a directions hearing. In multi-track cases, there will usually be at least one case management conference and a pre-trial review, both of which would almost certainly be good occasions to see whether ADR has anything to offer in that case. The Commercial Court, Chancery Division, and the Technology and Construction and Mercantile Courts all sensibly raise such a specific possibility in their Practice Guides, Protocols and in CPR Part 49.

Part 26.4 certainly does provide for the court *of its own motion* to order a stay where it thinks it appropriate, regardless of the wishes of either party.

It should be added that there is no particular need for existing proceedings to be stayed for ADR. If a party or the court believes that a request for ADR is another party's ploy to gain time by delay, the timetable for the action can, if desired, continue unobstructed, with costs continuing to be incurred meanwhile. It is only where all parties propose and engage in ADR in good faith that there is little point in expending more time and cost on forwarding litigation when there is a good chance that ADR will settle it.

4.3.4   Small claims track cases

The small claims track is the successor to the most successful innovation in the civil justice system in recent years, namely the county court small claims procedure. With virtually no legal costs capable of being awarded, it has been kept as a simple and accessible forum for low value disputes for which ADR is hardly necessary or in fact cost-effective. The current jurisdiction is up to £5,000 for money claims other than for personal injury. The ceiling for personal injury is much lower at £1,000. Claims higher than that level will normally be fast-track and will attract a costs award for the successful party in addition to damages.

4.3.5   Part 36 offers and settlement procedures

These are another useful innovation in the CPR, and on the whole have proved to be a success. Either party can now make an offer to settle before or after proceedings are issued, indicating what they would be prepared to pay or accept, and also specifying any acceptable non-monetary terms for a settlement agreement. Claimants who do better at trial than a defendant's Part 36 offer will normally get their standard costs in addition to their remedy. Those who do less well will normally (but not always) have to pay both sides' costs from the date of the Part 36 offer. Defendants who reject a claimant's Part 36 offer and do worse at trial can expect penal interest to be awarded on damages and costs, the latter probably being awarded on an indemnity basis.

Part 36 procedure has almost certainly led already to more settlements both before and after issue of proceedings. Mediations are often preceded by such offers and very often followed by them if a case does not settle. The mediation throws up more information upon which to assess the right level for such a proposal to be made. Nothing obliges a Part 36 offer to match what was offered at a mediation, and this brings a new tension into negotiations at a mediation.

4.3.6 Costs and proportionality

Lord Woolf regarded the problem of costs as 'the most serious problem besetting our litigation system'. As we have seen in relation to the pre-action protocols, the CPR give permission for judges to take pre-action unreasonable conduct into account in determining costs orders even against otherwise successful parties. The same range of tools is available to deal with post-issue unreasonableness. These include summary orders for costs on interim hearings, payable immediately; full information about costs expended and anticipated to be prepared and exchanged at every case management occasion; orders to be based on conduct, which is specifically said (in Part 44.3(5)) to include:

'(a) conduct before as well as during the proceedings and in particular the extent to which the parties followed any relevant pre-action protocol;

(b) whether it was reasonable for a party to raise, pursue or contest a particular allegation or issue;

(c) the manner in which a party has pursued or defended his case or a particular allegation or issue;

(d) whether a claimant who has succeeded in his claim, in whole or in part, exaggerated his claim.'

The other key feature to the new costs regime is the requirement of *proportionality* between the costs incurred and claimed by the receiving party and the litigation itself. Costs which are disproportionate to the amount or importance of the litigation may well be disallowed. CPR Part 44.5(1) provides that, in deciding how much should be allowed for costs, the court must have regard to all the circumstances in deciding (when applying the usual standard basis of assessment) whether costs were proportionately and reasonably incurred and were proportionate and reasonable in amount. It is only when costs are to be assessed on an indemnity basis that proportionality is ignored. This emphasis picks up on the provisions of CPR Part 1.1(2)(c) and the overriding objective. Dealing with cases justly is there said to include adopting ways which:

> '... are proportionate to the amount involved in the case, to the importance of the case, to the complexity of the issues and to the financial position of each party.'

The net effect of these linked provisions, put bluntly, is that a party can 'succeed' in litigation, but because of either unreasonable or disproportionate conduct of the claim may not 'win' in terms of obtaining all or most of the legal costs of winning. In an extreme case, the court even has jurisdiction to order the 'winning' party to pay a 'losing' party's costs.

The courts have already demonstrated their willingness to make tougher costs orders, sometimes much to the surprise of the party which might have thought it had 'won' under the old regime. The net result for mediators will be to provide ample grounds for testing whether success at trial might not be of doubtful worth. The attractions of settling a case on a party's own terms will increase in proportion to the uncertainty of the litigated outcome, and uncertainty and wide judicial discretion are found in the costs aspect of the CPR more than any other.

4.3.7   Court-referred ADR

As has been seen, the courts have so far shied away from truly mandatory ADR. Judges have, however, been making orders which put considerable pressure on parties to engage in ADR against the background that they might later regard reluctance or failure to have done so in good faith as a reason for a costs penalty. The orders do not actually spell this out normally. The wording is more or less persuasive, but remains tactfully silent over the consequences of refusal. Some judges have been prepared to be somewhat more assertive where parties have been shown to dally for ulterior reasons in co-operating over administrative arrangements for a mediation, for instance by not agreeing a mediator.

CEDR has circulated its publication *Court-referred ADR: a guide for the judiciary* to all full-time judges. This gives advice on assessing party and lawyer attitudes to ADR and supplies forms of order.

1 The range of court orders

Reviewing a range of ADR Orders made by a variety of courts since the CPR came into effect (and indeed made by the Commercial Court before that time), the basic framework utilised has been the draft Order contained in the Commercial Court Guide.

This takes the following shape:

1. On or before [Day 1] the parties shall exchange lists of three neutrals or identifying one or more panels of individuals who are available to conduct ADR procedures in the case prior to [Day 4].

2. On or before [Day 2] the parties 'shall in good faith endeavour to agree a neutral individual or panel from the lists so exchanged or provided'.

3. Failing such agreement [by Day 3], the Case Management Conference will be restored to enable the court to facilitate agreement on a neutral individual or panel.

4. The parties 'shall take such serious steps as they may be advised to resolve their disputes by ADR procedures before the individual or panel so chosen by no later than [Day 4]'.

5. If the case is not finally settled, the parties shall inform the court by letter by [Day 5 / a specified stage of the proceedings] what steps towards ADR have been taken and(without prejudice to matters of privilege) why such steps have failed. If the parties have failed to initiate ADR procedures the case Management Conference is to be restored for further consideration of the case.

6. [Costs].

2 'Good faith'

There is a good deal of unfamiliar language in this draft Order, such as 'shall in good faith endeavour' and 'take such serious steps as they may be advised', with even the court offering to 'facilitate agreement' if the parties cannot agree on a neutral. In fact no one seems to have found much difficulty in understanding what these concepts might mean, however difficult they might be to enforce.

In the Central London County Court, where an inexpensive mediation scheme has been run since 1996, a typical order (made at a case management conference or on an application for directions in a case started before April 1999) begins:

> 'The parties and legal representatives do now give serious consideration to using the mediation scheme at the court with a view to early settlement.'

In another county court, the wording used has been that 'there be a stay of proceedings to attempt a mediated settlement until' a specified date.

There has been some reluctance among judges to accept that there can be an enforceable duty to do things 'in good faith', as opposed to enforcing an obligation 'to use best endeavours'. Some of this debate emerges in Chapter 6 relating to the enforceability of ADR contract clauses. With a wide costs discretion, what is strictly enforceable as a matter of law may become less significant when sanctions can be imposed for unreasonable conduct.

3 Stay of proceedings

It should be noted that the normal form of order suggested by the Commercial Court (and often used word for word) does not specifically provide for a stay of the proceedings. What happens in practice very often is that the ADR form of words is embedded within the main timetable for an action, to minimise any delay if ADR does not settle a claim. This will provide sometimes for the completion of certain stages (such as amendment of statements of case or exchange of statements of witnesses of fact and / or some or all expert evidence) before the ADR order starts. It may then perhaps provide for a stay at that stage (though by no means in every case) for between a month and three months, and then for further directions in default of settlement, going so far as to fix a trial date or a trial window. Some orders are simply made on the basis of a stay for a fixed period to try ADR and adjournment of all other directions. Much depends upon the stage reached in the proceedings. It would appear that as many if not more orders are made at case management conference or on applications for specific directions as are made at allocation stage under CPR Part 26.4.

In one Queen's Bench action in which the judge ordered a defendant to pay into court £10,000 as a condition of setting aside judgment in default of defence, the judge additionally ordered that the action be stayed for 28 days from the payment into court 'for the parties to explore ADR'. Exchange of witness statements of fact was ordered to take place thereafter.

Typically a stay is ordered until a specified date, but occasionally a court will order a stay 'until the conclusion of the mediation'.

A Technology and Construction Court Order made recently by the assigned judge at his first consideration of the case observed that:

> '... mediation is not an alternative trial. Resolution of the differences between the parties seems to be a reasonable prospect by mediation without enlarging on the numbers participating and it should be attempted after close of pleadings.'

Following service of the Reply, the judge ordered a stay for eight weeks, which was not to affect dates already set in agreed directions. In the same order the judge, as is the practice in the TCC, set the trial date for just over 11 months time thereafter.

A stay may not actually be specified, but if a period is embedded in a timetable when only ADR is required of the parties (as sometimes happens), that really is as good as ordering a stay, since there are no other procedural deadlines during that period.

Liberty to apply in respect of the stay is often specifically ordered, though the CPR probably preserve an implied right to apply anyway.

4   Choice of mediator and machinery of mediation

The standard order visualises choice by the parties with the court facilitating any difficulty in reaching a decision. Some courts have been prepared to adopt a more robust approach, ordering that in default of agreement an ADR provider such as CEDR should have power to nominate a mediator. This happened in *Kinstreet Ltd v Balmargo Corpn Ltd*, an unreported decision of Mrs Justice Arden in July 1999, in which she also made an ADR order in the teeth of opposition from at least one of the parties. In one multi-party Commercial Court case in which the standard order was made, the parties failed to agree and on reference back to the court for 'facilitation', the parties' majority choice from a panel of three mediators was ordered by the same judge to act.

In one Chancery action, the judge ordered 'the parties to try to settle this case by mediation' specifying a date by which this was to have occurred and for a report back to the court. It provided that CEDR was to administer the mediation and was to be 'responsible for the appointment of the mediator after consultation with the parties'.

In a major multi-party action between a company in liquidation and its former employees, an interesting representative order was made 'in order that a process of mediation may be undertaken as soon as practicable in respect of actions . . . suitable for mediation' . . . between employer and employees. The lead solicitors for each side were ordered to make contact with CEDR to instruct them to administer the mediation, and apply jointly for the appointment of a mediator from CEDR's panel. A list of 10 actions in which the liquidator and employees were willing to submit to mediation was to be exchanged and four actions identified for mediation. In an interesting postscript to the order, it is provided that:

> '. . . whereas any ensuing mediations can only continue on a voluntary basis and subject to the terms of such mediation agreements as may be entered into, the Lead Solicitors . . . in consultation with the mediator as appropriate shall in good faith attempt to agree a time-table, venue and procedures for mediation . . .'

going on to make it clear that the mediation order was not to affect the operation of existing orders or the progress of the court action, thus not creating a stay of the action pending ADR.

Some county courts have also made orders that 'the parties try to settle this case by mediation' and identified a provider like CEDR to produce a list of potential mediators for agreement of a nominee by the parties. In default of agreement by a specified time and date the mediator was to be appointed by CEDR, the parties being bound by that appointment. In one such order a powerful extra paragraph was added which provided:

> 'Pursuant to the overriding objective and their duty to the court, both parties shall co-operate to implement the terms of this Order expeditiously and purposefully and without pre-conditions or qualifications. In the event of a party's default, the other party may apply forthwith for the defaulting party's Statement of Case to be struck out for judgment to be entered on that party's claim and for costs.'

A similar note of discipline was introduced into a District Registry Queen's Bench order which had stayed an action involving a building dispute for six weeks 'in order for a formal ADR to take place'. After providing that 'the expertise of the mediator should be preferably that of an engineer/surveyor' with a knowledge of the particular technical field 'rather than a lawyer', it went on:

'Any proposals in the mediation shall be without prejudice, but if as a consequence of one party's failure to co-operate and thereby sabotage the ADR, then either party can make an application to the judge with a view to lift the stay.'

The sanction visualised for non-co-operation was thus to be able to get on without further delay with the proceedings. The ground is probably being prepared for a fight over costs, if the recalcitrant party wins.

5   Costs of seeking an ADR order

Orders on applications for ADR have normally been for costs in the case. Orders dealing with the costs of ADR have normally been for each party to bear their own costs of the ADR process, though interestingly in one Admiralty case the judge ordered that the costs of ADR be reserved to the trial judge.

6   Sanctions for non-compliance or non-co-operation

This is a controversial area in which there is little if any indication of what the court will seek to do. The proviso in the standard Commercial Court order requires a report on a mediation which did not settle a case to set out 'what steps towards mediation have been taken and (without prejudice to matters of privilege (and confidentiality) [extra words sometimes added]) why such steps have failed'. These clearly presage possible sanctions for unreasonable failure to co-operate in setting up a mediation. They might also be used to justify an enquiry into unreasonable conduct at the mediation. As is discussed in Chapter 5, this is dangerous ground for mediation, since confidentiality is fundamental for it to be trusted as a process. It is to be hoped that judicial enthusiasm for requiring reluctant parties and lawyers to engage in ADR will be limited to behaviour before and outside the mediation process itself.

7   Future possible trends

Accounts have circulated about cases where the parties declined to try ADR and the judge indicated that, while a trial would be made available, there would be no order as to costs whoever won, and also about cases where judges have tried to investigate why

ADR failed and to apportion blame by looking behind the confidentiality curtain. Doubtless such hard cases will emerge and receive proper scrutiny. The only firm thing that can be said at present is that judicial ingenuity is considerable, as are the ideas submitted to judges by advocates.

There are bound to be new developments in the ways in which courts think it appropriate to generate pressure on parties to use ADR. The introduction of art 6 of the European Convention on Human Rights with its guarantee of a 'fair and public hearing within a reasonable time by an independent and impartial tribunal established by law' might put some fetter on mandatory referral, for instance. But it must be remembered that ADR does not exclude the court's jurisdiction. Parties are free *not* to settle within ADR and to move back into the litigation process. As we have seen, ADR and litigation are in effect alternative to each other. It would be surprising indeed if the human rights legislation was used to make settlement of litigation more difficult, in effect compelling litigants to incur the expense of trial. The full implications of the CPR have by no means yet emerged.

There is a brief discussion of the effect of the human rights legislation and its impact on ADR in Chapter 5, section **5.6**.

4.3.8 The specialist jurisdictions and court guides

One of the criticisms of the CPR has been that it is not the sole source of procedural wisdom for court users. Several specialist jurisdictions have published their own guides, sometimes establishing procedures quite different from the mainstream provisions of the CPR, the Commercial Court Guide being the prime example. This disapplies CPR Part 26.4 (which provides for a stay of proceedings while settlement by ADR or otherwise is explored), but reproduces and extends much of what was in the Commercial Court Practice Direction about ADR. Adjournment for ADR is preserved; the Commercial Court judges will in appropriate cases invite the parties to consider ADR and may make orders to encourage its deployment, setting out a draft order. Paragraph G1.4 provides that:

> 'Legal representatives should in all cases consider with their clients and the other parties concerned the possibility of attempting to resolve the dispute or particular issues by ADR.'

Similar provisions are to be found in Chapter 17 of the Chancery Guide and in the Guides from the Technology & Construction Court and Mercantile Courts. Even in CPR Part 49 there is found clear reference within the case management procedures of each of these specialist jurisdictions to the consideration of ADR.

4.3.9 Choices in litigation and ADR: which is truly alternative?

Translated into the ADR field, all these issues have important implications. The choice of methods to resolve a dispute is extensive – through the spectrum from direct negotiations to arbitration and litigation at the other end. A careful decision has to be made whether all proper avenues have been explored before issuing proceedings. Should negotiations be tried first? Should both claimant and defendant make a Part 36 offer first? Even if Part 36 offers have been tried and failed to produce a settlement, is it not right to try ADR then, before proceedings are started? Is it negligent, or at least risky, *not* to do so, bearing in mind the court's likely approach to costs? Certainly some more sophisticated parties are writing letters to opponents indicating willingness to mediate a case before issue if all other ways of settling have failed to produce a settlement, indicating that later reference will be made to that letter if the invitation is spurned. We have yet to see whether the court will make an adverse costs order on the basis of such an offer. An indication of their likely attitude is to be found in the 1999 unreported Court of Appeal case of *Dyson & Field v Leeds City Council* discussed at section **7.1.4** below.

Furthermore, the choice is not one to be made solely at the start of the claim and before issue of proceedings. It needs to be continually re-visited and re-made later in the litigation process. For example, when new information comes to light following disclosure of documents or witness evidence, there may be an increased desire either to settle, or, alternatively, to move away from settlement. Each time a choice of tactic has to be made, ADR must be one of the options to be considered. It should therefore be addressed with the client prior to the issue of proceedings and at regular stages during the process of litigation. There is nothing new or 'alternative' about the principle. It is simply an inherent feature of the lawyer–client relationship. What is new is the range of techniques available.

4.4 FUNDING LITIGATION AND ADR

This is a huge and rapidly developing topic, which can only be dealt with in outline because the full implications of what have been fundamental changes are only just emerging.

4.4.1 Public funding

As part of the review of civil justice, the Lord Chancellor has entirely reviewed the Legal Aid Scheme, introducing a whole new terminology and a fresh approach to funding itself. Gone is the term Legal Aid itself, to be replaced by LSC (short for the Legal Services Commission) funding, and gone too is the concept that public funds can be applied to finance only mainstream court litigation.

Any doubts as to whether solicitor's time in preparing for and attending a mediation on behalf of a legally aided person was allowable had already been finally removed by the *Wilkinson* decision of the Legal Aid Board's Costs and Appeals Committee in October 1998. The mediator's fees too were found to be payable as a disbursement. This enabled the Legal Aid Board and its 1999 Act successor, the Legal Services Commission (LSC) to begin the process of thinking how it would exercise its considerable regulatory powers over those it funds, so as to obtain the benefit of costs savings perceived to be available through ADR.

The answer emerged in the draft and final form of the Funding Code, the key source document to the Legal Services Commission's approach to public funding of civil litigation. The full details are outside the scope of this book, but a number of very important principles have been established relating to ADR.

1 Public funding of ADR

The Access to Justice Act 1999, s 4(4) sets out the LSC's intention to achieve swift and final resolution of disputes without any unnecessary or unduly protracted court proceedings, thus confirming and extending the application of the *Wilkinson* decision. Funding will therefore be made available for ADR, and particularly mediation, of non-family civil claims, with mediation fees and expenses being payable as disbursements, and lawyer's fees for preparation and attendance being allowable as ordinary preparation costs.

Funds may be provided for:

- *ombudsman* applications;

- *arbitration* if both sides agree, and it looks likely to be effective, though with no funding for representation at any hearing;

- *early neutral evaluation;*

- *mediation.*

4.4.1 *ADR and the courts*

Most importantly, the LSC now has power to restrict a certificate to cover participation in mediation only, though this will normally be triggered only by an opponent who reports that an LSC funded party has declined mediation in a suitable case.

2 Excluded services

Many areas of work where Legal Aid was formerly available are no longer eligible for LSC funding. The most important ones are personal injury (though it is still available for clinical negligence), boundary disputes, company, partnership and business disputes.

3 Cost benefit analysis

Claims will only receive LSC funding if they meet pre-set criteria for success, taking into account the cost of proceedings with the amount at stake and the chances of winning.

4 Very expensive cases

These will require individual budgetary control from the Special Cases Unit of the LSC, which may also pay and supervise funds for Litigation Support. This latter funding method is one of the few instances where personal injury claims of a particularly complex nature may receive public money to complement private or conditional fee funding for the core of the case. It will probably be in such heavier cases that ADR may become involved.

5 Continuing features of public funding

A number of familiar features remain the same, and may possibly arise in discussion during mediations, such as the statutory charge, by which the LSC Fund is entitled to recoup any shortfall in costs from any property recovered or preserved by or for the LSC funded party. Similarly, the rules relating to costs protection for a LSC funded party and the restrictions on obtaining an order against the LSC Fund continue much as before, with minor modifications. A defendant who successfully defends proceedings brought by an LSC funded party will still be highly unlikely to obtain an enforceable costs order.

It still remains open to an opposing party to offer to pay the LSC funded party's share of the costs and expenses arising out of a mediation as well as their own. This again points to the perceived value among some insurers and other commercial organisations of the mediation process.

4.4.2   Conditional fee agreements

As a replacement for public funding for the bulk of personal injury claims, and indeed as a means of funding virtually any claim for money, conditional fees are now permitted by law. They represent an exception to the rule which still prevails, namely that contingency fees are not lawful in contentious business in England & Wales. In effect the legal profession is now financing its work in progress in such claims itself and undertaking the risk of not being paid any costs if a case is not won. As the price for taking that risk, they are entitled to claim a success fee which amounts to a mark-up of up to 100% of their profit costs on a claim. This has normally been subject to a cap equivalent to 25% of the damages.

Until the Access to Justice Act 1999 and subordinate legislation came into effect in 2000, the success fee had to be borne by claimants out of their damages. But the new legislation has now provided that both success fees and the premium payable for any costs protection policy taken out by a claimant to cover liability for the defendant's costs if the case was lost are recoverable from the defendant (usually, therefore, the insurer backing the defendant).

The success fee represents a handsome premium for lawyers who get their risk assessment right, and who can defend the level of success fee sought against insurers keen to minimise what they have to pay. The collapse of the tobacco litigation in England, which was funded on a conditional fee basis, serves as a reminder that lawyers do not always get it right, and real losses can be sustained.

Although conditional fees have been permitted since 1995, it is still too early to predict all the consequences which will flow from this radical reform to litigation funding. Under old-style (pre-2000) CFAs, there is still likely to be a tension between claimant and lawyer over how much the claimant is actually going to recover from the damages agreed at mediation. The prospect of mediating between client and lawyer still looms in such cases, of which there must be many still to be resolved. Now that success fees and costs protection insurance premiums may be claimed from the defendant insurer, the focus of dispute shifts with it. There may be arguments over reasonableness of such fees and premiums for both parties and mediator to confront at the very end of an otherwise settled claim.

Other tensions will emerge in future mediations. A claimant's solicitor may be keen to settle a doubtful case at a discounted figure so as to make certain of 'success' and his marked-up fee, while the client may still want to take a chance on litigation. A weak case settled cheaply might justify a higher success fee and higher premium, whereas a case with little risk will certainly be argued by insurers only to justify a low mark-up and low premium. This will almost certainly provoke debate between parties if costs are dealt with at the end of mediation.

It also remains to be seen what role the insurers who back CFAs and 'no win–no fee' litigation will do about mediation. Before the event insurance – often sold as a bolt-on to household and motor policies – will have to be tried first, according to the rules. They often have a policy limit and may well want the insured claimant to try mediation early to avoid the embarrassment of refusing continuing policy cover because the indemnity limit has been reached. After the event insurers, who broadly take a premium to cover the claimant's liability for costs if an adverse costs order is made on failing to win, may have other commercial interests which are still hard to predict. Achieving certainty early is probably going to be their business aim. With litigation costs outcomes even more hard to predict than before the CPR, this is not an easy market in which to write business.

4.5 PILOT SCHEMES AND ADR RESEARCH

In parallel with the reforms in civil procedure, efforts have been made to investigate the effectiveness of ADR through a number of pilot schemes, two of which involved associated academic research to appraise effectiveness in a number of ways. We look very briefly at three of these schemes, though we recommend study of the published reports for detailed understanding of the findings.

4.5.1 The Central London County Court scheme

The Central London County Court is the premier County Court trial centre for civil cases for London, and can take cases from anywhere in the country, including transfers of High Court cases.

In 1996, the judges agreed to set up a pilot scheme which offered voluntary mediation in any defended case in the court involving claims of over £3,000. The scheme was appraised by Professor Hazel Genn over two years. Her report was published by the Lord Chancellor's Department in July 1998 (Research Paper 5/98, available free from the LCD). The scheme has continued with increased take-up and apparent benefit.

The model used was time-limited (three-hour) mediations at the court between 4.30 and 7.30pm. During the pilot period, take-up was low, but the report's findings indicated that mediation provided a satisfying way of settling disputes, reducing conflict and cost where it succeeded, with positive feedback from both parties and lawyers. Professor Genn's report addresses these issues in detail, but perhaps most tellingly she identified the need to:

'. . . focus on the value that mediation adds to normal settlement nego- tiations between solicitors, rather than simply setting up mediation in opposition to trial. The experience of the profession is that most cases are not, in the end, tried. Mediation *can* add value to the normal claims settlement process in civil disputes. It offers a cathartic pseudo "day in court" to parties; it gets cards on the table and all the parties around the table; and, with the help of a skilled mediator, it introduces some authoritative objectivity into the assessment of the strengths and weaknesses of the parties' claims.'

The scheme has outlasted its pilot period and remains in place. It is being used as a model for other schemes regionally.

4.5.2 The NHS pilot scheme and research report

In April 1995, a little before the Central London pilot scheme began, the National Health Service Executive initiated a pilot scheme to assess mediation as a tool for dealing with clinical negligence claims. Such claims are highly technical, usually funded on both sides out of the public purse, and have a relatively low success rate for claimants. Yet by 1995 there was a burgeoning interest in claiming against health professionals which has shown little sign of waning ever since.

This was a highly imaginative step, as there was virtually no track record for mediation of clinical negligence in the UK at the time that the pilot was set up. The investigation went in parallel with the implementation of new complaints procedures following the Wilson report. These were introduced in 1996, in the hope that they would provide the 'soft' remedies of apology, explanation, reassurance and so on, often regarded as fundamentally important to dissatisfied patients, though excluding consideration of monetary compensation, which was left to the litigation process.

Again, take-up of the offer of almost free mediation in the two Health Regions covered was very low, for reasons explained in Linda Mulcahy's report on the pilot *Mediating medical negligence claims: an option for the future?* (published by the Stationery Office in January 2000, though completed in late 1998). Yet the findings on those cases investigated were very positive. High levels of satisfaction were found among both parties and lawyers, as contrasted with high levels (about 70%) of considerable dissatisfaction among parties with traditional litigation, even where they had obtained compensation. The report concluded that:

> '... there are considerable benefits to mediated settlement and that plaintiffs [sic] in particular have much to gain ... It clearly has the potential to encourage more appropriate and effective resolution of disputes.'

4.5.3 The Court of Appeal mediation scheme

Perhaps the most surprising scheme to be tried has been the Court of Appeal scheme established in 1997. How can ADR really assist in cases where a judicial decision has already been made, which now is sought to be reviewed on technical grounds by a higher court? The simple answer is that many appeals are subject to compromise already.

By April 2000, nearly 40 cases had been through the scheme, with a settlement rate of about 45%, perhaps not surprisingly lower than settlement rates of cases before trial at first instance. A further 13% settled before the appeal was heard. Again there were clear signs of success. Unfortunately the scheme is poorly funded. Mediators act without fee and there were clear benefits for the scheme during the period when an administrator's salary was found. The scheme continues and ways may be found to enhance it.

CONTENTS

Chapter 5

ADR and its legal foundations

The legal status of mediation essentially derives from the mediation contract itself, but the contractual terms have begun to develop additional support from such legal principles as public policy. The courts have begun to make rulings which reflect public support for ADR processes in providing cost-effective and satisfying ways of settling disputes and minimising litigation. In the atmosphere engendered by the CPR, such judicial support can only be expected to strengthen. In this chapter we explore some of the legal concepts which are fundamental to ADR.

The CEDR standard form mediation agreement and the Model Mediation Procedure are found at Appendix A.

5.1 'WITHOUT PREJUDICE' STATUS

Paragraph 17 of CEDR's Model Mediation Procedure, incorporated into CEDR's standard form mediation agreement by Clause 7 states that:

> 'All information (whether oral or in the form of documents, tapes, computer discs etc) arising out of or in connection with the mediation will be without prejudice, privileged and not admissible in any current or subsequent litigation or other proceedings whatsoever. This does not apply to any information which would in any event have been disclosable in any such proceedings.'

Such a term will always be found in one form or another in mediation agreements. This is critical to the success of any mediation. It is an environment in which arguments, exploration of possible outcomes and firm offers (even if ultimately rejected) need to be aired with complete freedom, and clearly that will only take place on a 'without prejudice' basis. The contractual provision probably serves simply to restate the common law relating to settlement discussions. As the House of Lords made clear in *Rush & Tomkins v Greater London Council* [1988] 3 All ER 737, genuine negotiations with a view to settlement are protected from disclosure in any subsequent proceedings whether or not the 'without prejudice ' label has been expressly applied. This must be true of admissions and offers made at mediations.

Reinforcement to the status of 'without prejudice' negotiations in mediation was given in the case of *Instance v Denny Bros Printing* Times, 28 February 2000 in which protection afforded to communications made in a mediation which did not settle an earlier dispute was held to extend to later litigation connected with the same subject-matter. This case followed the Court of Appeal's review of the modern law relating to 'without prejudice' discussions in *Unilever plc v Procter & Gamble* Times, 4 November 1999, [2000] FSR 344, where a claim was struck out because it was based largely on communications made during without prejudice negotiations. The Court of Appeal founded its decision both on public policy considerations and also on express or implied agreement between the parties that such communications would not be admissible in any later litigation. Robert Walker LJ also emphasised that the court would not engage in a detailed analysis of what precisely constituted an admission or offer, as opposed to statements of a lesser or different kind which might arguably not have 'without prejudice' status accorded to them on a purist analysis. The need for free and wide-ranging settlement discussions which cannot be brought later into the litigation arena was clearly identified and supported.

It is worth remembering, however, that the 'without prejudice' rule will not sterilise or protect an admission of fact or a document which can be proved other than by reliance on that admission. This came to light in the Australian case of *AWA Ltd v Daniels* (24 February 1992, unreported) in the Commercial Division of the Supreme Court of New South Wales. During the course of a mediation, Party A disclosed the existence, expressly on a 'without prejudice' basis to Party B, of a certain document. The case was not settled in mediation and subsequently Party B made an interim application for an order forcing Party A to disclose a copy of the document, which was said to be germane to the case. Party A responded that, in making the application, Party B was relying on a 'without prejudice' admission as to the existence of the document made to it, which it was not entitled to do. Rogers CJ (now a respected mediator) heard the application and ordered disclosure of the document on the ground that the document itself was within the scope of the discovery process. The applicant was therefore not seeking to rely on the 'without prejudice' admission as a basis for requesting the document, but on the fact that it ought properly to be disclosed on discovery.

5.2 CONFIDENTIALITY

The issue of confidentiality goes beyond 'without prejudice' status, which is essentially a rule of evidence protecting admissions in settlement negotiations from being allowed in as evidence. A contractually binding confidentiality clause creates a specific duty as between signatories, breach of which gives rise to a potential claim for both damages and an injunction.

Clause 7 of the CEDR Mediation Agreement provides that:

'... the person signing this agreement on behalf of each party is deemed to be agreeing to the confidentiality provisions of the Model Procedure (paragraphs 16-19) on behalf of the Party he/she represents and all other persons present on that party's behalf at the mediation.'

Paragraph 17 of the CEDR Model Procedure is set out in the previous section, but para 16 reads:

'Every person involved in the mediation will keep confidential and not use for any collateral or ulterior purpose:

● the fact that the mediation is to take place or has taken place, other than to inform a court dealing with any litigation relating to the dispute of that fact; and

● all information (whether given orally, in writing or otherwise) arising out of, or in connection with, the mediation, including the fact of any settlement and its terms.'

Paragraph 18 makes a saving for information in so far as implementation and enforcement of the settlement agreement is concerned, and paragraph 19 deals with mediator immunity from giving evidence, which is looked at in more detail in section **5.3** below. The full text is to be found in Appendix A.

The confidentiality of a mediation is vital to its success. Many parties do not want their dispute aired in public, particularly where confidential commercial information is involved. Even the mere existence of a dispute can compromise some parties.

The confidentiality aspect operates on two levels. First, the mediation should be confidential as between the participants, preventing third party knowledge of the dispute, the attempt to settle it, and to all matters disclosed in the mediation. In this sense, other executives of a company which was a party to a mediation, or other partners of a firm would not be 'third parties'. Clearly, this provision will not prevent internal reporting of outcomes. Similarly, and by implication, a party must be free to take confidential legal advice on an outcome or a failure to achieve an outcome. The confidentiality of the lawyer–client relationship makes this possible. However, if a party authorised their solicitor (or a fellow employee or partner) to publicise a fact in breach of the terms of the confidentiality agreement, that party would undoubtedly be vulnerable to proceedings for breach of the agreement.

Secondly, matters discussed between one party and the mediator in private sessions or caucuses (see Chapter 11) should be confidential between them, and may not be disclosed to any other party without express consent. It is this feature, perhaps more than any other, which generates a frank and open discussion, in private, between the mediator and each party, and enables progress to be made towards settlement.

This extra layer of confidentiality, deeper than mere 'without prejudice' protection, might potentially create problems over a misrepresentation made within a mediation upon which any settlement agreement was based. The agreement itself is of course enforceable, and the court has always been prepared to look even at an agreement specifically expressed to be 'without prejudice' for the purposes of enforcement – see *Tomlin v Standard Telephones & Cables* [1969] 3 All ER 201, CA. The safest course, therefore, is to ensure that any material fact which leads to the settlement agreement should be incorporated as a term. If it proves to be untrue, a remedy for breach of that term of the settlement contract will arise. There would thus be no need to have an argument over whether a material misrepresentation conveyed unwittingly by the mediator from one party in private session to the other which induced the recipient to enter the settlement agreement is admissible in evidence.

In *Re D (Minors)* [1993] 2 WLR 721 the Court of Appeal found that statements made to a conciliator could not be introduced by one of the parties as evidence in proceedings under the Children Act 1989 other than in exceptional circumstances, such as where the statement indicates that the maker has in the past caused or is likely in the future to cause serious harm to the wellbeing of the child. Although the case dealt with children and was specifically stated to be limited to its particular facts, there are one or two very telling points in the judgment of Sir Thomas Bingham, then Master of the Rolls. First, he talked of the law as:

'... recognising the general inviolability of the privilege protecting statements made in the course of conciliation.'

More specifically, he was clear that the reason for the protection afforded to such statements is an independent head of privilege which has grown beyond the 'without prejudice' rule and is therefore not subject to the same exceptions. Thus privilege does not attach to a document described as such if it does not contain truly 'without prejudice' material, such as a genuine offer to settle, and he did not question that point. However, he continued:

'But we do not accept that evidence can be given of statements made by one party at a meeting admittedly held for the purposes of conciliation because, in the judgment of the other party or the conciliator, that party has shown no genuine willingness to compromise.'

Re D was of course a case involving suitability of a parent to have contact with children. But we expect that a similar response might be given by a court invited to hear evidence that a party was intransigent and had no genuine willingness to settle within the confidential confines of a commercial mediation.

Several cases abroad have upheld the confidentiality of what passed within a mediation. In *X v Y*, a decision of the Tribunal de Commerce in Brussels in 1999, the confidentiality clause in a CEDR mediation agreement was held to prevent a party from including mention of a mediation in subsequent proceedings. The Tribunal ordered the reference to be struck out and imposed stiff penalties for breach.

As might be expected perhaps, two decisions of the US courts illustrate their determination to penalise breach of mediation confidentiality. In *Parazino v Barnett Bank*, a 1997 Florida appeal case, the claimant who revealed to a newspaper that the bank had made an offer at a mediation which she had refused, hinting that this showed a degree of acceptance of her case, had her entire claim for $100,000 struck out 'with prejudice'. In *Bernard v Galen Group*, a New York appeal case, claimant's counsel, who had always opposed a court-directed mediation which failed, applied to the judge to end the mediation, quoting what had happened at the mediation (as he saw it) as evidence of the defendants' having not engaged seriously in the process. The defendant moved for sanctions, and the court imposed a $2,500 fine (payable personally) on the lawyer.

5.3 MEDIATOR IMMUNITY

Paragraph 19 of the CEDR Model Mediation Procedure reads:

> 'None of the parties to the mediation agreement will call the mediator or CEDR (or any employee, consultant, officer or representative of CEDR) as a witness, consultant, arbitrator or expert in any litigation or other proceedings whatsoever. The mediator will not voluntarily act in any such capacity without the written agreement of all the parties.'

The agreement should provide that the mediator will not be called as a witness by either party in any hearing pertaining to the dispute and that his notes are not disclosable by either party. Again this is vital in generating a level of trust between the parties and the mediator which will permit frank, private discussion. Some mediators, such as those operating on behalf of ACAS, are granted statutory immunity. That is not yet available for commercial mediators in the UK and the issue therefore has to be dealt with by contract.

Re D involved one party to the litigation seeking to adduce statements made to a conciliator, but not attempting to call the conciliator as a witness. In an unreported case in the Bristol County Court in 1997, *Bezant v Ushers Brewers*, District Judge Gillian Stuart Brown refused to hear evidence from a mediator who had been subpoenaed to give evidence about what had happened at a mediation, and upheld the binding force of the agreement negotiated at the mediation.

5.4 MEDIATOR COMPELLABILITY OVER DISCLOSURE OF UNLAWFUL CONDUCT

An ethical and legal topic which falls between the issues of confidentiality and mediator immunity potentially arises over whether a mediator can be compelled to give evidence in a civil or criminal trial about admissions made by a party during private meetings. What for instance if the mediator is told of matters relating to money-laundering or breach of national security or threats of future violence? This is an area in which it is difficult to make emphatic statements because of the dearth of experience of such problems in reality.

The issue is at heart one of the compellability of witnesses. The only absolute category of a contractually created immunity from giving evidence (also buttressed by common law and indeed public policy) is that of solicitor and client, where the privilege is the client's and not the lawyer's. The relationship of doctor or therapist with a patient is not ultimately sacrosanct, nor that of priest and penitent. The compellability of a spouse has been increased by the Police and Criminal Evidence Act 1984, and that of a journalist regarding a source reduced only to some extent by the Contempt of Court Act 1981, s 10. While the court has a discretion to respect disclosures made within confidential relationships and to excuse a witness from answering questions about them, this is bound to depend upon the importance of the answers to the issues being tried in the case in question. As Lord Wilberforce said in the House of Lords in *British Steel Corpn v Granada Television* [1981] 1 All ER 417 at 455, a civil case where a television company was compelled to disclose its confidential source of information to the claimants:

> 'As to information obtained in confidence and the legal duty which may arise to disclose it to a court of justice, the position is clear. Courts have an inherent wish to respect this confidence whether it arises between doctor and patient, priest and penitent, banker and customer, between persons giving testimonials to employees, or in other relationships ... But in all these cases the courts may have to decide that the interests in preserving this confidence are outweighed by other interests to which the law attaches importance.'

In civil cases, it is in our view extremely unlikely that any court would seek to extract confidences from a mediator or party about what transpired confidentially in a mediation, since there is a major public interest in making mediation work well in contributing to the settlement of civil disputes. *Re D* illustrates the likely approach that would be taken generally, with its proviso about child protection.

That public interest is of less direct interest to the purposes of the criminal courts. It is just not quite so easy to be dogmatic over whether proof of a serious crime like conspiracy to murder or breach of the Official Secrets Acts might not take priority over protecting mediator confidentiality. A mediator will have to exercise careful judgment over whether disclosure of such matters to the mediator justifies withdrawal from the mediation or even abrogation of the confidentiality provision of the mediation agreement. It may be wise for a mediator to decline to receive confidences of this kind, or to make it clear that immunity from being compelled to give evidence may not exist to protect such disclosures if made.

5.5 AUTHORITY TO SETTLE

Clause 3 of the CEDR Mediation Agreement identifies the lead negotiator by name on behalf of each party and provides that:

'Each of the lead negotiators will have full authority to settle on behalf of its party.'

The agreement reduces to the absolute minimum any risk that the person who attends the mediation does not have actual and ostensible authority in law to bind as agent the party represented. It is essential that each party should be represented at the mediation by someone with full authority to settle the dispute. Making this an express term of the mediation agreement helps to emphasise the importance of this principle to those representing each party.

Possessing authority does not of course mean that a settlement will be agreed. This may be because of a disagreement in good faith over an acceptable outcome. Sometimes, however, for a variety of reasons, a party may send a negotiator with limited or fettered authority, who is not authorised to deal at the level proposed, however much that level looks sensible. A company might send a manager or director; a partnership one or more partners. Either might send simply a lawyer, whether in-house or external, with a degree of authority to settle. The authority may extend up or down to a certain financial limit, or may require the representative to discuss the matter with others before concluding a settlement. This situation is by no means ideal. If a deal is struck after 12 hours of mediation, and final agreement is subject to a phone call to someone who has not been present, the latter may object to some proposals. Not having been present to hear all the debate and watch the deal slowly emerge, the absentee is not well placed to judge its terms properly from within the context of the mediation. If, however, this situation is genuinely unavoidable, then the parties and the mediator will simply have to work within that constraint.

Four further situations relating to authority to settle are worth bearing in mind.

5.5.1   Insured parties

Where the liability of one or more parties is to any extent covered by insurance, the insurer's consent will be required to any settlement, perhaps depending on the level of self-insurance or excess on the policy. If insurers carry the whole or the majority of the risk themselves, they will attend the mediation and control it as they would any litigation, having been subrogated to the rights of their insured. This is obviously the optimum solution. If the insurers are unable or unwilling to attend, the lines of settlement authority should be clearly set up in advance, but this is less than ideal.

If there is a dispute between insurer and party as to indemnity, the insurer ought to attend the mediation as an additional party, enabling the subsidiary dispute between insured and insurer to be settled at the same time. At least the presence of the insurer will allow the insured to settle the main dispute with the insurer's authority, leaving the indemnity problem between them to be sorted out later. In whichever capacity they attend, they should be bound into the other contractual provisions relating to 'without prejudice' status, confidentiality and mediator immunity.

5.5.2   Groups of companies and partnerships

Where a party is one of a group of companies, care should be taken to ensure that authority to settle is present on behalf of all those companies in the group who are likely to be involved in the settlement. This may well be a wider group than those who are party to the dispute. The same principle applies to appropriate channels of authority and consent in respect of a partnership. Again, with both companies and partnerships it is unlikely that the whole main board or all the partners will attend, giving rise to the need for care to be taken over authority to settle.

5.5.3   Public bodies

Complications may well arise with public bodies. Given the decision-making structures of national or local government, it is unlikely that any individuals will be able to attend a mediation with completely unfettered authority to settle. More likely, those who attend will be authorised to agree settlement terms subject to obtaining final approval from the appropriate committee, typically a finance committee. Although not ideal, for the reasons given above, mediation can and does still operate effectively in these circumstances. It may be helpful, however, to obtain a commitment in advance that the appropriate committee will meet within a specified and short period following the mediation, so that the matter is not left unresolved for too long. Additionally, the mediator may even be asked to attend that meeting to assist in explaining (and if necessary justifying) the settlement terms.

5.5.4 Parties under legal incapacity

It is clearly impossible for a binding agreement to be made at a mediation which affects the rights of a party to a dispute who does not possess legal capacity to contract. This may well arise in mediations relating to personal injury and clinical negligence claims, where there may be claimants who are infants or who have suffered serious brain damage. This is not to say that such cases cannot be effectively dealt with by mediation. Terms that are agreeable are worked out and agreed conditional upon court approval. Application is then made to the court for approval by the judge.

For this reason, as we suggest in Chapter 9, it is wise to have counsel, who is to advise for this purpose on any settlement, actually present at the mediation, so as to take a full part in the debate which leads to the terms to be referred to the court. Counsel can then give due explanation to the judge from direct knowledge over any appreciable discount for litigation risk.

5.6 EFFECT OF THE EUROPEAN CONVENTION ON HUMAN RIGHTS ON ADR

The European Convention on Human Rights (the ECHR) entered into domestic jurisdiction as from 2 October 2000 as a result of the Human Rights Act 1998. In Scotland, implementation into domestic legislation occurred in May 1999 as part of the devolution process.

Article 6(1) of the ECHR provides in essence as follows:

'In the determination of his civil rights and obligations . . . everyone is entitled to a fair and public hearing within a reasonable time by an independent and impartial tribunal established by law.'

There has been some debate about whether compulsory court referral of claims into ADR or, by analogy, the enforceability of ADR clauses will be affected by this provision of the ECHR as in some way interfering with the citizen's right to a fair trial. The point is put into sharp focus by the position of arbitration. This is distinguishable from non-binding ADR processes like mediation by the fact that it does indeed offer a *binding process* for 'determination' of civil rights and obligations, but in an essentially private hearing before an arbitrator. Could an arbitration be impeached for infringing the art 6(1) requirement for public determination?

The answer is that it is plain that the European Court encourages parties to settle disputes extra-judicially, thus relieving the courts of excessive strains. Submission to arbitration is just one way in which this encouragement is manifested, and other forms of ADR should prove to be another. In the case of arbitration, this is by recognising the right of disputants to waive their rights under the ECHR. It is, however, clear from authority and commentary that the court might consider intervention in a case where there was any undue pressure into a non-judicial process such as arbitration, or no real opportunity for a party truly to agree (or not) to such a term in a contract. Such waiver was expressly approved by the European Court in the case of *Deweer v Belgium* (1980), a case involving a quasi-criminal administrative intervention in a butchery business. In that case, though, M. Deweer was held not to have waived his right to go to court by paying a penalty sum in composition of his liability (a form of settlement). There was a degree of constraint imposed in inviting him into composition rather than facing a criminal proceeding.

So far as *non-binding* ADR is concerned, it is difficult to see how this could be regarded as anything approaching a 'determination'. By definition a decision is not made in the process by the neutral; the parties alone decide whether to settle. They remain at all times entirely free to withdraw from the process and return to the path which leads to actual determination of their civil rights and obligations by the independent and impartial tribunal established by law, namely the relevant court.

Indeed, Clause 10 of the CEDR Mediation Agreement specifically states:

> 'The referral of the dispute to mediation does not affect any rights that may exist under Article 6 of the European Convention on Human Rights. If the dispute is not settled by the mediation, the Parties' rights to a fair trial remain unaffected.'

The only possible argument to the contrary might be that, particularly if a stay is ordered in the litigation, mediation might be regarded as hindering a public hearing 'within a reasonable time'. However, a stay is not a necessary component of a court-referred mediation, and even if a stay were granted, it is highly unlikely that the kind of delay that this would create would be regarded in the general scheme of litigation progress as an infringement of such a right. The cases decided by the European Court so far deal in much longer delays than is likely to be generated by a referral to ADR, particularly mediation, which often takes no more than four weeks from initial referral to outcome.

CONTENTS

Chapter 6

Contracting in advance to use ADR

We discuss the role of the non-contentious lawyer in some detail in Chapter 15. This chapter is of particular relevance to them in terms of the options available to both in-house and external lawyers in providing in advance in contract terms and conditions that ADR is to be used as the primary means of resolving any disputes which may arise in the future.

This is an area which is not free from legal controversy, and the experience of other common law jurisdictions more advanced in ADR than the UK suggests that we can expect the law to develop and change over future years. For this reason, we look in some detail at a parallel jurisdiction, namely Australia, in considering some of the arguments deployed in the debate over whether such agreements are enforceable.

6.1   WHAT IS AN ADR CONTRACT CLAUSE?

An ADR contract clause is a clause in an agreement by which the contracting parties agree to attempt to resolve any disputes between them by the use of one or more ADR processes. It may be a very simple, short clause, or alternatively set out a lengthy and complex process. It may specify a particular ADR procedure, such as mediation; or leave the parties to agree on one as and when a particular dispute arises. Where it contemplates the use of a *non-binding* ADR procedure, such as mediation, mini-trial, judicial or expert determination, it can clearly only require the parties to *attempt* resolution. A clause containing a *binding* ADR procedure, such as expert determination or adjudication can oblige the parties to abide by any award which results from it. Arbitration clauses, which we do not consider in their pure form here, were the earliest form of clause of this type which in effect sought to exclude or at least delay the involvement of the courts in determining a dispute.

6.2 WHAT DO ADR CLAUSES AIM TO ACHIEVE?

The whole thrust of ADR tends towards a non-binding, 'without prejudice' approach, designed to provide an opportunity for the dispute to be discussed, and resolution explored, in a relatively risk-free and confidential environment. The use of a contract clause to *compel* parties to take part in, for example, mediation might therefore be regarded as contrary to the essential philosophy of ADR. After all, if the parties are only attending a mediation because they are contractually obliged to do so, it may be difficult to achieve settlement. Mediation presupposes some degree of willingness on the part of both or all parties at least to explore the various settlement options and to listen to the other side's arguments, whatever view is eventually taken. This may be absent among parties compelled to attempt ADR. Similar arguments arise in the debate over whether the courts should compel disputing parties into ADR by order.

However, the primary value of an ADR clause lies not in its element of compulsion, but in the fact that it puts ADR on the agenda. It is a reminder to the parties that, when they signed the agreement, ADR was viewed as a sensible step to take in the event of a dispute arising. It may even helpfully remind them that there was a time when relations between them were better! Most importantly, it overcomes any reluctance to suggest ADR when a dispute arises, for fear that such a suggestion may be viewed as an indication of weakness. ADR can be discussed and attempted merely because it is in the contract. It is difficult to overstate the importance of such clauses in enabling parties to set up an ADR procedure. There has been a widespread assumption that the suggestion by one party of a willingness to use ADR will be perceived by the other(s) as a sign of weakness. Whatever the truth of this since the CPR were introduced, such a fear acts as a significant barrier to many disputes reaching mediation (or other ADR processes). ADR contract clauses constitute by far the most effective way of circumventing this fear. The existence of the clause provides ample justification for mediation to be suggested, discussed and entered upon freely and voluntarily and on an equal basis without any assumptions about relative strength of each party's position. If ADR is not felt suitable, the parties can always agree to waive the requirement. Indeed, since many ADR clauses may not be enforceable as a matter of law (see section **12.4** below), either party can often unilaterally avoid the obligation in any event.

In fact, the inclusion of ADR clauses in contracts is a vital element of good dispute systems design and management. It is an attempt to pre-empt future disputes by putting in place the appropriate resolution structure while the parties are still on good terms. At the very least, it provides yet another argument to deploy before the court in inviting the judge to refer a case to ADR, because the resistant party already signed up to its use before the dispute began.

For this reason it is important to note that consideration of ADR begins at the contractual, non-contentious stage. Those involved in drafting and preparing contract documentation need to be as informed and aware of the various ADR possibilities as those who will eventually handle the resulting disputes. Creative design and mobilisation of contractual dispute systems ought to be considered the responsibility of non-contentious lawyers and contracts managers.

6.3 TYPES OF ADR CLAUSE

There is a wide variety of types of ADR clause, some examples of which are set out in Appendix B. Although the precise wording of the clause may seem to matter less if it is unenforceable, the clause should nevertheless be the subject of considerable thought. If the parties do choose to implement it when the dispute arises, it will need to meet the demands of their situation effectively. The nature of the agreement in which the clause appears may well have a bearing on the choice and drafting of the clause. For example, a partnership agreement would suggest the use of a very flexible, facilitative process such as mediation, whereas a highly technical engineering contract might call for an expert determination, adjudication, or early neutral evaluation.

6.4 CONSIDERATIONS

There are a number of considerations to bear in mind.

6.4.1 Length and detail

Essentially, the clause merely needs to stipulate that in the event of a dispute arising, the parties will attempt to resolve it by ADR. A very short form of clause can accomplish that with ease (see

6.4.1 *Contracting in advance to use ADR*

Appendix B). However, such a clause may beg as many questions as it answers, such as which ADR process will be used, who will the neutral be, is the ADR process a condition precedent to litigation or arbitration, what (if any) should the timetable be for carrying out the ADR process, and so on.

Surprisingly, this may in fact be of benefit. It leaves the details of the process open for the parties to decide at the time the dispute arises. The most appropriate type of ADR process might only become clear at that time, and the parties would not want to be restricted by reference to an earlier stipulation. Furthermore, some contracting parties might find it distasteful to draft too detailed a disputes clause at a time when no dispute exists between them. On the other hand, leaving the parties with a choice when the dispute arises can also present problems. If they are unable, when a dispute does arise, to agree the requisite details, the whole value of the clause may be lost. Furthermore, parties wanting some objective justification for not complying with a clause will find it easy to disagree on the details and hence prevent any progress.

The drafting of each clause should therefore be approached freshly each time, with thought given to the context in which disputes will arise, each party's likely attitude, the results which the clause is intended to achieve, and so on. In fact, the principle that contracting parties should discuss the resolution of any disputes *at the time of contracting* is a sound one, and is more likely to increase rather than diminish the trust between the parties, since the otherwise taboo subject will be brought out into the open. That discussion will serve as a much more solid base for the parties to refer to when the dispute does arise. Ideally, the drafting of ADR clauses should be much more than the reproduction of a standard form ADR clause, and in particular the parties themselves, and not just their advisors, should be drawn into discussion about the optimum dispute resolution structures.

Drafting should also be approached with imagination. There is no reason why each contractual context should not have its own dispute resolution process (see sections **2.4** and **3.6** on dispute systems design above). Parties will become increasingly aware of the approaches that prove most effective for them through a process of trial and experience.

6.4.2 Content

In terms of the detailed contents to be included in an ADR clause, the following points at least should be considered:

- Will the clause refer to an ADR process to be agreed, or stipulate a particular one (eg mediation)?

- Is there to be a timetable for compliance with the clause or with procedural stages within the clause (eg appointment of a mediator, exchange of case summaries etc)?

- Is the ADR process intended to be a condition precedent to the commencement of litigation or arbitration proceedings, or not? (See section **6.5** below for the implications of this.)

- Is the identity or discipline of the neutral or mediator to be spelled out in advance? If not, what provision should there be for appointment?

- Is an ADR organisation to be used to nominate or appoint a mediator and administer and supervise the process?

- How will any costs of the process be apportioned?

- Is a tiered process to be used, eg direct negotiations, followed (if necessary) by mediation, followed (if necessary) by adjudication, arbitration or litigation?

6.4.3 Tiered or stepped clauses

ADR clauses present an opportunity for the use of a 'tiered structure' within the clause – that is, a series of steps in the overall dispute resolution process, each designed to handle the dispute if it has not been resolved by the previous step. These can be particularly effective. Indeed, this approach has already been widely used in the past, for example in the introduction of a negotiating phase as a prerequisite to the commencement of litigation or arbitration, and the 'engineer's decision' in some construction contracts. ADR techniques allow for this principle to be developed and used in greater detail.

The principal strengths of a tiered structure are:

- The dispute resolution mechanism in use at any particular stage of a dispute will be the one most likely to resolve it. For example, it may be that the issue of proceedings too early in a dispute will drive out certain settlement possibilities which have not been achievable through initial direct negotiations. The introduction of a mediation phase between the negotiation and litigation phases may well provide a process more capable of teasing out a settlement in that particular environment.

● The resolution processes can increase in formality and structure as it becomes clear that the dispute itself requires that. All the benefits of the litigation/arbitration processes remain available to the parties, but the formality and rigidity they bring is delayed until it is considered indispensable.

Some detailed examples of tiered ADR clauses are set out in Appendix B. In terms of drafting, the guiding principle should again be an attempt imaginatively to anticipate likely dispute scenarios, and to match them with relevant methods of resolution.

It is also worth noting that the choice of dispute clause can constitute a powerful form of policy statement to those with whom one deals. The tiered ADR clauses all anticipate mediation being attempted before litigation or arbitration has been commenced, but not thereafter. This reflects the policy approach not to commence litigation until other avenues have been exhausted, but equally not to use any ADR processes once proceedings have been commenced. Those advising government departments or their contractors clearly need to be aware of this approach.

6.5 ENFORCEABILITY

We suggested earlier that the primary value of an ADR clause does not necessary lie in its enforceability as a matter of law, but rather in its role as a pretext for discussion of possible ADR solutions. Indeed, even before addressing the legal position on the enforceability of such clauses, there is considerable debate on whether it is appropriate or even desirable for ADR clauses to be enforceable and enforced. The arguments were neatly summarised by Giles J in the Australian case of *Hooper Bailie Associated Ltd v Natcon Group Pty Ltd* (unreported, 12 April 1992 at pp 24–25):

'Conciliation or mediation is essentially consensual, and the opponents of enforceability contend that it is futile to seek to enforce something which requires the consent of a party when co-operation and consent cannot be enforced; equally they say that there can be no loss to the other party if for want of co-operation and consent the consensual process would have led to no result. The proponents of enforceability contend that this misconceives the objectives of alternative dispute resolution, saying that the most fundamental resistance to compromise can wane and turn to co-operation and consent if the dispute is removed from the adversarial procedures of the Courts and exposed to procedures designed to promote compromise, in particular where a skilled conciliator or mediator is interposed between the parties. What is enforced is not co-operation or consent, but participation in a process from which co-operation and consent might come.'

6.5.1 The position under English law

Two decisions at first instance have now considered the enforceability of ADR clauses in English law: firstly, Judge Hegarty QC sitting as a High Court judge in Liverpool District Registry in *Cott (UK) Ltd v F E Barber Ltd* [1997] 3 All ER 540; and then McKinnon J in *Halifax Financial Services Ltd v Intuitive Systems Ltd* [1999] 1 All ER Comm 303. So far no higher court has directly ruled on such clauses apart from the House of Lords in *Channel Tunnel Group Ltd v Balfour Beatty* [1993] 1 All ER 664, dealing with a very narrow type of expert determination clause. Before we look at these recent cases, it may help to review the legal position from first principles.

1 An agreement to negotiate is unenforceable

Until the decision of the House of Lords in *Walford v Miles* [1992] 1 All ER 453, there was still some doubt about this proposition, stemming from the dictum of Lord Wright in *Hillas & Co v Arcos Ltd* (1932) 38 Com Cases 23. However, the position following *Walford v Miles* is clear, namely that an agreement to negotiate is not enforceable in law. This case followed and endorsed the decision of the Court of Appeal in *Courtney & Fairbairn Ltd v Tolaini Brothers (Hotels) Ltd* [1975] 1 All ER 716. It is worth looking at *Walford v Miles* in some detail.

The case concerned the sale of a photographic processing business, and the central issues were the enforceability of a contract to negotiate and the terms of a 'lock-out' agreement (ie an agreement not to negotiate with any other parties whilst negotiations were continuing with one party). In 1986 the vendors decided to sell the business and received an offer of £1.9 million from a third party. In the meantime new purchasers (the later claimant in this case) had entered into negotiations with the vendors and in March 1987 the vendors agreed in principle to sell the business and premises for £2 million. It was also further agreed in a telephone conversation that if the purchasers provided a comfort letter confirming that their bank had offered them loan facilities, the vendors would 'terminate negotiations with any third party or consideration of any alternative with a view to concluding agreements' with the purchasers, and that even if the vendors received a satisfactory proposal from any third party before that time they would 'not deal with that third party and would not give further consideration to any alternative'.

Subsequently the vendors withdrew from negotiations and decided to sell to a third party. The proposed purchasers brought an action against the vendors for breach of a lock-out agreement under which the proposed purchasers had been given an exclusive opportunity to try to come to terms with the vendors and which was collateral to the 'subject to contract' negotiations which were proceeding for the purchase of the business and the premises. The proposed purchasers alleged that it was a term of the collateral agreement, necessarily to be implied to give business efficacy to it, that so long as the vendors continued to desire to sell the business and the premises, the vendors would continue to negotiate in good faith with the proposed purchasers. It was contended that the consideration for the collateral contract was the proposed purchasers' agreement to continue negotiations.

On appeal, the Court of Appeal held that the alleged collateral agreement was no more than an agreement to negotiate and was therefore unenforceable. On further appeal, the House of Lords held that a lock-out agreement, whereby one party for good consideration agreed for a limited specified time not to negotiate with anyone except the other party in relation to the sale of his property, could constitute an enforceable agreement. This was confirmed by the Court of Appeal in *Pitt v PHH Asset Management* [1993] 4 All ER 961, where Sir Thomas Bingham MR's lead judgment found that a lock-out agreement for a period of two weeks relating to the sale of land was enforceable. However, an agreement to negotiate in good faith for an unspecified period was not enforceable, nor could a term to that effect be implied in a lock-out agreement for an unspecified period, since a vendor was not obliged under such an agreement to conclude a contract with a purchaser and he would not know when he was entitled to withdraw from the negotiations. Furthermore, the court could not be expected to decide whether, subjectively, a proper reason existed for the termination of the negotiations. It followed that the alleged collateral agreement was unenforceable.

Lord Ackner gave the lead judgment in *Walford v Miles*. In it he said (at 459):

'Mr Naughton accepted that as the law now stands and has stood for approaching 20 years an agreement to negotiate is not recognised as an enforceable contract. This was first decided in terms in *Courtney & Fairbairn Limited v Tolaini Brothers* where Lord Denning MR said:

> "If the law does not recognise a contract to enter into a contract (when there is a fundamental term yet to be agreed) it seems to me it cannot recognise a contract to negotiate. The reason is because it is too uncertain to have any binding force . . . It seems to me that a contract to negotiate, like a contract to enter into a contract, is not a contract known to the law . . . I think we must apply the general principle that when there is a fundamental matter left undecided and to the subject of negotiation, there is no contract." '

In the *Courtney* case Lord Denning rejected the dictum of Lord Wright in *Hillas & Co v Arcos Ltd* as not well founded:

> 'There is no bargain except to negotiate, and negotiation may be fruitless and end without any contract ensuing: yet even then, in strict theory, there is a contract (if there is good consideration) to negotiate, though in the event of repudiation by one party the damages may be nominal, unless a jury thinks that the opportunity to negotiate was one of some appreciable value to the injured party.'

Having considered a proposition put forward by Bingham LJ in the Court of Appeal in *Walford v Miles* that there was an obligation upon the vendors not to deal with other parties which should continue to bind them 'for such time as is reasonable', Lord Ackner concluded:

> 'However, as Bingham LJ recognised, such a duty, if it existed, would indirectly impose upon the respondents a duty to negotiate in good faith. Such a duty, for the reasons which I have given above, cannot be imposed. That it should have been thought necessary to assert such a duty helps to explain the reason behind the amendments to paragraph 5 and the insistence of Mr Naughton that without the implied term the agreement, as originally pleaded, was unworkable – unworkable because there was no way of determining for how long the respondents were locked out from negotiating with any third party. Thus, even if, despite the way in which the *Walford* case was pleaded and argued, the severance favoured by Bingham LJ was permissible, the resultant agreement suffered from the same defect (although for different reasons) as the agreement contended for in the amended Statement of Claim, namely that it too lacked the necessary certainty and was thus unenforceable.'

In essence, then, *Walford v Miles* confirmed that a contract to negotiate is unenforceable since a court cannot say with sufficient certainty what the obligations are that it is being asked to enforce, and in any meaningful way monitor or assess compliance.

2 A court can require compliance with certain procedures as a condition precedent to issue of litigation or arbitration proceedings

This general principle was established in the case of *Scott v Avery* (1865) 5 HL Cas 811, 10 ER 1121. Whilst the eventual jurisdiction of the court cannot be ousted, it can nevertheless be validly delayed or stayed, in that the parties can properly impose on themselves, by way of agreement, a series of intervening steps which have to be completed as a condition precedent to either party commencing litigation or arbitration.

This principle translates easily into the ADR arena. Many ADR clauses simply require parties to attempt resolution by an ADR process (see, for instance, the short-form clauses in Appendix B). However, it is equally possible (indeed, increasingly common) for the clause to express compliance with, and exhaustion of, the ADR phase as a condition precedent to the issue of any proceedings, usually with a specifically timed moratorium. Such a clause at least has the effect of introducing a slightly clearer, and therefore more certain, set of steps into the process, which arguably a court might find easier to enforce, though on the clause used in *Halifax Financial Services v Intuitive Systems*, as we shall see, the court did not find that the steps specified were clear, or even whether they had been implemented or breached. Thus, unless drafted with great care, the uncertainty problems raised in *Walford* persist, since the court still has to determine whether compliance with that condition precedent had been achieved, so that proceedings could be validly issued. For example, would a party who attended a mediation but terminated it by leaving after an hour be said to have 'attempted to mediate'?

Whilst it may be difficult to produce a set of criteria or rules by which compliance can be judged in every situation, it is in practice often very clear to the parties whether they have attempted to settle a case through ADR or not. It is, of course, even clearer to the mediator, who is not in a position to confirm or deny compliance after the event, partly because of the contractual commitment to confidentiality and partly because his role during the mediation would be fatally compromised if the parties felt that the mediator could eventually pass judgment on their conduct.

The problem is, of course, exacerbated by a lack of comprehension of what ADR actually involves. Thus, the uncertainty argument is strengthened because it is assumed that ADR procedures are inherently either too unclear or too flexible to be able to require compliance. As ADR use has grown, however, this argument has lost some of its impact, since there is greater familiarity with ADR practice and the processes themselves have become more regularised. Indeed, although mediation is a very flexible and adaptable process, it is already possible to say with some consistency what constitutes, in procedural terms, a 'typical' mediation. It must also follow that the more detailed the ADR process spelt out in an ADR clause, the greater the likelihood of its being enforceable. Thus a simple commitment to attempt an ADR process leaves unresolved too many procedural issues (not least which ADR process will be used). Conversely an agreement to use mediation, under the auspices of a particular ADR organisation, or using a certain individual mediator, where the procedural requirements for the process (eg timetable for submitting case summaries and holding the mediation, who will attend the mediation, etc) are spelt out in detail, must inherently be more capable of enforcement.

It is worth noting, however, that such detail may in fact be counter-productive. Mediation (of all the ADR processes) has a unique flexibility to respond to the very particular exigencies of a given situation. The greater the emphasis on a pre-arranged structure, the less the opportunity to adopt a particular approach and format of mediation which the situation demands. There is therefore some measure of balance to be achieved in the drafting of such a clause.

It is also important to distinguish between various kinds of ADR process. Some, such as early neutral evaluation, contain no element of negotiation about them. There, the parties simply make oral and/or written submissions to an agreed neutral, who makes a non-binding evaluation, which the parties can then use to inform their negotiations. There is no reason in principle why the uncertainty objections raised in the *Walford* case should apply to such a process. Indeed, since the process is not inherently one of negotiation at all, the *Walford* case is not relevant to any assessment of it.

Finally, the uncertainty objections in *Walford* can be very largely minimised by the use of specific time periods, or 'lock-out' agreements. For example, rather than requiring the parties to mediate prior to issuing proceedings, an ADR clause may simply impose a time period between the dispute arising and proceedings being commenced. Provided it follows the *Scott v Avery* form, there is no objection to such a clause. During the intervening time period, the clause can either impose an obligation to use ADR, or simply offer it as an option, subject to the parties' consent at the time (see

111

6.5.1 *Contracting in advance to use ADR*

Appendix B, clause 2, long-form clauses). As a matter of law, this changes little. An obligation to use ADR would still be vulnerable to the uncertainty arguments and an option to use ADR is in fact no more than the parties already have in any event, even without such wording.

In practice, however, the position is very different. A specific breathing space is created, during which the parties are unable to issue proceedings. ADR is on the agenda during that period, whether by obligation or option, and there can therefore be little concern about raising it with the other side. Many parties, faced with an intervening period during which they may either negotiate and/or use ADR, or do nothing, will sense the value in trying to use all available means to resolve the dispute. If the breathing space were not imposed on them, it is likely that some of them would be tempted to miss out the ADR, and even the negotiation, phase, and a valuable settlement opportunity might be lost.

Finally, where there is a concern that the imposition of a 'breathing space' may prejudice a party's position in the event that, for example, immediate injunctive relief is required, express provision for that can easily be made in a clause giving rights to by-pass the ADR or negotiation phases in such circumstances (see for example Appendix B, short-form clauses, additional clause).

3   Is ADR equivalent to negotiation, such that the law regarding agreements to negotiate applies equally to ADR?

So far in this section, we have assumed largely that ADR is a form of negotiation, and thus that the law regarding the enforceability of agreements to negotiate applies equally to agreements to use ADR. However, we have already drawn a clear distinction between ADR processes which involve a large element of nego-tiation (eg mediation, mini-trial, etc) and those which do not (eg judicial appraisal, early neutral evaluation, etc). Clearly, the latter category is exempt from any of the problems relating to agreements to negotiate. The remainder of this section therefore applies to the former category of ADR processes.

On the face of it, those processes are extremely similar to negotiation. Indeed, their aims and objectives are almost indis-tinguishable from those of direct negotiations. Both seek a consensual result, with no ability to mandate any concession or change of position from the other side. Both can be abandoned by either party at any time. Neither requires or permits the imposition on the parties of any form of binding judgment. The outcome of both types of process is either a mutually acceptable agreement (which the parties can agree should have binding or non-binding status) or no agreement at all. Following this rationale, the law applicable to negotiation should also apply to ADR.

However, whilst ADR and negotiation may share the same aims and objectives, there are fundamental differences of process. Anyone familiar with both will immediately appreciate this. The introduction of a third party (a mediator/neutral) fundamentally changes the terms and conditions of the negotiating process. The parties submit themselves to management by a third party in a process with an independent dynamic and momentum of its own, to a far greater degree than they do in direct negotiations. Indeed, the mere fact that the process has such a momentum and a structure beyond that generated by the parties themselves, distinguishes it very significantly from direct negotiations. The process elements of a mediation are to a large extent governed by the mediator's own input and perceptions of what will prove effective, even allowing for the fact that the parties must at least consent to any such process decisions.

It is therefore possible to say, at least to some extent, that ADR processes exist as structures independent of the parties themselves. The implication of this is highly significant. If it is possible to identify such processes or structures with sufficient clarity, the uncertainty objections raised in the *Walford* case begin to fall away. By agreeing to use ADR, the argument runs, the parties are not agreeing to negotiate, but rather to submit themselves to a series of objectively definable processes, the effect of which is likely to be greater on them than if they merely entered the direct negotiation process. To quote again from Giles J in the *Hooper Bailie* case:

> 'What is enforced is not co-operation and consent, but participation in a process from which co-operation and consent might come.'

If that rationale is adopted, it becomes much easier to countenance enforcement of an ADR clause.

To use an analogy, assume that a husband and wife have a particular problem in their marriage. They may agree between themselves to attempt to resolve it by discussion. Clearly they cannot be compelled to resolve the problem. Realistically, neither can they be compelled to 'discuss it' since that is too vague an obligation to define effectively. How productive do discussions have to be in order to constitute compliance? If they set aside an hour to do so, and simply sit in silence, or scream at each other, have they complied? And for how long do the discussions need to continue? On the other hand, they might agree to attempt to resolve the matter by seeking the assistance of a counsellor. Even more expressly, they might commit to have 10 weekly sessions with the counsellor. This is an easy obligation to monitor. It contains no assumptions that they will succeed in reaching resolution but merely a commitment to submit themselves to a particular and definable process. Implicit in it is an assumption that the counselling process constitutes something independent of the parties, a pre-existing structure into which the parties will submit their differences.

Necessarily, the counselling process itself is not easy to define in advance, in terms of the detail of how a particular session will progress. But that does not mean that it does not have enough of a structure of its own to enable the parties to know in advance what obligations they will take on when they agree to use it. Exactly the same is true of, for example, the mediation process. Indeed, the only difference between the two (in terms of ensuring compliance) is that counselling is currently better known and more widely used than ADR and thus more easily permits an immediate and objective recognition of what is involved.

In summary then, we tend to the view that ADR is 'more than' direct negotiation, in a way which tends to distinguish the two processes and therefore the law applicable to each. We can envisage circumstances in which an ADR clause requiring mediation might be enforceable. Perhaps with its new-found mainstream status under the CPR, the courts might confer that degree of authenticity on ADR as a separate entity over and beyond ordinary negotiation.

4   The practicality of enforcement

How then could a party enforce an ADR clause? Could a stay be obtained from the court to enforce such a clause? Subject to the arguments set out above, there happens to be one specific statutory provision which specifically provides for such a step to be taken, albeit by a side-wind. The Arbitration Act 1996 made sweeping changes to the framework for arbitration. Section 9 of the Act provides:

'(1) A party to an arbitration agreement against whom legal proceedings are brought (whether by way of claim or counterclaim) in respect of a matter which under the agreement is to be referred to arbitration may (upon notice to the other party to the proceedings) apply to the court in which the proceedings have been brought to stay the proceedings so far as they concern that matter.

(2) *An application may be made notwithstanding that the matter is to be referred to arbitration only after the exhaustion of other dispute resolution procedures* [our emphasis].

(3) An application may not be made by a person before taking the appropriate procedural step (if any) to acknowledge the legal proceedings against him or after he has taken any step in those proceedings to answer the substantive claim.

(4) On an application under this section the court shall grant a stay unless satisfied that the arbitration agreement is null and void, inoperative, or incapable of being performed.

(5) If the court refuses to stay the legal proceedings, any provision that an award is a condition precedent to the bringing of proceedings in respect of any matter is of no effect in relation to those proceedings.'

This provision was inserted to reflect the effect of the House of Lords decision in *Channel Tunnel Group v Balfour Beatty* [1993] 1 All ER 664. In theory, therefore, if a contract contains a stepped clause which provides for, say, mediation to be followed by arbitration, and one party issues proceedings without using either mediation or arbitration, a court would be bound to order a stay under s 9(4).

Enthusiasm about this provision has to be tempered by the decision of McKinnon J in *Halifax Financial Services v Intuitive Systems Ltd* [1999] 1 All ER Comm 303, in which he held that the stepped ADR/arbitration procedure devised for a contract between the claimant and a software designer did not make compliance with its procedures mandatory. More importantly, he held that it was doubtful whether such clauses were enforceable. He drew a distinction between determinative procedures such as arbitration or binding expert determination as against non-determinative procedures such as negotiation, mediation, expert appraisal and non-binding evaluations. This contract had a series of non-binding processes coupled with a series of moratoria on issue of proceedings, leading towards permission to issue proceedings unless arbitration was agreed. No mention was made of s 9 of the Arbitration Act 1996 in the judgment, but he distinguished the case before him from *Channel Tunnel Group Ltd v Balfour Beatty* on the grounds that the *Channel Tunnel* case involved a clause which was 'nearly an immediate effective agreement to arbitrate, albeit not quite.' The *Halifax* clause could not be construed as close to being 'nearly an immediately effective agreement to arbitrate'. He drew comfort from the judgment in *Cott (UK) Ltd v F E Barber Ltd* on the basis that, although the judge had been prepared in principle to order a stay for ADR, the relevant clause required the case to be referred to an expert whose decision was to be final and binding, and was thus a determinative rather than non-determinative outcome.

In truth, McKinnon J in *Halifax* felt that the stay sought by the defendant by means of the ADR clause was being used as a device to delay the start of proceedings and keep the claimant unjustifiably out of his claim. If the decision had gone to mere exercise of discretion as to whether to grant a stay or not, he would have found against the defendant, because he felt it was time for the claim to continue. He found specifically that the claimant 'has not rushed to litigation or refused to consider a negotiated settlement'. If the claimant had rushed to issue, it is clear that the CPR give ample grounds to a court to penalise such an approach.

This underlines what the true incentives and disincentives are for unreasonable parties since the CPR came into effect. A rogue party who issues court proceedings too early, especially in the face of a pre-agreed commitment to ADR, is going to face a serious risk of costs sanctions under CPR Part 44.5, for ignoring the spirit of the pre-action protocols and the overriding objective in CPR Part 1, extending as they do to pre-issue unreasonable conduct. The party aggrieved simply needs to point out to the court, even where the aggressor 'wins', that there was no good reason for failing to try ADR first, and a court should be prepared to be sympathetic over the costs order to be made.

6.5.2 Enforcing ADR clauses under Australian law

Whilst obviously not binding in any way on the English courts, the legal status of ADR clauses in Australia nevertheless sheds considerable light on the central issues concerning the enforceability of ADR clauses in England. There are two schools of thought there. For some time the established position was that an ADR clause (requiring conciliation or mediation) was not binding. There were two principal reasons for this:

    (a) An ADR clause may be unenforceable because it seeks to achieve too much, by ousting the jurisdiction of the court (per the Supreme Court of Queensland in *Allco Steel (Queensland) Pty Ltd v Torres Strait Gold Pty Ltd* (unreported, Supreme Court of QLD, 12 March 1990, Master Horton QC). In that case, the court refused to stay proceedings in that court while a contractual conciliation clause was implemented.

(b) An ADR clause is no more than an agreement to negotiate and is therefore unenforceable because it lacks the necessary certainty required to create legally binding decisions (per NSW Court of Appeal in *Coal Cliff Collieries Pty Ltd v Sijehama Pty Ltd* (1992) 24 NSWLR 1). The reasoning here is, of course, essentially the same as that followed by the House of Lords in *Walford*.

However, doubt has since been cast over the application of both principles to ADR clauses. A decision by the New South Wales Supreme Court held that an agreement to conciliate, in the form permitted by *Scott v Avery*, would be enforced by the court staying arbitration proceedings under the contract until the conciliation phase had been properly concluded. Furthermore, the judge (Giles J) expressly stated that such a stay would also have been granted had there been court proceedings on foot equivalent to the arbitration proceedings. The case in question was *Hooper Bailie Associated Ltd v Natcon Group Pty Ltd* (supra). The facts of the case were summarised as follows (from Robert S Angyal in the 'Mediation Agreements and Enforceability of ADR Clauses' paper to the First International Conference in Australia on Dispute Resolution):

'Hooper Bailie was the Contractor for the construction of dry wall partitions and ceilings of the New Parliament House Building in Canberra and Natcon was sub-contracted to perform that work. Disputes arose under the Contract; the disputes were submitted to arbitration; and in that arbitration Natcon claimed more than $3,000,000 from Hooper Bailie. Before the arbitration could start, it was found by Giles J that the parties reached agreement that they would conciliate a number of issues and that the arbitration would not take place until the conciliation had concluded. A conciliator was retained and a series of successful meetings took place in which the conciliator took the role of facilitating the voluntary agreement of the parties without making any determinations in relation to disputed items. Before the conciliation could conclude, Natcon was wound up. About a year later, the liquidator of Natcon sought to proceed with the arbitration rather than continuing with the conciliation meetings. At that point Hooper Bailie commenced proceedings to establish that Natcon was unable to continue with the arbitration basing its claim in part on the argument that the parties had agreed that the arbitration would not continue until the conciliation had concluded, and that it had not concluded.'

The judgment of Giles J contains a lengthy and detailed analysis of the issues, out of which the following principal points arise:

(i) The *Allco Steel* case had found that a conciliation clause could not operate as a pre-condition to litigation. Part of the rationale for this seems to have been a belief that conciliation was futile in view of the apparently entrenched and divergent positions of the two parties. In *Hooper Bailie* the judge found no evidence to suggest that further conciliation meetings would not prove fruitful (earlier ones had been fruitful) and even the fact that Natcon would not participate in the conciliation without an order to do so did not necessarily imply that the process was pointless.

(ii) This point was substantiated by remarks of Rogers CJ in *AWA Limited v Daniels* (unreported, NSW Supreme Court, 24 February 1992). In that case, Rogers CJ concluded that there was 'utility in requiring parties, who are clearly bent on being difficult, to submit to conciliation processes . . . In my view initial reluctance is not necessarily fatal to a successful mediation. If the parties enter into [it] as they all said they would, the skill of the mediator would be given full play to bring about consensus'.

(iii) Rogers CJ also criticised the *Allco Steel* decision on the basis that 'the Master ought to have required the parties to adhere to their freely agreed contractual obligations'. This argument has, in our view, quite some force. Where parties, particularly sophisticated commercial ones, have freely constructed for themselves a dispute resolution procedure which they clearly anticipate should be used in the event of a dispute arising, the courts should be straining wherever possible to give effect to their intentions.

(iv) Giles J assessed the English authorities on the question of an agreement to agree, acknowledging that the established position (following *Walford v Miles, Courtney v Tolaini* and *Paul Smith Ltd v H&S International Holding Inc* [1991] 2 Lloyds R 127 was that an agreement to negotiate was not enforceable. However, he drew a clear and important distinction between a contract to negotiate and a contract to mediate or conciliate, and accorded to the latter process sufficient procedural certainty to permit enforcement.

> 'An agreement to conciliate or mediate is not to be likened (as Lord Ackner likens an agreement to negotiate, or negotiate in good faith) to an agreement to agree. Nor is an agreement to negotiate, or negotiate in good faith, perhaps necessarily lacking certainty and obliging a party to act contrary to its interests. Depending upon its express terms and any terms to be implied, it may require of the parties participation in the process by conduct of sufficient certainty for legal recognition of the agreement.'

He then applied that consideration to the present case and held that:

> 'There was a clear structure for the conciliation for which Natcon was to attend before Mr Schick [the conciliator], put before him such 'evidence' and submissions as it desired and receive his determinations. As has been seen, ancillary to this arose an exchange of information between the parties for the purposes of the conciliation and there were no determinations in any sense other than in the sense of suggested solutions. In my opinion, Natcon promised to participate in a conciliation by doing those things and the conduct required of it is sufficiently certain for its promise to be given legal recognition.'

It is also worth stressing that the judge did not impose any obligation to compromise any of the matters which would be the subject of the ensuing conciliation, nor did he express any view on whether there was an implied term that the parties would conduct themselves in good faith during that conciliation.

(v) The judgment in *Hooper Bailie* also expressly reflects a recognition of the increasing profile and usage of ADR in Australia and, in particular, the enactment of legislation enabling courts to refer cases to mediation in certain circumstances. Whilst it remains unclear what view an English court might take of a similar case, the position in Australia does reflect the way in which the increased use and profile of ADR has begun to have an impact upon the law relating to it.

(vi) In *Aiton Australia Pty Ltd v Transfield Pty Ltd*, a 1999 decision of the Supreme Court of New South Wales, Einstein J disagreed with part of the reasoning of Giles J in the *Hooper Bailie* case and another of his decisions, *Elizabeth Bay Developments v Boral Building Pty Ltd*, in which Giles J had doubted the enforceability of a contract term requiring good faith efforts of each party in negotiation or mediation. The judge in *Aiton* believed that it is possible to enforce good faith negotiation, which –

'. . . is not the equivalent of agreement, is not a synonym for settlement and does not require any particular outcome . . .'

though he made it clear that the duty to mediate must be sufficiently precisely defined by the agreement to be certain and therefore enforceable. As it turned out, Einstein J found that the particular agreement in the *Aiton* case was not enforceable, for the somewhat striking reason that there were no provisions for remuneration of the mediator, or for appointing an alternative to the mediator nominated in the contract if he declined. The judge refused to imply a term that the parties would share the mediator's fees equally.

6.6 AREAS OF RELEVANCE

ADR clauses of different types are being used in a wide variety of contexts. Examples of these include general commercial contracts, partnership agreements, terms and conditions of business, construction contracts, development contracts, and so on. In each new application, thought should be given to the type of ADR process most likely to generate resolution.

It is also important to remember the value of ADR clauses in corporate policy statements. Thus many large American companies have adopted a public 'corporate pledge', to use ADR processes in appropriate situations. Although not legally committing the company to the use of ADR in any particular dispute, this pledge has been used to send a powerful message to those with whom this company deals, and promote the company's public image. This is similar in concept, as we have noted, to Accords, by which parties, insurers, lawyers and others engaged in a particular area of dispute state their intention to use ADR when problems arise.

Part C

The practical framework of ADR

CONTENTS

Chapter 7

Advising the client on ADR

7.1 THE DUTY TO ADVISE THE CLIENT ABOUT ADR

7.1.1 Is there such a duty?

A client approaches a lawyer in the expectation of receiving advice on the best method of achieving what the client wishes. On most occasions, the client wants the resolution of any dispute by the quickest and most cost-effective means available and on the best terms available. In many cases, this will be achieved by the lawyer through correspondence and, not infrequently, by negotiation with the other side. In such circumstances there is no need to resort to the formal methods of the dispute resolution process through the courts, tribunals or the arbitration process. Normal negotiation and settlement procedures often work perfectly well, so long as the client has obtained what was really wanted.

What happens, however, if the settlement process does not work, breaks down or drags on? Perhaps the client becomes impatient with the rate of progress and feels that the issue of proceedings will concentrate the opponent's mind.

At this stage another set of choices faces the client and lawyer. A solicitor is obliged by Solicitors Practice Rule 15 and the Solicitors Costs Information and Client Care Code to give 'the best information possible' to the client about the implications of starting litigation – the risk, the likely costs, the cost-benefit and risk, different tactical approaches, the forum, and so on. These duties are ongoing, and require updated information throughout the claim.

Once the prospect of litigation or arbitration has loomed large, it is not uncommon for differing perceptions to arise in the mind of lawyer and client. The lawyer may tend to view the litigation in terms of the process itself, as a series of procedural steps and a timetable to be adhered to. By contrast, the client still has in mind those initial aims and priorities – to resolve the matter as quickly and cheaply as possible and on the best available terms. While these views will often coexist comfortably, most lawyers (and many commercial clients too) will be no stranger to court actions which 'take on a life of their own'. They acquire an inherent momentum focused on the next procedural step, often losing sight of the wider commercial or personal picture.

The lawyer's duty is always to safeguard and pursue the client's own priorities and aims. Litigation, or indeed any other legal process which a lawyer can offer to clients, is really only justified to the extent that it seeks to achieve that. Thus at all stages during litigation, procedural and tactical choices should be exercised in the light of the client's overriding goals. The process, be it litigation or anything else, is the means but never the end.

7.1.2 Other sources of the duty

There is now an additional overriding objective for a lawyer to bear in mind, as we have seen in Chapter 4, namely that of the civil court system itself. This began with the Commercial Court and High Court Practice Directions, and has been continued in the pre-action protocols and the Civil Procedure Rules themselves.

What we now have, as we have seen above, is an integrated set of Civil Procedure Rules which embody an overall framework and spring from the philosophy enunciated in the overriding objective defined in CPR Part 1. Thus specific duties are now laid on the court, which parties and lawyers are required to help discharge (see CPR Part 1.3) to encourage the parties to co-operate with each other, to use ADR, to help the parties settle and to undertake cost-benefit analysis. It is a rash lawyer who fails to do this.

Non-compliance with (or mere lip service paid to) such obligations is almost certain to open a lawyer to valid criticism and probable costs sanctions from the court and thus from the client, even to the extent of wasted costs orders against the lawyer personally.

7.1.3 What is the scope of the duty?

The Law Society's Guide to Professional Conduct of Solicitors and the Solicitors Practice Rules are the prime source for defining solicitors' duties and obligations to clients, though many of these are regarded as originating from the common law itself. Both the CCBE Code of Conduct for EC Lawyers and Solicitors Practice Rule 1 requires that a solicitor shall not do anything in the course of practice which compromises the solicitor's duty to act in the best interests of the client or the solicitor's proper standard of work. There is no specific professional obligation imposed by the Solicitors Practice Rules to advise clients on ADR. The section in the Guide to Professional Conduct dealing with ADR primarily covers the duty of solicitors acting as mediators to avoid conflicts of interest, and introduces Codes of Practice for solicitor mediators. However, in the commentary on the CPR, the Guide reminds solicitors that helping the court to further the overriding objective may include encouraging the parties to use an ADR procedure. Its commentary on CPR Part 1 concludes:

> 'The court also has wide powers to take into account the conduct of the parties, including the conduct of their legal representatives, both pre-action and during the conduct of the proceedings. The particular responsibility placed on the parties to help the court to further the overriding objective is a development of the duty of solicitors to act as officers of the court.'

This is in effect an express professional duty to advise on ADR. Whether failure to do so could amount to a basis for disciplinary proceedings against a solicitor might still be arguable. But there are many sanctions which a court might deploy, especially in relation to its jurisdiction to order penal interest and indemnity costs and wasted costs to make this almost an unnecessary refinement. The courts are well placed to police this area of advice-giving, as they represent the final venue for solving the problem, either if ADR is not tried or it is tried and does not lead to settlement.

The duty clearly extends to giving full advice on ADR to one's own client. This advice should include:

- the full range of ADR techniques available;
- the legal and financial implications of each;
- whether the case is in any way unsuitable for ADR;
- whether it is ready for ADR yet;
- how best to approach the other side;
- when the best time to attempt it might be.

Similar considerations apply to meeting the requirements of the Commercial Court, Chancery, Technology & Construction Court and Mercantile Court Guides, discussed above.

7.1.4 Implications of the duty

It is fair to say that the existence of the duty to advise on ADR has not yet been directly tested in the English courts. However, extremely persuasive comment on this topic is to be found in the unreported decision of the Court of Appeal (which included Lord Woolf) in *Dyson and Field (Executors of Twohey Dec'd) v Leeds City Council* 22 November 1999, in an appeal by claimants against an adverse judgment on an asbestosis claim on the ground that the judge had failed to spell out why he had preferred the defendant's expert. In remitting the case back for further hearing, Lord Justice Ward said:

> 'Since damages had been substantially agreed, it seems to the court that this is pre-eminently the category of case in which, consistent with the overriding objective of the Civil Procedure Rules and the court's duty to manage cases as set out in Rule 1.4(2)(e), that we should encourage the parties to use an alternative dispute resolution procedure to bring this unhappy matter to the conclusion which it now deserves sooner rather than later.'

Having mentioned that ADR had been proposed by the claimants, but counsel for the defendant was unaware of how insurers had responded, he went on:

> 'If it be that the overture was rejected, we urge the defendants to think again. In the light of the unfortunate history, I would add that the court has powers to take a strong view about the rejection of the encouraging noises we are making, if necessary by imposing orders for indemnity costs or indeed ordering that a higher rate of interest be paid on any damages which might at the end of the day be recoverable. With that warning of dire consequences but essentially with a note of encouragement, I would allow this appeal and remit the matter back to the County Court.'

Lord Justice Laws and Lord Woolf agreed with Lord Justice Ward and particularly associated themselves with his remarks about using ADR.

Supposing that a case takes the traditional course taken by at least 90% of cases following the issue of proceedings, and settles, whether before or perhaps even at the door of the court. Even if the deal done there includes payment of costs on the standard basis to be assessed if not agreed, it is well known that recovery may not be more than two-thirds to three-quarters of the costs expended by a winning party. It is impossible to recover anything to reflect the lost management time and sheer stress, strain and uncertainty of the case hanging over the parties' heads. If, following a settlement at the door of the court, a party were to learn for the first time of ADR, would a claim in negligence succeed against a lawyer for failure to give advice about the option (subject of course to proof of causation and loss)? Such a claim has succeeded in the USA, and one day the UK may follow suit. This is even more likely if the lawyer is shown to have been in breach of the Commercial Court's Guide or any other duty to advise.

What still remains to be tested in the new post-Woolf era is whether judges themselves are going to remain prepared simply to accept and ratify court-door settlements. What if a judge enquired into why a case had only been settled that late, and insisted on operating on the assumption that cases settled then are almost always capable of earlier settlement through ADR? It is open to the court to apply the principle of proportionality as it affects other court users, to whom the facilities of a court-room and a properly prepared judge have been potentially denied by failure to address settlement earlier in the settled case before the court. In doing so, a judge could well be tempted to impose penalties on court users in the absence of proper justification for late settlement. Lost costs in those circumstances would undoubtedly be regarded by the client as something for which the lawyer should take responsibility, if adequate ADR advice had not been tendered earlier.

In a sense it is disappointing even to have to address the issue of a formal *duty*. ADR is inherently a process in the client's interests, which should and will come naturally to many lawyers and parties. The developing attitude of the courts in favour of its use is consolidating that view.

7.2 WHEN TO ADVISE ON ADR

It will be apparent from section **4.1** above that ADR options can and should be considered at all stages of a dispute, before proceedings are issued right though to immediately before trial. The most effective use of ADR will often depend on the client receiving advice on it as early as possible, ideally before any dispute has arisen, but certainly before proceedings are issued, as required by the spirit of the pre-action protocols and the CPR.

7.2.1 Dispute system design

Bitter and costly experience of disputes has caused parties to give serious thought to putting into place a system designed to cope with and manage the breakdown in a relationship so as to avoid subsequent unnecessary and time-consuming confrontations. The particular strength of this is that the parties address the whole issue of disputes before one arises, and thus at a time when they are able to approach the subject more dispassionately and indeed together. If an effective mechanism is put in place at that stage, much of the acrimony and defensive posturing so characteristic of disputes can be avoided. The growth of this area is reflected in the increased number of attempts to design dispute systems.

In the early 1980s a major contract for the construction of the El Cahon dam in South America introduced a Disputes Review Panel. This consisted of two independent nominees, one chosen by the owner and one by the contractor, who together then chose a third neutral chairman. Members of the panel were sent the site minutes and all relevant contract documentation and viewed the construction site on a regular basis. Disputes arising under the contract were put to the panel who gave an interim adjudication. At the conclusion of the contract there were no outstanding claims. Building on this experience the American Society of Engineers introduced such a panel on a number of its underground sewage works projects. It was also used on some harbour projects, particularly in Boston.

In the UK the first high profile use was on the Channel Tunnel. Decisions by the panel were binding on the parties unless they gave notice of arbitration within a certain period. The matter then became subject to arbitration in the normal way. This structure is to be seen set out in the report of *Channel Tunnel Group Ltd v Balfour Beatty Ltd* [1993] 1 All ER 664 and it was duly supported by the House of Lords. More recently, such hybrid schemes have been designed for the Hong Kong Airport and the Channel Tunnel Rail Link.

Not only on construction contracts but also in other contexts, one of the problems with disputes is allowing them to fester until the conclusion of the commercial venture. With the passage of time attitudes harden, positions become more entrenched and there is a general reluctance to back down from a position for fear of it being taken as a sign of weakness or considered as a loss of face. The introduction of an intermediate panel allows for an early determination of the dispute, thereby nipping any potential problems in the bud. The nature of such a panel can be flexible. In its simplest form it can consist of a nominated executive from each of the contracting parties: indeed such a version is commonly found in joint ventures and commercial shareholders' agreements.

7.2.2 At the contract stage

There is a temptation amongst non-contentious lawyers to assume that ADR solely concerns litigation and is therefore not within their concern or province. It must be remembered that it is the non-contentious lawyers who are responsible for drawing up the commercial agreement. Often one of the few clauses that is not argued over is the disputes resolution clause. Many non-contentious lawyers put in such a clause, often choosing arbitration, without proper consultation with their litigation colleagues as to what would be the preferred method of dispute resolution. These days, a standard-form arbitration clause is not always in the parties' best interests.

The introduction of an ADR clause into the contract at a time when the parties' relationships are at their best, with the hopes and aspirations of both sides looking towards a beneficial commercial agreement, is an effective way to introduce the concept of ADR. Most such clauses provide that in the event of any dispute the parties will attempt to resolve their differences through mutual discussion, failing which, the parties will attempt to resolve their dispute through mediation or some other ADR means. A more detailed discussion of such clauses, together with some sample clauses, can be found in Chapter 6 and Appendix B.

It is difficult to overstate the value of an ADR clause. Its introduction into a contract overcomes one of the fundamental difficulties that one party faces when attempting to suggest ADR to the other – the fear that the suggestion of ADR will be regarded as indicating lack of confidence in their own case. If ADR arises contractually, no such fear need exist.

7.2.3 After an alleged breach of contract or tortious duty

It has to be remembered that many disputes do not even get to the stage where proceedings are issued. Many disagreements are settled amicably between the contracting parties before even reaching an external lawyer. Lawyers only see the tip of the iceberg. Even then, of the claims that reach lawyers, whether for breach of contract or damages for some actionable wrong, many settle then through negotiation, long before any need to consider litigation may arise. Most lawyers find that negotiation is a key professional activity and skill throughout their careers, and spend much time engaged in it, be it discussing the terms of a conveyancing transaction, a commercial agreement or the settlement of a piece of litigation.

Yet, as we have seen, even the best negotiators may find it difficult, through no fault of their own, to achieve agreement through direct talks or contact. It may well be that before the next stage of the dispute resolution process is mobilised, the introduction of a third party facilitator could break what is otherwise a negotiating impasse. One of the recurrent themes of the ADR process is that the earlier it is introduced the better, and the greater the savings in time and cost. While many traditional litigators are reluctant to embark upon a full negotiation without many of what they perceive are the essential facts at their fingertips, nevertheless it must be remembered that the majority of commercial disputes settle prior to litigation, and without necessarily having assembled every last piece of information. Company executives and insurers repeatedly take decisions to settle matters often with only the information available from their own side. The introduction of a mediator may cause the parties to re-assess their positions and possibly widen the scope of the negotiations. Mediation itself very frequently provides a very efficient occasion for information exchange and clarification of positions in any event.

7.2.4 Entering the litigation or arbitration stage

The parties have failed to reach agreement through negotiations. There seems to be no other alternative but to issue proceedings. Especially where the lawyer consulted has not been involved in the contract or dispute negotiations hitherto, the range of options open to the client should be explored thoroughly at this stage more than any other. Few lawyers will ever advise their clients to issue proceedings solely in the hope that it will bring the opponents to the negotiating table. Very often, the issue of proceedings is the defining act in solidifying the dispute. Litigation should rarely be embarked upon unless there is a willingness and an ability to carry the matter through to its ultimate conclusion. Thus, quite apart from the implications of the CPR and pre-action protocols, it makes considerable sense to try one final attempt to conclude matters by agreement before embarking upon the long and expensive litigation trail. The introduction of a neutral third party into the negotiation dynamic is usually a new idea and can easily be seen to be a worthwhile extension to what has been tried in negotiation hitherto. Especially if ADR has not been raised before, it should be discussed with the client at this stage.

Once the litigation process starts up, it is extremely difficult to stop the machinery from grinding remorselessly on. This is perhaps particularly so where the court is repeatedly imposing target dates by reason of its active case management responsibilities, let alone where the case is allocated to the county court fast-track. There is also the temptation always to want to go on just to the next stage, be it sight of the opponent's defence, disclosure of documents, exchange of witness statements or expert's reports, before deciding that the moment is right to open or resume negotiations. All these sub-processes cost time and money. The sooner the suggestion of ADR is made and taken up, the better. The likening of litigation to dancing with a gorilla, whilst well aired among advocates of ADR, is nevertheless a neat metaphor of the experience – you only stop when the gorilla wants to stop.

7.3   WHEN TO USE ADR

It is sometimes assumed that a case will *either* go to ADR *or* to litigation or arbitration, perhaps as a consequence of the word 'alternative' in the acronym. This is quite incorrect. Many if not most mediations concern disputes in which proceedings have already been commenced and in some cases trial is due very shortly. In other cases, the disputing parties may not even have consulted lawyers and may regard the use of ADR as a way of avoiding that altogether. It follows that there can be no universal right time to take a case to ADR. However, the following general principles should be borne in mind at least as a starting-point.

7.3.1   The earlier the better

This is true not just because the cost and time savings are at their greatest, but because parties tend to become more entrenched the longer the dispute lasts. The scope for a genuinely constructive settlement may decrease as time goes by, and the recovery of escalating professional costs will increasingly distort the substantive issues.

In relation to the use of mediation prior to the issue of proceedings, it is of course important to remember the operation of any statutory time limits under the Limitation Acts. The use of mediation (or any other ADR procedure) will not of itself prevent these from running. In circumstances where the period is about to expire, it would be prudent to issue proceedings as a protective measure, or to enter a binding agreement to postpone their operation, then allowing attempts to be made to mediate the dispute before proceedings go any further.

7.3.2 Some disputes may have to run for a time before the parties will agree to ADR

It is not unusual for some parties not to countenance ADR (or any settlement discussion) until they have 'fought' for a period of time. This may stem from tactical considerations, perceptions of relative merits, or even pride or the desire for revenge. In terms of the timing of ADR, this needs to be borne in mind. Refusal to entertain ADR early in a case may well not equate with unwillingness to use it at all, though it is wise for parties to try to avoid even the impression of intransigence in the light of the possible costs penalties that might emerge from CPR Part 44.5. In fact, as a case progresses, perceptions of merits and risks change, new information emerges, costs and delays increase, and the parties may have vented their initial spleen, all of which can increase readiness for settlement exploration.

7.3.3 Enough information needs to be available to permit a realistic assessment of the case

This is dealt with in more detail in section **7.3.6**. Suffice it to say here that unless sufficient information is available (or potentially available through a chosen ADR process) to enable parties to establish in their own minds the parameters for settlement, it may well be difficult and even imprudent to settle the case, by ADR or any other means. This may be their own information (counsel's opinion, medical or experts' reports and so on) or the other side's (available through disclosure of documents or exchange of evidence).

That said, two qualifications should be borne in mind:

1   Many disputes are actually settled by the parties even before lawyers are consulted. The benefits of an early settlement must be weighed against the risks of doing so without (perhaps) all the information that litigation might produce, and a commercial judgement made. Neither option is objectively 'right'. An early settlement may ultimately prove to be on less advantageous terms than would subsequently have been available (though how will this be discovered?), but with savings of time and cost and with relationships preserved. Conversely, litigation may provide an ultimate victory, but with loss of other commercial opportunities for the parties as a consequence, or maybe intervening financial failure by the unsuccessful party will render it a Pyrrhic victory. It falls to the lawyer and particularly the client to make this judgment in each set of circumstances.

2   The question of available information usually centres on disclosure of documents. The argument is sometimes made that ADR should not be attempted before that stage because settlement discussions may otherwise be ill-founded. Sometimes this will be true. Often, however, disclosure does not reveal anything of sufficient importance materially to change the nature of a case. The desire to complete disclosure may reflect the lawyer's very understandable desire to keep immune from criticism (and an action for negligence) in relation to the terms of settlement. This needs careful advice from lawyer to client, but a decision can then be made by the client, who may be best placed to know if disclosure will or will not be helpful first. In many actions, the issues and relevant information are clear long before disclosure. Disclosure of relevant documentation is not, therefore, a pre-requisite for ADR, but should reflect a reasonable assessment of what information is really needed for effective case evaluation and negotiation.

7.3.4   Assessing case value and risk

Assessing case value from a risk management point of view is clearly a key element of dispute handling, and the assessments reached will necessarily affect the choice of dispute resolution process. The structure of litigation and arbitration tends to defer a detailed consideration of the case until much nearer to trial (and indeed many clients do not want to face the uncomfortable realities of their positions). ADR necessitates a disciplined focus on the case

7.3.4 *Advising the client on ADR*

whenever it takes place, often long before trial. Thus an assessment of case value is both a part of the decision about whether to take a case to ADR, and also a likely product of doing so.

The Heilbron Report (yet another report into civil justice reform and published in 1993) criticised the lack of early assessment of issues in litigation (para 4.1(ii)):

'Often insufficient time is spent in preparing cases. The result is that lawyers do not get fully to grips with the issues in a case. Thus, they cannot give their clients realistic advice until nearer to the trial itself. This protracts litigation and delays the chance of compromise. Although initially reducing costs, it more often has the reverse effect and increases the costs of the resolution of the dispute. To counter these disadvantages, more thorough preparation at an early stage with consequent "front loading" of costs is required. The actual or imminent risk of having to pay costs as opposed to the distant prospect of having to do so, coupled with realistic legal advice, is as good a recipe as any to make litigants focus on the matters in issue, rather than to postpone decision making.'

The front-loading foreshadowed by this report has been one of the main practical results of the CPR and the pre-action protocols.

1 Aim

In litigation terms risk management breaks down into two elements:

(i) *A claims/recovery analysis:* an assessment of one's own likely recovery and that of the other side.

(ii) *A costs/risk analysis:* an assessment of the cost of pursuing the various options, and the attendant risks of each.

2 Claims/recovery analysis

It should be possible though a systematic and methodical approach to carry out a detailed analysis of each item of claim assessed against a degree of possibility and probability of success. The need for a high/low bracket is to allow for the uncertainties of litigation such as the ultimate performance of the witness in the box, the quality of the case presentation and the judge's reaction to it. Having assessed each and every claim in percentage terms, they can then collectively be averaged out.

Obviously, such an analysis would not be complete without carrying out a similar exercise upon any counterclaim. In addition, if a broader view is required, the exercise can be repeated based upon differing 'what if' scenarios.

3 Costs/risk analysis

A similarly detailed and methodical approach, coupled with a litigator's experience and a great deal of realism, can produce a reasonably likely forecast of the costs of an action. Indeed, summaries of future anticipated costs are now required by CPR to be produced for the court and the opponent at several key stages of any action. Inaccuracy in producing these may have an influence on whether costs are awarded in full or only in part once the action is determined. Each stage of the litigation (summons, particulars of claim, defence, allocation, case management conference, disclosure, evidence exchange, pre-trial review and trial) needs to be analysed, and a calculation of the cost of each stage in terms of minima and maxima of work and cost produced. Figures for counsel, court and expert fees and other disbursements must be ascertained and included. The figure can then be worked through to the conclusion of the trial. This will be of great use both to the party (for cash-flow purposes) and his adviser. The likely shortfall between standard costs and solicitor and client or indemnity costs on detailed assessment even in the event of the client succeeding at trial needs to be borne in mind.

4 Updating

For such a piece of management information to be fully accurate and useful, this exercise and evaluation needs to be carried out on a regular basis throughout the course of the litigation. The discipline imposed by the CPR and Solicitors Practice Rule 15 will make it an ordinary part of case management and client care anyway. The factors to be taken into account will change and vary in the light of the experience gained during the conduct of the litigation. Lawyers are often criticised for inability or reluctance to give their clients accurate quotations for the cost of litigation. This can thus become a useful marketing tool for professional advisers, quite apart from assisting the client in evaluating the most cost-effective time to attempt to settle the case.

Clients in any complex action should ensure they receive a regular update on cost levels, predictions of success in the action and review of appropriateness of ADR, including potential cost-saving benefits.

7.3.5 Direct negotiations between the parties or their advisers are not succeeding

Direct negotiation between parties and their advisers is clearly the most efficient and effective method of resolving a dispute. Generally, parties should have attempted these before attempting ADR, not least because it is cheaper. The negotiations may take the form of direct talks or (usually less effective) an exchange of correspondence, perhaps including 'without prejudice' offers. However, it is important to remember that:

- Some direct talks may in fact drive the parties further apart, particularly if there is personal animosity between the protagonists.

- Some direct negotiations are obviously not succeeding after a couple of hours, whereas others may prove very effective if left to continue for several days, or even over a period of weeks or months. It is not always easy to assess when talks are not in fact producing results.

- Since most litigation cases settle before trial, on the basis of direct negotiations, it is tempting to assume that most settlement negotiations work. However, the crucial question is not whether they work (in the sense of ultimately producing a negotiated settlement), but whether they work well. It is not the hallmark of an efficient process if to generate settlement the negotiations have to take place over a number of years, whether or not against the back-cloth of expensive litigation, if in fact a mediation might produce settlement in a few days. ADR will usually concertina the negotiation process into a much tighter time frame, because of the inherent nature of the ADR processes.

7.3.6 Selecting individual cases

There have been long debates, often among those with little or no experience of ADR, as to how to assess whether a case is suitable for ADR. The experience of ADR usage and practice built up in this jurisdiction alone for over 10 years, let alone the much longer experience of other common law jurisdictions, has not identified a large tranche of cases which are inherently unsuitable. Indeed, some sophisticated repeat users of ADR in the UK have reversed the normal question and self-imposed onus of proof by asking 'is this case unsuitable for ADR?', and this may well be a much sounder approach. Very often the right question is not 'is it suitable?' but 'is it ready' for ADR. Section **7.4** sets out some reasons for not using ADR immediately in a given case, but here we set out a rule of thumb which can at least act as a starting-point for consideration of a given case.

The rule is that a case is, on the face of it, suitable for ADR if:

- *each party has sufficient information regarding the case to enable it to make a reasonable assessment of its position; and*

- *direct negotiations are not proving effective in generating a settlement; and*

- *none of the reasons set out in section* **7.4** *applies.*

It will be apparent from this that large numbers of disputes, perhaps even most disputes, will be suitable for resolution by ADR at some stage in their life-cycle. This counters the common perception that only the occasional dispute will be suitable. The onus is on lawyers and parties to ascertain the correct moment for ADR to be tried.

7.3.7   Systematic case selection

Much current ADR use in the UK at present is on an essentially case-by-case basis. Parties and advisers discuss ADR in relation to a given case and in due course agreement is reached (or not) with the other side to use it.

From the point of view of a client with a large through-put of litigation (typically insurance companies, banks and some other large corporations), the real benefit of ADR is to be obtained through much more systematic use. Some insurers are choosing to use ADR in a consistent and planned way for their claims work, in an attempt to reduce their overall claims handling expenses by achieving earlier and better outcomes, thus minimising their exposure to legal costs. This is a lesson long since learned by many US carriers and large corporations with heavy involvement in claims settlement. Typically in such cases, no assumption is made that ADR will emerge as an option at some unspecified future point. Instead, a policy is implemented which imposes a formal requirement that the initial and regular subsequent reports on each case from its in-house or panel lawyers contain a proper review of ADR possibilities. It presumes that all cases within certain pre-selected criteria are suitable for ADR (usually mediation), unless specific justification is given to the contrary.

These might include:

- all claims over two years old which are not dormant or allegedly fraudulent;
- all new claims above a certain value;
- all multi-track claims;
- all fast-track cases where liability is significantly at issue;
- all cases where the difference in valuation between claimant and defendant exceeds a certain figure;
- all claims within a certain category of risk (professional indemnity, construction, brain damage);
- any other criterion that fits the insurer's particular claims philosophy.

The use of a more systematic approach to case selection, whilst not removing the need for individual consideration of each case, has a number of benefits:

- it is likely to generate a much higher level of ADR use;
- it will therefore maximise the benefit delivered to the client;
- it transfers the onus of responsibility and judgment over case selection from individual case handlers to objectively established systematic criteria;
- it swiftly builds up data to form an empirical basis by which to measure the benefit that ADR is delivering to that company;
- it may enhance that company's claims handling reputation in the market-place.

A number of such schemes are being developed in the UK, and have been in place for many years in other parts of the common law world.

7.4 WHEN NOT TO USE ADR

It should be clear from the above that ADR is not a universally applicable procedural remedy, nor is it intended to replace the litigation and arbitration systems in their entirety. The key to the successful use of ADR is to know when, and when not, to use it. Again, it is unwise to be too prescriptive, but the following general principles should be borne in mind in relation to when ADR is not suitable.

7.4.1 Negotiations proving effective

If the negotiation process is already working there is no need to introduce the agency of a third party. It should be remembered that even taking into account the vast number of litigated cases that settle prior to trial, the majority of disputes do not even reach the stage where proceedings are issued. Countless commercial disputes are settled perfectly adequately without recourse to the courts.

7.4.2 Need for court assistance/protection

If there is a need for an injunction or some other form of relief available only through the court procedure (such as a declaration), then ADR will not be appropriate. Clearly, the need to protect or seize assets will require a court-based approach. However, it may well be that once such protection or seizure is obtained, the underlying issues can be resolved through ADR.

7.4.3 Need to set a precedent

ADR cannot deliver a precedent decision and in circumstances where that is required ADR is clearly inappropriate. For example, an insurance company might litigate over the interpretation of a policy condition, and require the finality of a court decision in order to substantiate its stance towards all policy-holders. Similarly, a commercial precedent might be required for reasons of corporate policy or image. For example, a company might wish to assert the primacy of a form of conduct – eg a firm commitment to dismissals for theft – or send a particular message to its marketplace competitors. In these circumstances, ADR is unlikely to be used, except perhaps as an aid to streamlining the issues for trial.

It is important to remember, however, that a precedent can be a two-edged sword. If the insurance company litigating over a policy-term is unsuccessful, it not only loses that action, but also publicly declares to other holders of a similar policy that they too have a right of redress against the company. Where such concerns exist, the privacy afforded by ADR can be attractive. The safest test for a litigant who wants a precedent is for the question to be asked whether the precedent will be valuable, *win or lose*. If losing a case and thus setting an adverse precedent would be painful or dangerous, settlement by ADR or any other means may be preferable.

7.4.4 Publicity

Sometimes a party may perceive that one of the major benefits (perhaps the only benefit) of litigation is the publicity that it can attract. This can be used to apply commercial pressure, or the pressure of public opinion, which can be a very powerful weapon. The public vindication of a reputation is often the primary objective of a libel action. The privacy and confidentiality of most ADR processes does not generally permit such publicity. However, libel actions are themselves being mediated now, often involving a planned move from private negotiation to an agreed public declaration of outcome.

Interestingly, however, ADR techniques (primarily consensus-building) have been used to great effect in environmental disputes, where the publicity element is often regarded as very important, and provision for it can be made in the design of the process itself. This is a useful reminder that the flexibility of ADR techniques permits a matching of the chosen process with the priorities and aims of the parties.

7.4.5 Economic power

Litigation can often be used by the commercially stronger party in an oppressive way. A party which is perceived to have limitless resources to pursue or resist litigation can often exploit its advantage, thereby forcing the weaker party into a compromise at a figure below that which they could reasonably expect in litigation. The weaker party either cannot wait or simply does not have the resources to take the matter right the way through to a conclusion. The risks involved are too great. Often, in addition, merely to sue invites a cessation of commercial relations. This is one reason why many large oil companies appear to have a relatively litigation-free existence. Some of their smaller suppliers simply do not dare issue proceedings. Economic power may therefore be used to prevent, inhibit or determine litigation outcomes. Whether this is an appropriate strategy is a wider issue than the question of ADR use. However, some companies have begun to set up schemes with distributors as a way of deflecting just such criticism.

7.4.6 Summary judgment available

Where summary judgment is available (whether to claimant or defendant by virtue of CPR Part 24) and attainable, there is an argument for seeking it as an end in itself. Alternatively, it might be sought so that, should there be any subsequent negotiations, perhaps over enforcement or terms of payment, the claimant can operate from a position of strength. Thus, in a straightforward debt recovery action with no substantive defence, ADR is not often used.

Similarly, if a defendant can get rid of an unmeritorious claim once and for all by using Part 24, there is little point in considering ADR.

However, even in those situations, there are still valid arguments for using ADR, for example the desire to maintain good commercial relations with customers or suppliers. In this context, ADR usage has to be viewed in the light of wider corporate policy or image, and not solely as a question for that particular dispute. ADR is sometimes used by a party who thinks that it has an unanswerable case simply to meet with the opposition to explain that view to them and to listen to any persuasion to the contrary. It is best to discover at the earliest possible time that a case thought to be cast-iron, or a defence thought to be just plausible, is less so than hoped. If this can be done in a principled and respectful way, future relationships if any may well be able to be preserved.

In any event, there are many actions where summary judgment is not obtainable. If a claimant, or indeed defendant, applies for it and fails, that may well be an appropriate juncture to try ADR.

7.4.7 No genuine interest in settlement

ADR processes are consensual, and to that extent require all parties to be interested at least in exploring settlement opportunities (though that is by no means tantamount to a willingness to settle on any terms). If one or more parties to a dispute can genuinely be said to have no interest in settlement, then manifestly ADR is unlikely to work, except to the degree that such an attitude may itself change as a result of an ADR process.

However, it would be unwise to assume too readily that any party is genuinely uninterested in settlement. Very few parties litigate for the sake of the process, unless perhaps motivated by a desire for vindication or revenge. Most parties are interested in the substantive outcome, not the process. If terms can be found that satisfy their demand (in the light of the strengths and weaknesses of their position) then settlement can be achieved. The question is simply which process will be more likely to generate such terms.

Therefore, great caution should be applied in interpreting the inevitable posturing of both the other side and indeed one's own client. Such behaviour is by no means necessarily inconsistent with a willingness to settle.

7.5 BENEFITS OF ADR

Any advice to clients on whether or not to use ADR will need to contain an assessment of the benefits and risks of doing so. Although these are touched on in other parts of this book, it is useful to draw those strands together and summarise them. Clients for whom ADR is new will almost certainly want to address these at some length.

7.5.1 Cost

It is self-evident from the informality and speed of ADR processes that the costs are likely to be significantly less than commencing or continuing with litigation or arbitration. The costs element is dealt with in more detail in section **7.6.3** below.

7.5.2 Speed

The speed with which ADR can achieve solutions is in marked contrast to litigation or arbitration. A typical mediation lasts one day. Infrequently a mediation may extend to two days, and an exceptionally lengthy one might last five days. Moreover, mediations can be set up as quickly as the parties require, the only constraint being the availability of those who will attend. Especially since court-referred mediations under a CPR Part 26.4 order or at case management conference, involving a stay for one month or more, have become increasingly common, the time from referral to mediation has been reduced as a matter of course from six to eight weeks to three weeks or even less.

The importance of speed cannot be underestimated. Commercial disputes take place in a commercial context, not a vacuum. The inability of business managers to plan for the future because of the uncertain outcome of a dispute, which in litigation may remain uncertain for many months and even years, can be a major problem, touching not only on cash-flow, but often on much wider issues of corporate planning and strategy. Similarly lay claimants often find the slow nature of litigation incomprehensible, painful and unacceptable.

7.5.3 Control

Businessmen (and many lay people) are used to the negotiation process, in which they retain a large measure of control over both the process and the outcome. In litigation they find they have very little, if any, control, and that in itself is immensely frustrating. The process is largely dictated by pre-determined court procedures, and the outcome is dependent on the presentation of their case, the performance of their witnesses, and the opinions of the judge, all of which are largely beyond their control.

ADR returns the element of control to the parties (in conjunction with their advisors). The process is not pre-determined, but open to the parties to decide. Thus a process can be chosen or even designed to reflect their intentions and priorities, as well as the nature of the problem. The similarity of mediation (in particular) to normal methods of direct negotiation means that many clients are instinctively familiar and at ease with the process. The outcome, too, remains entirely within their control, in the sense that terms cannot be imposed upon them, but only arrived at through negotiations. Furthermore, the informality of the process, and its similarity to direct negotiations, makes their active and confident participation far more likely, and compares very favourably to the experience of being in the witness box!

Court trial can be a very unpleasant environment for any party, whether the case involves commercial or personal issues. Control is in effect given over to the professionals. This is in marked contrast to the centrality of parties within mediations, both physically to the mediator in joint sessions and also at the heart of the discussion and decision-making process.

7.5.4 Relationship

The adversarial nature of litigation and arbitration forces parties into confrontation. Not only does confrontation not always generate results efficiently or effectively, it may drive the protagonists further apart. In some cases this may not matter, since the parties have no ongoing relationship to consider. In a commercial context, however, the effect on business relations can be a major disincentive to, or a detrimental by-product of, litigation or arbitration.

By contrast, ADR is an approach far more likely to minimise the deterioration in relationships, and in some cases may even provide a forum for new and more creative future working relationships to be established. That is not to say that the atmosphere of a mediation is not a tough and often aggressive one, but rather that the process itself is contributing to, rather than destroying, the parties' relationship.

This can also have implications for a company's image or reputation. Consistent and fair use of ADR (where appropriate) may be used to send a significant message to business suppliers, customers, and others. The use of ADR should, at best, go far beyond consideration of individual cases, and inform a company's approach to its corporate image. A good example of this is the corporate ADR pledge, used to good effect by leading companies in the US. This involves a public commitment to the use of ADR in appropriate cases. In reality, the discretion over ADR use is left entirely to the company, on a case-by-case basis, but the message sent to the market-place is an important one. Furthermore, it is much easier for a party in dispute with such a company to suggest ADR in the light of such a pledge.

The practice of entering into non-binding statements of intent to mediate or use other forms of ADR has become more popular. For example, the Market ADR Commitment (MAC) is an Accord which commits signatories, all of them significant participants in the professional indemnity insurance market, to utilise ADR where possible to resolve such disputes.

7.5.5 Creative and forward-looking solutions

Litigation and arbitration are historical exercises, based on an analysis of rights and obligations. The focus of any search for a solution, or the final judgment, tends to be based solely on what happened (historical facts) and what rights and obligations attach to the parties as a result (law).

These elements certainly feature in ADR, but other elements are also involved – in particular, the parties' interests and needs. Necessarily, therefore, the scope for settlement is wider, generating more possibilities and making settlement more likely. Settlements reached in ADR will often reflect much more than a straightforward payment of damages. A typical example in a commercial dispute is terms of settlement including an agreement for A to supply B with certain products at discounted rates (say, cost price). B will then receive something with a value of, say, 100 units, which only costs A 50 units to supply.

Furthermore, it is entirely logical that a settlement should reflect not only the strict legal position (or rather the parties' perceptions of it), but where possible their personal or commercial interests and needs as well. There are often situations where the payment of damages, whilst always welcome, does not in itself address the underlying commercial problem. Such interests and needs are simply not relevant as far as a judge or arbitrator is concerned, in arriving at a decision, but are highly relevant in ADR.

Such innovative and wide-ranging solutions are particularly to be found in personal injury, clinical negligence and employment mediations. Those who bring such claims often labour under a major sense of grievance. They may want to know why a catastrophe (as they perceive it) happened to them, whether any changes have occurred to ensure that no one else goes through the same experience, or whether any disciplinary steps are to be taken against someone who discriminated against them. Even receiving an expression of regret can help.

More tangible outcomes can be negotiated, such as:

- an assurance of future employment;

- the restructuring of a department or of a hospital's procedures;

- compensation in kind, such as treatment or care or a written expression of regret for delay.

The list is potentially endless, and illustrates the scope for imagination in devising ways of meeting the true interests of those involved in disputes.

7.5.6 Confidentiality

There will often be situations where, for example, commercial considerations demand confidentiality. Litigation is almost always a public forum, and arbitration can become public on appeal. ADR is a private process, and this is frequently cited by parties as a reason for using it. For example, a company may wish to settle with a certain litigant without that information becoming known to other litigants with similar claims. A charity might fear the effect on its donation income if it is seen to be involved in a bitter and costly dispute. A professional partnership may wish to deal with a negligence claim against it without any public knowledge that the claim was made, not least for reasons of professional reputation.

Equally, it is open to parties at a mediation to discuss and plan any necessary publicity for the outcome of the mediation. ADR is now being used for defamation claims, the outcome of which might well require public statements as part of the settlement terms. The parties can therefore agree within the entirely confidential process which led to settlement precisely how retractions, apologies and agreed statements are to be given due circulation.

7.5.7 Discipline and focus

The CPR have injected the concept of active case management into the litigation process. This means that even the heaviest case will move from case management conference to case management conference with the court keeping an eye on progress. The whole jurisdiction of striking out cases for want of prosecution, so beloved of defendant lawyers, is largely irrelevant and defunct now. However, there is still no doubt that the time-scales at which litigation and arbitration move are much slower than ADR. While litigation and arbitration might not be able to drift along quite so much as they could before the CPR, it is still by no means rare that it is relatively late in the day that the case begins to be analysed in full. The pre-action protocols will help in advancing information exchange, of course, but there is always a temptation to want to extract yet more information (by disclosure, exchange of evidence and so on) before the case can be properly and fully appraised. This can also be a symptom of an unwillingness, sometimes on the part of the lawyer and sometimes the client, properly to focus on the case, to address the issues and take decisions.

Ultimately, the only procedural step (in litigation or arbitration) which forces them to do so is the final hearing or trial – hence the tendency for such focused analysis to happen late, and probably the reason for many court-door settlements. ADR engenders the same effect, forcing the pace of rigorous analysis, debate and decision-making, but it can do so at any stage, though preferably sooner rather than later. It operates as an artificial court-door, creating much of the atmosphere and focus associated with an imminent trial, but doing so much earlier and without all the expensive trappings of trial such as fully paginated bundles of evidence and attendant counsel and experts waiting to contribute. As we have seen, it is possible that settlement at the real court door may be made less attractive as the implications of the CPR and its costs sanction regime are worked through in judicial decisions.

7.5.8 Satisfaction and consequent compliance

ADR processes are often more satisfying to the parties than a trial or hearing, for many reasons. The fact and relief of reaching settlement, and of doing so by consensus, coupled with all the other attendant benefits referred to in this section, tend to generate very high levels of satisfaction. Inevitably, some of this will reflect well on their advisers, and furthermore, the parties are much more likely to return to those advisers with future disputes if the whole experience has been a positive one.

Secondly, ADR is likely to provide a much more satisfying day in court than a real day in court. The informality means that parties can participate fully, rather than solely through their advocate, and there is none of the stress of cross-examination by the other side. They can, and often do, speak their minds, and indeed some element of venting of emotion may be vital in generating settlement.

Finally, since any settlement is reached by consensus, it follows that implementation or enforcement is much less likely to be a problem than it is where judgment is imposed.

7.5.9 Effectiveness

Finally, ADR processes do have a remarkable track record in generating settlements. Whatever the arguments, this fact alone suggests that the use of ADR should always be considered.

7.6 RISKS OF ADR

It is generally accepted that ADR is not, on the whole, a risky process. The fact that it is voluntary, confidential and 'without prejudice' leaves little real scope for parties to be exposed or prejudiced as a result. However, such concerns as there are do need to be addressed, not least because clients may well wish to discuss them.

7.6.1 'I will disclose my hand'

The trend towards 'cards on the table' litigation has been confirmed and consolidated by the CPR. The components of the overriding objective, embodying concepts of an equal footing between parties, fairness, proportionality, cost saving and so on mean that a party who endeavours to take an opponent by surprise at trial is likely to find such a tactic back-firing. A prime example of this is found in the case of *Ford v GKR Construction* [2000] 1 All ER 802, a personal injury case in the Court of Appeal, where the claimant still received her full costs despite failing to beat a Part 36 offer. During an adjournment of her trial for two months, the defendants obtained video evidence showing that she was capable of doing more than she claimed in her evidence. This was disclosed before the hearing was resumed some weeks later but the defendants declined to negotiate. The judge accepted the evidence of the film but was supported by the Court of Appeal in declining to give the defendants their costs from the date of the Part 36 offer. They had chosen not to video her before and then refused to negotiate. The implication was that the continued trial had in effect been their fault. Thus a party conceals their true case in order to ambush their opponent at trial at their peril, at least in relation to costs orders.

All procedures within both the mainstream CPR and the specialist court jurisdictions now require exchange of witness statements and experts' reports well in advance of hearings. The pre-action protocols even require a substantial degree of frankness about each party's position before proceedings can safely be issued at all. The Personal Injury Protocol calls for a detailed letter of claim setting out a full factual summary, the nature of any injuries suffered and financial loss incurred. The defendant must respond within three months: if liability is denied, reasons for doing so must be given, and a list of relevant documents sent. There is also provision for medical evidence to obtained either jointly or separately. The Clinical Negligence protocol additionally deals with disclosure of medical records.

The same spirit of pre-action frankness is demanded of all litigants in whatever type of case by para 4 of the Practice Direction to the Protocols, which reads:

> '... the court will expect the parties, in accordance with the overriding objective ... to act reasonably in exchanging information and documents relevant to the claim and generally in trying to avoid the necessity for the start of proceedings.'

In such circumstances, it is unlikely that resort to an ADR process will have what is perceived to be the adverse effect of giving the other side early notice of one's 'clever points'. Furthermore, the reluctance to disclose one's hand contains an underlying logical flaw. The only way to make no disclosure at all is to have no contact with the other side (a risky omission in the light of the CPR anyway), by making no attempt to settle. This will virtually guarantee that the case will be tried. Perhaps it is only where one side intends to argue that an available document or a piece of evidence has much greater significance and effect on a dispute than an opponent seems to anticipate that legitimate reluctance over disclosing such a position arises.

Once it is accepted that some degree of communication and discussion, and therefore disclosure, is necessary, the argument is simply one of degree. All potential disclosures will be subjected to a cost-benefit analysis. What is the perceived or likely benefit of making this disclosure, in terms of generating movement towards settlement? What is the potential risk if settlement is not achieved? Those familiar with mediation will be aware that parties frequently conduct such an analysis during the mediation itself.

Furthermore, mediation contains a structural feature which enables, in effect, partial disclosure. A matter can be disclosed to the mediator, but without giving the mediator permission to disclose it to the other side. This enables hitherto highly secretive points or concerns to be raised for discussion, and exposed to neutral third party input, without the risk of raising them directly with the other side. In addition, the mediator may well be in a position to assist that party in assessing the value of extending the disclosure to the other side, and is more likely to know how such a point would be received.

Finally, the following points are worth noting:

- If a party has a strong case, what is the point in keeping all those strengths hidden? If the intention is to encourage or force the other side to change its position, early disclosure is likely to assist.

- If a party has a weak case, how much advantage is there in prolonging the agony? Of course there will always be instances where, for tactical, financial or commercial reasons, one party perceives it necessary to prolong the litigation process for as long as possible. However, that has to be offset against the ultimate and far greater exposure of losing at trial. Furthermore, discounted settlement terms may be available in exchange for a quick settlement.

- In practice the majority of cases are not sufficiently strong or weak to be able actually to guarantee an outcome with certainty. If they are, summary judgment is always available to claimant or defendant. If either party seeks and fails to obtain summary judgment, there is almost by definition enough doubt about the outcome of the case to justify consideration of ADR.

7.6.2   'ADR is merely a delaying tactic'

Another perceived risk is that ADR can be used merely as a delaying tactic by the other side. Some litigants try to use CPR Part 26.4 to obtain a stay of proceedings while ADR is explored but with the ulterior purpose of buying time. Some of the tactics experienced by mediation providers to delay by declining to agree on a mediator or making difficulties over finding a date are perhaps further illustrations of this.

However, ADR should not be allowed to delay the overall prosecution of a claim. The maximum compulsory stay provided for by CPR Part 26.4 is for one month, and all parties must consent to that. Otherwise the court must consider a stay to be appropriate. The Commercial Court Guide specifically provides that an ADR order can be made without adjourning a case, and goes on 'the parties should give careful consideration to the possibilities of fitting ADR into the pre-trial timetable without the need for any or much delay to it'.

The court has ample power to penalise and pressurise tardy parties. If one party delays in agreeing a mediator or a date or venue for mediation, applications back to the court have resulted in tough orders, on occasions conferring power on the ADR provider to nominate a mediator and to fix arrangements in default of agreement. A party or lawyer may try to delay once or twice, but it will be difficult to escape a developing reputation for such tactics, against which opponents will take steps.

The defendant can therefore be made fully aware that the claimant has every intention of vigorously pursuing the claims timetable set by the court. If the litigation clock is still ticking and costs rising, this will provide useful concentration on the need to consider reaching a solution to the dispute.

7.6.3   'There are no real costs savings'

Another objection to mediation is that it can only be usefully deployed once the whole panoply of the various litigation steps have been completed (statements of case on each side, disclosure, exchange of lay and expert evidence). Thus, it is said, savings in cost and time will be minimal. It is often said that the primary factor which contributes to settlement at the door of the court (certainly in English procedure) is that it is only shortly before trial that the barrister who is to conduct the case is fully briefed with all the relevant information to hand. Counsel is thus in a position (some would say for the first time) to make a detailed and informed assessment of its merits. As we have seen, this may prove a dangerous approach in future under the CPR.

The question of what stage a case needs to reach before it can be referred to ADR is dealt with above. In this particular context, the following observations can be made:

- Even where a case is referred to ADR shortly before trial, the costs of doing so will frequently compare very favourably with the costs of trial itself. With counsel and experts often not required at a mediation, and nothing like the formality of preparation associated with a trial, major economies are available.

- Where a case does not settle in ADR, on the face of it increased costs have been incurred. However, most cases do settle in ADR. Of those that do not, many settle shortly afterwards, as a result of input in the ADR process. In the remainder, much of the preparatory work for ADR can be used at later stages. Finally, it may well be that following unsuccessful ADR, the resultant litigation is on narrower or more clearly-defined issues than before, thus making it cheaper to conduct.

- Finally, a company whose policy is to use ADR where possible will almost inevitably find overall cost-savings. Even if one particular case fails to settle in ADR, and thereby generates increased costs, others will settle and the overall result is likely to be a net saving, rather than a loss. Several repeat users of ADR have now given details of major savings to their claims costs accounts.

7.6.4 'There is too much pressure to settle'

Those who experience mediation for the first time often reflect that they had not appreciated how much the process builds up a 'pressure to settle'. The combined effects of the parties' thinking about settlement objectives and the structure of mediation in a skilled mediator's hands mean that a considerable momentum builds up towards settling the case. This is seen in the high percentage of cases which settle in mediation, which is normally regarded as a virtue of the process.

However, there may be cases where clients need to be advised that they can achieve better settlement terms, or even maybe a better result at trial, than those finally on offer in a mediation (assuming that the advice is sustainable, and that 'better' takes into account the wider considerations of uncertainty, commercial risk, the stress of continued litigation, and so on). Alternatively, a period of reflection might be more appropriate than signing up to a late-night agreement.

The pressure or momentum built up during mediation is not so much a risk of the process, but rather a warning to parties to ensure that they are properly advised in relation to settlement proposals.

7.6.5 'I will give the impression of weakness on liability'

It is a common problem in many disputes that when each party has taken up its position, neither wishes to suggest any form of settlement discussion (including ADR) for fear of appearing weak or exposed. However, the CPR has done much to rid parties of any such fear. It is now entirely congruent with the thrust and purpose of the overriding objective that ADR be proposed by any party weak or strong. Because ADR is recognised as a full component of active case management by the court, anyone proposing it is simply acting consistently with that duty to assist the court in achieving the overriding objective.

That being so, the sooner the problem is addressed the better, otherwise the parties may find themselves committed to a trial they may not want.

CONTENTS

Chapter 8

Approaching the other parties

8.1 SECURING THE INVOLVEMENT OF OTHER PARTIES

Certainly, until the CPR came into force on 26 April 1999, it used to be true that one of the most difficult problems connected with ADR was to persuade an opponent into the process. This is still the case in a number of litigation sectors, notably in personal injury and clinical negligence. There is after all a dispute. Commercial relationships have broken down. A serious injury has been caused, said to be the other party's fault. An insurer has declined to pay a claim promptly. Feelings for a variety of reasons are running high. In such circumstances, it is unsurprising that one party's suggestion of a conciliatory process will be viewed with considerable suspicion by the other. Even when relations are reasonably good, the common reaction in litigation is that if one party suggests something new, in all probability it is to their advantage, and therefore to your disadvantage.

Why should proposing mediation be any different? The problem is still exacerbated by the fact that knowledge and experience of ADR remains relatively limited even now. While a number of the larger law firms and their clients have become sophisticated repeat users, the large bulk of law firms have still not been involved or undergone any training in ADR. Why should either party, or their lawyer, risk a process about which they know so little? Furthermore, there is no rule book, no CPR Practice, as there is for litigation. The absence of rules for a process not previously experienced may understandably provoke suspicion, insecurity and reluctance to engage in it. Coupled with the need to assimilate, understand and utilise the radical reshaping of the system produced by the CPR, let alone the new co-operative culture which they were intended to create, even now it is difficult for experienced litigators to embrace a yet further demand on their ability to cope with change.

ADR is now undoubtedly part of the mainstream of litigation practice, and these problems of unfamiliarity can be expected to ease increasingly. There will still remain the question as to how and when best to persuade the other side to engage in mediation, and considerable thought is still required to ensure the best approach. It is certainly true that there is no universally right method or time: each case will depend upon its particular facts, circumstances and personalities.

8.2 METHODS

Choosing between each of the following suggested methods for raising the ADR option with an opponent will turn on prior planning or on the assessment by lawyer and client as to which is the likeliest to succeed.

8.2.1 ADR contract clauses

The problem is largely eradicated if there is a contract between the parties containing a clause referring the dispute to ADR. The importance of such clauses in promoting an effective dispute resolution avenue, and therefore in helping to ensure the smooth performance of the contract, cannot be overemphasised. These clauses are dealt with in detail in Chapter 6. For the present, it is important only to note:

- It is largely irrelevant whether, as a matter of law, the clause is enforceable or not. (The debate about enforceability is also set out in Chapter 6.) The primary value of the clause does not lie in giving either party the right to mandate the other to attend a mediation. Indeed, one might readily conclude that a mediation taking place in such circumstances would have lost much of its potential for successful resolution.

- The value of the clause is that it enables the subject of ADR to be raised without any fear of indicating a concern about the strength of one's own case.

- The clause also reminds the parties that, at the time the contract was signed and relations were better, ADR was generally perceived to be a sensible route to take.

- The responsibility for the inclusion of these clauses rests with the non-contentious lawyers, being those charged with drafting the agreement in the first place. ADR is not only a proper concern for litigators.

8.2.2 Court-related ADR

As with contract-derived ADR, the suggestion by a judge or arbitrator that ADR might be attempted in effect does the job for the parties. There was much debate associated with the Woolf report which is still rumbling on as to whether ADR should be made mandatory, with the court having power in effect to direct that parties engage in it. The clear decision at the time of drafting the CPR was that ADR should not be made mandatory. Its tradition has always been one of voluntary engagement, and the fact that the parties chose to engage provided evidence of their commitment in good faith to exploring settlement. The first moves by the Commercial Court to increase pressure on parties to try what was seen as a very useful tool for dispute resolution were embodied in their Practice Note of 1995. The judges of that court developed the concept of persuasive orders to parties to try ADR, falling short of mandating it, but leaving the parties in no doubt that careful consideration would be given to exercise of the court's costs jurisdiction in relation to any party who declined to engage in the process or failed to do so in good faith.

The CPR have not extended their scope to incorporate the full force of the Commercial Court's approach, even though this has been reproduced in the Commercial Court Guide, with similar provisions in the Chancery Guide, and to be expected in the forth-coming guides to the Technology & Construction Court and the regionally based Mercantile Courts. Rather the CPR provide windows of opportunity for ADR to be considered, buttressed by the generalised threat that unreasonable conduct, whether before or after proceedings are issued, can in the discretion of the court be met with costs sanctions.

It is undoubtedly hoped that the information exchange generated by the letter and spirit of the pre-action protocols will enable a good number of cases which do not settle through direct negotiations before issue of proceedings to settle at that stage through ADR. The question of ADR is then raised specifically in the Allocation Questionnaire sent to all parties when the statements of case (formerly called pleadings) have been filed and served. The CPR Part 26.4 stay for one month for ADR or other settlement processes can then be tried if both parties agree, or the court thinks it appropriate. The court therefore can raise the issue of its own initiative.

Allocation is the last time that a case is likely to come before the court for an ADR direction on the fast-track, unless a special application is made. On the multi-track, opportunities arise to propose ADR at both case management conferences and pre-trial review. The court's power to intervene enables the issue to be raised in a relatively neutral way, not necessarily through actually imposing an obligation

Mandatory ADR as a feature of the court process does exist in some US Canadian and Australian jurisdictions. Contrary to what might be expected, surprisingly high settlement rates are achieved in such circumstances. In the English courts, the first signs are that court-referred mediations have no lower settlement rate than those initiated voluntarily.

8.2.3 Persuasion

Assuming that there is no contractual or court-derived obligation to use ADR, the only route to the mediation table is through persuasion. This is a skill in itself, requiring considerable thought and diplomacy. There is almost certainly very little to be gained from a demanding or heavy-handed approach; a subtler approach is more likely to bear fruit.

The opening approach can take place at various levels.

1 Party to party

If parties to a dispute have not yet consulted lawyers, any suggestion of ADR will be made directly between them. If lawyers are already involved there may still be good reasons for introducing the subject party to party rather than lawyer to lawyer. Lawyers often discourage direct client to client contact when a case is in litigation so that rights are not prejudiced. However, a direct contact between clients may be one of the primary ways to help people restore negotiating momentum. It is the clients who can really take decisions to progress the dispute. One of the reasons third party ADR methods are often successful is that the resultant meeting produces client contact, often for the first time in many months or even years.

Furthermore, where, for example, talks between lawyers have failed to produce agreement to go to ADR, a subsequent dialogue between chairmen of the disputing companies, or their managing directors, may offer a second chance. Indeed, disputes are not infrequently disposed of in their entirety at this level, after previous settlement negotiations have failed.

2   Lawyer to lawyer

If litigation or arbitration is under way, the majority of formal contact between the parties (whether concerning settlement or not) will be directly between each side's lawyer. Thus, if the suggestion is to be made that ADR be used, it can very properly be made through the lawyers. This has the advantage of introducing ADR within the context of the litigation or arbitration process, and thus avoiding the (false) impression that it is not part of the mainstream. Furthermore, it enables the lawyer to whom the approach is made to feel that the process is not one which will exclude him, a common fear amongst some practitioners.

3   Good offices

This expression is commonly used in international diplomacy where a third party country intervenes to act as a channel for making contacts and re-opening discussions between parties. The same role in commercial disputes can be performed by contacts which are common to the parties involved, such as a business associate, an acquaintance, an industry association or other interested third party. A good example of this was in the dispute between Euro Tunnel and TML over claims towards the end of construction of the Channel Tunnel. There was pressure from the governments of Britain and France and shareholders for the two parties to negotiate a settlement which they had failed to do. The Bank of England stepped in to 'hold the ring' while the parties met and ultimately achieved a settlement that at least allowed for completion of the Tunnel, although it did not resolve every disputed claim.

4   Formal ADR approach

One of the benefits of ADR organisations is that they can take over the task of reopening bridges or making contacts to facilitate further negotiations. If one party approaches an ADR organisation, most such organisations will offer to contact the other side.

8.2.3 *Approaching the other parties*

In some disputes they may even initiate contact with both parties in order to encourage a more beneficial settlement. Where neither party has invited this approach, it has the added advantage that neither loses face by agreeing to further discussions under the auspices of the organisation.

In the right circumstances, an indirect approach to the other side through an ADR organisation can succeed where a direct approach has failed, or is likely to fail. An ADR provider is often perceived as more independent or neutral. The party receiving the approach has the opportunity to discuss its misgivings or anxieties about ADR more openly, as well as to inform itself about the process in more detail. In short, some of the inherent strengths of the mediation process can be used even before the mediation itself formally takes place, in winning the consent of all parties to participate.

8.3 CHOICE OF APPROACH

Given the difficulties often experienced in getting other parties to the table, the choice of approach should be informed by the likelihood of success. A certain amount of forethought may be important and the following considerations may assist:

- Is there any objective information to refer to? For example, does the other side have any form of corporate pledge or public statement on its use of ADR? Is the other law firm a member of an ADR organisation and/or has it a track record of using ADR? In particular, it is worth noting that if a government department is involved in the dispute, the Central Unit on Procurement Guidelines can be referred to. These establish best practice for all disputes involving government departments and encourage the use of ADR where possible. (These are subject to review and thus have not been reproduced in the Appendix to this edition.)

- Is the suggestion most likely to be well received by the parties, their lawyers or other advisors? Are the lawyers likely to have to persuade their clients, or the reverse?

- Will the use of a third party approach make the suggestion seem more independent, and is that particularly important in this case?

- Do the other side and their lawyers understand what ADR is about? At all costs, avoid putting the other side or their lawyer in a position where they have to respond to the suggestion of ADR without having time to inform themselves. Ideally, once the suggestion has been made, they should be encouraged to discuss the matter with an ADR organisation, before giving a response.

- What factors would make ADR unattractive to you if you were advising the other side, and can they be met or addressed in any way?

- Offer 'talks about talks'. These can be very effective in obtaining unanimous consent to mediation. They will often consist of a meeting of all parties and advisers together with the ADR organisation which has been engaged, often on a 'without prejudice' basis. Views can be canvassed as to the most appropriate ADR process (mediation, executive tribunal, expert or judicial appraisal, etc), the ground rules that would be acceptable, a proposed timetable, and so on. A standard form of mediation agreement makes a useful focal point for discussion. The mediation process can be explained and discussed with reference to each clause of the agreement. It soon becomes apparent that the nature of the obligations that the parties are being asked to accept under the agreement are not particularly onerous. The process then becomes much less intimidating. Furthermore, the mere fact of bringing parties together for discussions (albeit not of the substantive claim) creates a constructive momentum and opportunity to re-open settlement discussions which may lead to an agreement without further third party intervention.

- Emphasise that the likelihood of both parties' gaining from the outcome is greater than in litigation, or at least that an effective review of each party's case will result.

- Emphasise that the offer of ADR should not be taken as a sign of weakness. Contrary to much expectation, the offer of ADR can in fact indicate, and be read as, a position of strength, especially since the CPR came into effect. What need is there to camouflage the factual and legal issues of the case behind the procedural technicalities of litigation? Surely the confident party will be willing to discuss the issues fully and frankly?

- Emphasise also a genuine willingness to hear the other side's arguments.

161

- Indicate, if your mind is not made up, that the approach does not prejudge the nature of the ADR process to be used, nor does it commit to the selection of a particular mediator or neutral – these can all be the subject of genuine dialogue.

- Recognise in particular that parties reluctant to use ADR at first may agree to it months or even years later. Many disputes have their own momentum, and will only come to ADR (if at all) once that force has been spent.

- Be thick-skinned! If you want to use ADR, accept the fact that not all the offers you make will be accepted. This is not a flaw in the process, but simply a fact of life. Your position after a refusal is unlikely to be materially worse than if no offer was made.

- Consider the balance between a consensual and a threatening approach. It would be perfectly possible to write to an opponent saying 'I wish to engage with you voluntarily in mediation, as this is the best way. If however you decline, I will draw this letter to the court's attention at trial. Unless you have achieved something wholly beyond what mediation might have supplied, we will invite the judge to make no order as to costs from the date at which mediation might have resolved the case.' This power-play approach is probably only going to work if all else fails, and even then it may not allow the mediation to set off in an atmosphere of harmony. However, it is often the case that mediations make good progress despite a difficult opening. Quite often the reason for having come to mediation has been forgotten by the time it starts, at which point the settlement dynamic may create its own momentum.

- Since the Access to Justice Act 1999, Legal Services Commission (LSC) funding (the new style for Legal Aid) is likely to be relatively rarely encountered except in clinical negligence claims. However, if the opponent has LSC funding, a refusal to mediate proposed by the unassisted party can be referred to the Legal Services Commission, who have made it clear that they might in those circumstances require the LSC funded party to mediate before permitting further progress with litigation.

CONTENTS

Chapter 9

Setting up a mediation

Once all parties have agreed to participate in a mediation, there are a number of issues to be dealt with and in most cases agreed with the other side. However, as with all approaches to ADR, flexibility is critical. It may be, for example, that many of these points need to be discussed and agreed before a party will give final consent to participating in the mediation. A rigid procedural approach should therefore be avoided. Whilst the various points below do need to be addressed, this can easily be done conditionally upon final consent to mediate being given. Indeed, receiving satisfactory answers to these points may be what finally brings a reluctant party to the mediation table.

9.1 CHOOSING A MEDIATOR

9.1.1 Sources of mediators

A mediator may be selected either through an ADR organisation or independently. In the latter case it may be, for example, that an obvious candidate suggests himself to one or both sides, perhaps someone they have worked with in the past, or whose role is in any event inherently 'in the middle'. Obviously if it is someone whom the parties already trust and respect, his role as a mediator will be enhanced to that degree before the mediation even begins.

An ADR organisation provides a useful source of mediators. Most will have available a range of individuals trained as mediators who mediate for the organisation as and when required. The advantage of this approach is that the organisation takes responsibility for ensuring the quality and ability of its mediators and ideally should have been involved in their initial mediation training. They therefore come with a certain (unofficial) seal of approval which can be comforting to the parties. Furthermore, it helps to ensure that matters such as mediator's professional indemnity insurance cover are addressed. Also the organisation's staff can help deal with general administrative arrangements, preliminary issues or with sensitive issues concerning the mediator's handling of the case, in a neutral capacity.

9.1.2 What qualities are you looking for?

The role and therefore the required qualities of a mediator are set out in some detail in Chapter 10. You will seek a mediator who you feel suits your needs and the particular characteristics of the dispute. It is also wise to think about what kind of mediator your opponent needs. It is important to remember that the mediator will almost certainly be having private consultations with your opponent in private. During these, the mediator will in effect be presenting your case and testing out your opponent's case in the light of your case, but clothed with the power and status which neutrality confers. Hence your choice should be one which fits your opponent's needs as well as your own. After all, the mediator will of course be doing exactly the same presentation of your opponent's case to you.

9.1.3 Subject-matter expertise or mediation skills expertise

Given the relative inexperience in mediation even now of many parties and advisers, it is perhaps inevitable that the request for a mediator should sometimes be accompanied by lengthy and detailed requirements as to his expertise in the subject-matter of the dispute. One ADR provider reports having received a request for a mediator with eight different specialist qualifications, and the likelihood of finding any individual who combined them all was negligible! This approach tends to reflect a preoccupation with an essentially arbitral (or at least very heavily evaluative) approach, where (albeit under the guise of mediation) the mediator is expected to give a view on the merits of the case – hence the importance of someone with expertise in the given area. Indeed, if the parties in fact want an essentially evaluative, as opposed to facilitative, mediation, then the requirement may be more justified.

The heart of mediation, however, tends to lie in a more

facilitative approach. In that case, the priority for a mediator should be strong 'mediation process' skills. These are addressed in more detail in Chapter 10, although in reality entire books could be devoted to discussing and analysing them. To a great extent, too, these skills are partly innate (in terms of the personality of the individual) and partly acquired by knowledge and experience. They are certainly not a product of mere book knowledge.

So in selecting a mediator, some useful questions to ask may be:

- What kind of mediation, primarily facilitative or evaluative, do I want?

- How vital is subject-matter expertise of the mediator? Am I looking primarily for an answer or a negotiating opportunity?

- What other factors might suggest the importance of strong process skills? For example, are there strong or difficult personalities involved which need to be handled well?

As professionals and parties become more experienced in mediation, the choice seems less daunting. Although it is difficult to generalise, it is likely that most people currently underestimate the importance of process skills and overestimate the importance of subject-matter expertise. This is partly due to immersion in arbitration or litigation processes, with their preoccupation in finding a factual or legal answer to a specific question, and partly because the nature of the mediation process is widely misunderstood. Much, if not all, of the subject-matter expertise required in a mediation is provided by the parties themselves, together with their respective advisers and experts. The mediator's role is much more concerned with working with their input, than with providing his own. In reality, of course, many good mediators will have some combination of the two skills, albeit in differing proportions.

9.1.4   Other ways of balancing skills

A number of options are available where a combination of mediation process skills and subject matter expertise is insisted upon.

1   The use of experts

A good process mediator can be selected to lead the mediation, assisted by a subject-matter expert in whom all the parties have confidence, who will provide specific expert input. This method has been used to great effect in a number of mediations in which we have been involved. It has similarities with the process of early neutral evaluation, or expert appraisal, referred to in Chapter 3, but with the additional benefit of a mediator present to negotiate with the input provided by the parties and the neutral expert. However, there are obvious cost implications of having an additional professional on the mediation team.

2   The use of co-mediators

Two mediators may be able to work together effectively on a dispute, by bringing to it a combination of differing skills and personalities. This can be a useful way of resolving a dispute between the parties as to the kind of mediator each wants, although great care has to be taken to ensure that the co-mediators can establish a realistic joint working method in advance of the mediation itself. That is particularly the case in mediation, where each mediator tends to have his own style and approach, which may not be shared by the other, and of course their ability to work together is central to their effectiveness. Again there are cost implications too.

3   The use of assistant mediators

As part of its training programme for would-be mediators, CEDR pioneered the approach of using assistant (originally called 'pupil') mediators. These are trained but inexperienced mediators who work alongside experienced mediators for a number of cases. Apart from its value to the individual, it can also be a useful way of combining different professional expertise in the mediation, in all probability without the cost implications of formal co-mediators. Mediators with some experience may also have a supervisory mentor at the mediation who is there to give additional feedback and advanced training, as well as offering input to the process. Such an arrangement is always disclosed to the parties and requires their consent.

9.2   ESTABLISHING THE GROUND RULES

Whilst the flexibility of mediation is rightly emphasised, there are nevertheless some fundamental ground rules which should govern the process. These are designed to provide a necessary level of protection for the parties, in terms of confidentiality and the 'without prejudice' nature of the process, so as to give the parties confidence in it and generate an environment for frank discussion.

9.2.1 The mediation agreement

For the sake of clarity, the terms on which the mediation is to take place should be agreed in writing between the parties and the mediator. A short mediation agreement is the most common format. CEDR's standard form mediation agreement is set out at Appendix A, and is discussed in detail in Chapter 5.

9.2.2 Codes of conduct

In addition to the mediation agreement, many mediators operate under written codes of conduct, and indeed ought to do so. These govern the ethical position of the mediator in various situations. An example of such a code is set out in Appendix C. The neutral and confidential position of the mediator is one which may create difficult ethical scenarios for him and it is as well to have thought those through and be able to rely on a written code of conduct should the need arise. Indeed, some mediation agreements incorporate an ethical code of conduct into their terms by reference. It is also important that the parties have the opportunity to consider the terms of any code prior to appointment of the mediator, so that their consent to its terms is obtained.

An example of the kind of ethical problem which might arise is the situation where one party discloses to the mediator, in a confidential private session, that the bridge which it has built (the final account for which is the subject of the mediation) may have a design fault. Although the chances are very slim, it is conceivable that the bridge may collapse in certain circumstances. The mediator is instructed not to divulge this information to the other side. What does he do? Clearly he has a contractual and tortious duty of confidentiality to the disclosing party. But what kind of duties does he have to the other party and to third parties and members of the public? At what point, if at all, is he released from his duty of confidentiality? Should he merely resign from the mediation and inform no one? This is discussed further in Chapter 4.

Another important issue would be in relation to conflicts of interest. In view of the importance of the mediator's neutrality, mediators should also operate under a duty not to act in circumstances where any conflict might arise. For example, if in the past a mediator has acted as an advisor to one party, is he prevented from ever mediating a case in which they are involved? Or is this merely for a period of time, and if so for how long? And at what point should he be influenced if his firm has acted for one of the parties in a related matter? These are all issues which a code of conduct will try to cover.

9.3 COSTS OF THE MEDIATION

9.3.1 Who pays?

The costs of a mediation can be divided into two elements – the costs of the mediation itself (mediator's fees and expenses, neutral venue hire, etc) and the associated costs for each party (preparing for, and having legal or other representation during, the mediation etc).

The most common position is for the former to be split equally between the parties while each party bears its own costs in relation to the latter. This reflects the fact that parties to a mediation are, in essence, buying a 'negotiating opportunity', and that opportunity applies equally to both or all parties.

There is value too in each party investing financially in the mediation as well as in terms of time and effort. Experience and common sense tend to show that those who have invested their own money in the process will approach it with a greater commitment to making it work than those who have not.

9.3.2 Variations on who pays

As is typical of ADR, flexibility is the key. If one party simply cannot afford the cost of a mediation, or is unwilling to because it is not convinced of the likelihood of success, it may be worth the other party paying all the fees. This is a relatively common practice, usually where the paying party has previous experience of mediation and therefore of its value, and the non-paying party does not. It is an indication too of the perceived value of the process that one party is prepared to pay both sides' fees simply to get them 'to the table' to talk. A variation of this is for one party to pay the other side's fees (as well as its own), but with the proviso for reimbursement in the event that settlement terms are (or alternatively are not) reached in the mediation. If the settlement terms involve any payment being made, the reimbursement can easily be built into it.

Those steeped in litigation will often instinctively want to apply a 'costs in the cause' approach to ADR. This is very unlikely to prove workable, since it presumes that one party will be the designated 'winner' in the mediation and the other the 'loser'. This can very rarely be said to be the case in any negotiated settlement, whether in ADR or in direct settlement negotiations between the parties.

The relative informality of ADR means that the negotiations can include a wide range of matters, including costs. The starting point for setting up a mediation may have been that each party has paid its own share of the mediation fees. However, there is no reason why the terms of settlement reached should not include, for example, reimbursement by one party of the other's mediation fees (and indeed of their legal costs of preparation for and representation during the mediation). This is purely a matter of negotiation.

In certain cases the mediator may agree to accept payment (or higher payment) only if the process achieves a settlement during the mediation (or within a defined period after the mediation). This is, however, not a common practice and any financial involvement of the mediator in the fact or terms of settlement may entail an unacceptable compromise of his position.

9.3.3   Costs of the litigation or arbitration

If a dispute has been in litigation or arbitration for some time, each party may have incurred very substantial legal and other professional fees, and the question of who eventually pays for these will usually be a substantive part of the terms of any settlement negotiated through mediation.

9.3.4   How much?

Most mediation fees are charged on a similar basis to any other professional fees, that is an amount per hour, per day, or whatever. However, the very short time periods required for a mediation (often only one day) mean that the costs are never likely to be that high.

The advantage of a daily, as opposed to hourly, rate is that it frees parties from the pressure of watching costs rise as each hour of the mediation passes. Some take the view, however, that such pressure is effective in terms of making the parties, and therefore the whole mediation process, more focused on their priorities and negotiating stances and preventing it from dragging on. Whatever the amount and basis of charging, fees will usually be agreed (and often settled) in advance of the mediation.

Public funding and conditional fee agreements are dealt with more fully in Chapter 4.

9.4 WHO SHOULD ATTEND THE MEDIATION?

The effectiveness of a mediation can be enhanced or reduced by the choice of who attends, and careful thought should be given to it. This applies to which parties attend, as well as to which of their representatives and advisers.

9.4.1 Which parties should attend?

1 Two-party disputes

Clearly in a two-party dispute both parties need to be present at the mediation. They will be signatories to the mediation agreement and should play an active role in the process. This is of immense importance. Mediation provides the parties with an opportunity to take control of, and 'own' their dispute and any solutions reached. It is these elements of control and ownership that are so often squeezed out by the formal litigation process. The temptation to think that the legal advisers alone can attend the mediation, and then report back to the clients by phone for final approval of the terms of settlement, should be resisted. Settlement terms emerge during a mediation, and in order to be acceptable to parties, they will often need to have seen them emerge, and to understand them in the context of all the discussions in the mediation. Full participation by the parties is essential for successful mediation.

2 Multi-party disputes

Similarly, in a multi-party dispute, it is important for all parties to take part in the mediation. Indeed, resolution of the dispute may only be possible if all do (for example, because the terms on which A settles with B may depend on the terms which B can agree with C and so on).

Similarly, a first defendant may only agree to pay the claimant £X if the second and third defendants also accept a proportion of the liability. In fact, mediation can often be particularly effective in multi-party disputes because the process is one in which all the various permutations of settlement can be explored with all the parties present.

However, if some, but not all, parties in a multi-party dispute want to mediate, and the remaining one(s) cannot be persuaded to take part, the willing parties can still use the mediation process to great effect. This feature is often overlooked. For example, three defendants to an action might easily mediate as between themselves on the question of how any settlement with the claimant will be apportioned amongst them. This may then put each of them in a much stronger position with the claimant, focusing all their attention on defending or negotiating the question of liability to the claimant, rather than defending their positions with each other as well.

The same logic applies to the issues which parties wish to address in mediation. Most mediations aim to achieve permanent and binding settlement of all the issues in dispute between the parties. However, many disputes contain an array of different issues. If agreement cannot be reached to attempt mediation in respect of all of them, it is entirely valid to agree to attempt resolution of only some.

3   Groups or associated companies

Mediated settlements can be wide-ranging in nature, sometimes touching on new commercial arrangements in their terms. Where a subsidiary company in a group is involved in a mediation, it is worth bearing in mind the possibility that another group company might ultimately be involved in any terms of settlement, and that representation of that company at the mediation (with appropriate settlement authority) might therefore be useful. However, that may be difficult to predict.

4   Insurers

Where a defendant is indemnified by an insurer in respect of any liability in a claim, it is the insurer who will in effect conduct the litigation by subrogation. The defendant may still have some interest by virtue of an excess or deductible, but the more the insurer has a financial stake in the outcome of a claim, the more essential it will regard it to be at a mediation to agree the terms of settlement. Where risks are shared between insurers, each will be represented.

As we shall see below, it is vital that sufficient authority to settle is given to those who attend on behalf of a commercial party. The same is true of an insurer. It is vital that the claims staff attending a mediation have enough authority to agree any sum which might have to be paid. This must be distinguished from what the insurer hopes the outcome will be, doubtless a much lower sum. The easiest way to be sure is to attend with sufficient authority if necessary to pay what the claimant's best case figure is. This is respectful to the claimant, for whom it may be very important to hear that someone with authority to pay his claim is sitting at the table for discussions. Conversely, to learn that the insurers have sent someone with limited authority is highly disrespectful and likely to antagonise the claimant, who may think (with some justification) that the claim is not being taken seriously.

9.4.2 The composition of a mediation team

1 Individual parties and negotiating teams

As has been touched on in relation to insurers in the previous section, one of the most important elements of a successful mediation is the presence at the mediation of those with full authority to settle the matter, on behalf of all the parties to the dispute. (It is interesting how often a mediation is the first occasion on which all those with such authority have met with a view to settling the case.) For individuals and sole traders, that should not present any problems. For companies, partnerships and other bodies or legal entities, the appropriate delegation of authority may need to be considered, such as board minutes, etc. Many mediation agreements contain express provisions confirming that those attending have full authority to settle (see Clause 3 of the CEDR model mediation agreement, at Appendix A). Other questions relating to authority to settle are addressed in Chapter 5.

2 Legal advisers

If there ever was a time when there was a body of opinion that suggested that commercial clients at least did not require lawyers at a mediation, that time has gone. Of course it is open to sophisticated parties to choose to dispense with lawyers. If a mediation is to be in effect a business negotiation with a purely commercial interest-based objective, the process is likely to be essentially non-legal, at least until settlement terms are reached, when lawyers might well be required to check the legal implications or draft a legally effective agreement. But it is certainly unusual for commercial parties not to have lawyers present, sometimes in-house, sometimes external, and sometimes both. Some insurers choose to represent their insured at mediations using claims staff and dispensing with lawyers, particularly in cases before issue of proceedings.

Individuals unused to litigation, like claimants in personal injury or professional negligence claims, should certainly have a legal adviser present at a mediation, and indeed the general guidance should always be for any party to have such advice available at a mediation. Very often the purpose of a mediation is to try to settle a claim which, if not already well into litigation mode, is likely to switch into litigation mode very quickly. The legal adviser is there to help assess the best choices to be made, advise on whether terms on offer might be bettered at trial and generally to keep the whole picture clear for the client. The mediator cannot fulfil that role of giving objective advice in the sole interests of each individual party: indeed it would be wrong for a mediator to do so, especially to an unrepresented party where this can give rise to real difficulties in mediations, as we shall see below.

Normally the lawyers who attend mediations are solicitors, but in heavy cases a party might choose to have a barrister present also. This needs some examination. Mediation is an informal forum, with very limited opportunity for forensic advocacy. One of its main virtues for lay participants is its very informality, and the centrality given to parties themselves. The more lawyers there are to get involved, the higher the risk that the parties will be marginalised in just the same way as occurs in litigation or arbitration. There is little extra value in bringing a barrister merely to be an advocate. If the case is sufficiently complex in terms of legal issues, then it might be warranted, but the days of solicitors feeling the need to 'take counsel's opinion' as a kind of insurance policy to protect themselves ought to be over. Such a view is in any event bad law: solicitors must take responsibility for the totality of advice given to a client and are not protected from liability in negligence by counsel's opinion. Furthermore, there is now no distinction between a lawyer's preparatory and advocacy roles in terms of exposure to claims for negligence, since the

House of Lords in *Arthur J S Hall & Co (a firm) v Simons* [2000] 3 All ER 673 reversed the principle of advocate immunity from suit for negligence or breach of contract.

Mediation is a forum in which a solicitor's skills ought to be well adapted. While an ability to advise authoritatively on the litigation alternative is of importance, it may prove just as important in a complex commercial case to have a non-contentious commercial lawyer at a mediation to help with constructing and drafting a workable commercial outcome.

In one circumstance, it is crucial that counsel for a party is at a mediation. This is where the interests of a party who is under a disability are involved, so that any settlement could only be provisional and subject to the approval of the court. Most typically this will involve children and head-injured claimants in personal injury claims. It will be counsel who will advise the litigation friend as to whether what is proposed is acceptable, and will have to take responsibility for persuading the court to approve the settlement. In such cases, there may have been an appreciable discount from the sums claimed to reflect a real litigation risk. It is much better for counsel to have taken an integral part in the debate which led to such concessions, so that a convincing case can be put to the court to give approval.

3 Expert and factual witnesses

It can come as a surprise how often cases which at trial would turn on testing out and resolving differences in expert evidence are mediated successfully without the experts there. The truth is that parties and lawyers are always taking a view on the strengths and weaknesses of expert evidence when they settle cases before trial, and very much the same happens at mediations. Besides the expense factor of having an expert witness present, when the debate turns to commercial and personal interests and away from legal rights and the prospects of success at trial, the details of the likely trial evidence, expert or lay, become less significant.

In theory it would be perfectly open to the parties to agree to have a trial cross-examination of expert or lay witnesses at a mediation. Mediation practice is flexible enough to allow for any such sub-process if the parties and the mediator see that it would help. As an alternative, it can be wise to have witnesses attend at a mediation to test their evidence out in private against whatever emerges to challenge that witness's evidence, and thus decide in privacy whether it will be persuasive at trial.

Another option in cases where there is a dispute between experts seen as crucial to the outcome of litigation already commenced is to hold the CPR Part 35 meeting of experts at the same time as the mediation. The results of that meeting can then be fed into the mainstream of the mediation.

A highly technical dispute, for example one involving computer software or a complex clinical negligence claim, might well benefit from the presence of each side's expert, and this approach is relatively common. The only question over that is whether the experts themselves are prepared to adopt a constructive and open approach to the discussions, or whether they are themselves part of the problem in being too partisan or losing sight of their clients' commercial agenda. Of course experts who are going to give evidence at trial will have to guard against such partisanship. A mediation could provide a safe forum for finding out whether they will approach their role appropriately if a trial takes place. A similar approach can be taken with lay witnesses.

A further alternative is to have an expert available at the end of a telephone to confer over any points that might arise, either throughout the day or at a specific time. While there should be no difficulty over confidentiality, especially where an expert has already had a report disclosed as part of the claim, it may be wise to clear such an approach with the mediator at least and probably also with the other side.

4   Unrepresented parties

Having an unrepresented party, or one who is not sufficiently sophisticated to appraise their rights, obligations or negotiating position, can present considerable difficulties to a mediator. Every effort should be made to persuade such a party to have legal advice available to them. Such a problem quite often arises where the claim is for professional negligence against one or more former solicitors. For entirely understandable (even if misguided) reasons, a claimant suing a former solicitor may well have no wish whatsoever to trust yet another lawyer as a representative and adviser. Sometimes such a party can be persuaded to use counsel instead.

With a mediator's obligation to be impartial and not to advise, it can be very frustrating and puzzling for an unrepresented party when the mediator declines to help with such problems. It can be very difficult for a party to make sound decisions, especially with such difficult issues as causation of damage to disentangle. There is also the very real problem of how to ensure that a settlement is not unfair to the unrepresented party in terms of how it reflects their actual rights and obligations in the dispute.

It is not the mediator's responsibility to determine or impose fairness, though that responsibility certainly extends to guarding the parties against the adverse effects which can arise from a significant imbalance of power. Even a friend who is not legally qualified can help to add perspective for an unrepresented party. Ultimately it may be wise for a mediator to suggest that a cooling-off period is written into a settlement agreement for the protection of both parties. Even with a neutral mediator, there is still perhaps the risk that an obviously unfair agreement proposed by a strong party and accepted by a weak party might be set aside as unconscionable. However, it must be remembered that what might appear to be unfair to one party may yet be acceptable to that party because of other factors of which the mediator is unaware.

9.5 DOCUMENTATION

In most disputes, there will be some relevant documentation which it will be important for the mediator to see prior to the mediation itself. In addition, it is common practice for each of the parties to submit to the mediator a brief written summary of the dispute and its position. This helps to inform the mediator in advance. Furthermore, in a complex case, drafting such a summary may be a valuable exercise in itself for those concerned, since it requires reducing extensive statements of case, schedules, chronologies and witness statements to a brief format.

The emphasis in preparing documentation should be on brevity, in keeping with the whole thrust of mediation towards ascertaining key and fundamental issues. Additional documentation can always be produced during the mediation if necessary, since there are no rules governing the inclusion or exclusion of documents. Thought must be given to what the mediator *really* needs to see in order to be informed about the dispute, and to which documents reflect the *key* issues and arguments that need to be addressed. Equally, however, in cases of extreme complexity, it may be that more extensive paperwork is necessary, not least so that the mediator can understand the situation in advance of the mediation. Even here, though, it should be remembered that the purpose of the mediation is not to generate a binding decision, and therefore the documentation is likely to play a less important role than in litigation or arbitration.

Once the parties' case summaries have been prepared, with relevant documents appended to them, they are exchanged between the parties and copied to the mediator. This is normally done expressly on a 'without prejudice' basis.

Various options are available in relation to documentation:

- Each party can produce its own case summary and related documentation.

- The parties can agree a joint bundle of relevant documents, and even a joint case summary or list of key issues.

- The parties can have joint or separate summaries and documentation which they are prepared for the other side to see plus further private summaries, position papers or documentation which they can send in advance to the mediator or bring to the mediation for the mediator only to see, such as counsel's opinion, experts' reports not yet exchanged, etc.

Again, the flexibility of the procedure permits these and other options.

A copy of CEDR's advice to parties in preparing a pre-mediation written submission is to be found in Appendix D.

CONTENTS

Chapter 10

The roles of mediator, lawyer and party in a mediation

10.1 THE BROAD SHAPE OF THE MEDIATION PROCESS

Unless defined otherwise by contract or court order or rule, there are no strict legal requirements on the procedure by which a mediation or indeed any ADR process is to be conducted. The management of a mediation is thus very much within the mediator's discretion, subject only to appropriate consultation with the parties and any preliminary agreement. As will be seen in detail in later chapters, a typical structure has evolved, comprising:

- an opening joint meeting;

- a series of private meetings (or caucuses) with each party;

- (optionally) a further joint meeting or meetings;

- a final joint meeting to sign the settlement or (again optionally) to plan the future in the absence of settlement.

The process for the mediation can usefully be discussed at a pre-mediation meeting or contacts between the mediator and ADR provider organisation and the parties. This can be used to agree the legal framework or ground-rules for the conduct of the mediation itself, including the terms of the mediation agreement by which it is to be conducted.

This chapter will look at the roles of each of the major participants in a mediation in general to ensure that all concerned fully understand what is going to happen, their own role, and the different perspectives which the other party is likely to have during the process. Subsequent chapters will look in detail at each stage of the process.

10.2   THE ROLE OF THE MEDIATOR

In clarifying the role of the mediator, it is vital to distinguish between the two fundamental elements of a mediation, or indeed any dispute resolution process, and where responsibility for each lies. These are *process* and *outcome*.

10.2.1   Responsibilities for process and outcome

As we have seen, responsibility for *process* in mediation lies with the mediator, just as it lies now with the court in litigation. This encompasses the nature of the event, whether each of its possible component parts are used at all in a given case, and if so in what order and involving which participants.

Responsibility for the *outcome* of mediation and indeed the outcome of the dispute rests always with the parties, as advised by their lawyers. The mediator is not a judge or arbitrator and makes no findings as such. The parties are free to negotiate or not, make offers or not, or settle or not. It is their dispute and it needs to be their solution. This very control over the outcome is what makes mediation an attractive process for many who ultimately might feel they would prefer not to confer responsibility for making a major business or personal decision on their behalf on a third party stranger. Whether this is a judge or an arbitrator, the person who decides the case has absolutely no personal or legal responsibility for any later consequences of that decision, subject only to any right of appeal.

Of course parties have a contribution to make to decisions about process and the mediator to discussions about outcome. The mediator will obviously consult with the parties to make sure that decisions about the order of joint and private meetings, opening presentations and so on are made as far as possible to suit the particular needs of participants. Ultimately though, it is for the mediator to determine these issues. Equally, the mediator will stimulate debate and analysis of the issues and possible solutions, though being careful not to cross the boundary into expressing a view on the merits unless clearly asked to do so.

These parameters explain differences in approach of mediators on various matters and at various stages within the mediation process. A mediator may well be firm and authoritative (but not domineering or autocratic) in managing the process but much less assertive when it comes to dealing with the issues at stake in the dispute. Especially with parties and (perhaps even more) lawyers inexperienced with the mediation process there is a need for careful handling and explanation of procedural decisions. This applies too in novel or complex cases and / or where issues of public accountability arise. But a mediator must take responsibility for ensuring a fair unbiased process and if this is not secured, a disadvantaged party may well quickly object.

A mediator is unlikely to bring the same style to the issues. Mediators will probably avoid arguments with parties and advisers, and should not give approval to one or other party on the merits of their case. The aim is to establish a working atmosphere in which the parties sense that the mediator is working alongside them in a joint problem-solving venture with each side. This may well involve testing reality in a direct and probing way, but should be challenging rather than confrontational or judgmental. The key is to be able to address the issues with each party in an analytical and objective way which will help that party to reach a better understanding of the strengths and weaknesses of their position. They have to feel that the mediator has not judged them or 'come down in favour of the other side'. It is not for mediators to ensure that the outcome is what *they* consider to be just. It is always for the parties to decide what is fair for them, though they are free to seek as much perspective from the mediator on what is fair as they wish.

A mediator will almost always seek to explore the interests of each party (what that party really needs and is looking to achieve from the situation of dispute) as well the pure legal rights which underpin the dispute, and which doubtless they are claiming. In most mediations, settlement is reached without determining or reaching a final decision as to what the purely legal rights are. Indeed, very often the final outcome falls somewhere between two diametrically opposed outcomes (one party wins, the other loses) which is all that a court could decide.

It is a vital skill for any mediator to gain the trust of all present at a mediation. Until there is a good level of rapport between mediator and party or advisers, any venture even into entirely objective reality-testing may be viewed suspiciously as evidence of having taken sides. This means that a mediator may need to spend some time on apparently inconsequential or marginally related topics with a party if that necessary degree of confidence in the relationship has still not been established.

Mediators must also judge the balance to be struck between dwelling on the strict legal position and investigating and mobilising interests. Parties may well need the occasion provided by the mediation to give vent to their feelings about what has happened, both to the other party and to the mediator. Such catharsis may well prove fundamental to that party's ability to move on from the past in order to find a solution to the present and future. A skilled mediator will allow just enough of that to happen to be effective without being destructive.

The mediator must judge:

● how much the legal issues themselves are really responsible for the deadlock in negotiations, rather than lack of information about the other side's case or unrealistic negotiating positions: this can be a function of excessive lawyer control over the content and balance of the dispute and might as a result need reassessment with the party direct; and

● the strength of feeling the parties have about them: if strong, more time for review may be needed until the party feels they have been given due respect and attention, before turning to what might be a sensible or commercial way of trying to solve the problems.

10.2.2 Mediator intervention

Intervention by a mediator to influence the substantive outcome should be limited to exceptional cases, where the integrity and reputation of the process may be at stake, such as the following:

1 The need for a workable agreement

The terms of agreement emerging seem to be acceptable, but the mediator may have a strong sense that it will break down soon afterwards or has omitted a crucial term or consideration. This needs to be carefully tested out in private sessions first: it is possible, for example, that one party does not expect workability but is using mediation to achieve a simple agreement on which to sue for summary judgment.

2 Protection of unrepresented parties

Unrepresented parties can present a significant challenge for a mediator, unless they are obviously sophisticated enough not to need representation. There is a temptation for mediators to be drawn into 'advising' them, albeit informally, and so to depart from their neutral role. Mediators will have their own views in dealing with this, but as a general rule should confine themselves to ensuring fairness of process, not outcome. A degree of imbalance of power between parties is almost always manifested at a mediation. However, a mediator ought to intervene where power is obviously being abused or undue influence exercised by a strong party against an unrepresented party. In any event, an unconscionable bargain can sometimes be set aside by a court on established legal principles. The fact that such a bargain was struck at a mediation will probably not of itself legitimise it. A mediator will therefore want to ensure that the good faith approach inherent in the mediation process is not subverted.

3   Unethical conduct

A mediator should not *aid* a party to lie or make misrepresentations in negotiating with the other side. No mediator expects to be told everything by a party or for that party to be entirely frank with either the other side or the mediator, but that does not go so far as in effect colluding with a party who reveals an intention to mislead.

4   Protection of third party safety or property

There may be isolated cases where information emerges in mediation which indicates imminent danger to the health, lives or property of third parties (for example disclosure of a defect in new vehicle equipment). In such instances mediators arguably may be under a legal or moral duty, higher than their duty of confidentiality, to ensure that appropriate third party agencies are informed by the party or themselves. This is one of the most difficult ethical situations for a mediator to face, and fortunately likely to be a rare occurrence. Mediator codes of ethics may address this concern, and it may be incorporated as a term in the mediation agreement. The CEDR Code of Conduct is set out in Appendix C. The legal arguments relating to this conflict of duty are set out in Chapter 5.

10.2.3   Some role models for mediators

Mediators may undertake a wide variety of roles in a single mediation process. These will vary in balance and intensity

10.2.3 *The roles of mediator, lawyer and party in a mediation*

according to the needs of the parties and the context of the dispute. Some of the more usual ones are set out here, with brief critiques.

- *Process manager*

We have looked at this role above. Exercising this role effectively frees the parties and their advisers to concentrate on the problems

- *Facilitator*

There is always an important job to be done in easing communications by defusing a hostile or provocative atmosphere, channelling exchanges into a constructive mode, clarifying complex points and allowing or discouraging discussion of sensitive areas.

- *Problem-solver*

As someone with no stake in the outcome, the mediator can assist the parties to explore potential areas for solution, and to review obstacles and options for overcoming them. The mediator can help identify where expert advice may be worth calling in, review previous proposals for settlement and discover if adjustments can be made to make these more acceptable.

- *Information-gatherer*

There is much that can be achieved at a mediation by way of filling gaps in knowledge in a way that improves the parties' assessment of risk. Mediators may well be used for this process through private sessions, or may convene a joint meeting as a more efficient and responsive method of information exchange.

- *Reality-tester*

The mediator's neutrality is very important. It allows each party to have someone independent reflect on their case. While a mediator should generally avoid giving opinions, he can help shift party positions by questioning and reviewing their evidence and arguments (in a non-partisan manner) as a 'devil's advocate'. This can bring a greater sense of perspective to the existing views of clients or advisors. Mediators chosen for their expertise in a field may have been given an even clearer role of case assessment and evaluation and more scope to challenge each party's case. They should still avoid doing this until they have a good sense of the issues from both parties, and should preferably acknowledge that any views they express are based on the limited evidence presented to them.

● *Scapegoat/lightning conductor/sponge*

Mediation gives aggrieved clients and their advisers their 'day in court' more frequently than settlement negotiations within traditional litigation. It certainly provides a more satisfying 'day in court' than a court hearing (which is in any event very often forestalled by settlement at any stage up to the court door), since the informality of the process allows for a much freer and franker exchange in the parties' own words. There is a neutral third party to 'hear' the case and the problems and damage caused by the other side, and even possibly to 'blame' for a poor settlement when reported back to the company. By acting as a lightning conductor for feelings which permeate even the driest of commercial disputes, let alone personal injury, clinical negligence or employ-ment disputes, the skilled mediator will provide a useful safe outlet, capable of allowing and acknowledging the strength of views and feelings held.

● *Observer and witness*

This is not a witness for the sake of any future litigation, but someone silently watching parties as they deal directly with each other, able to control and step in if matters go wrong, but being able also to reflect back to each party in later private sessions what went on during the joint meeting.

● *Messenger*

This tends to be a less welcome role for mediators. Whilst there will be messages to be conveyed from one room to another, mediators who limit their role to this are unlikely to be very effective. Further-more, responsibility for the contents of messages lies with parties sending them, and a mediator may feel it more appropriate for a message to be conveyed by the sender direct. The mediator should arrange a carefully prepared environment for this to take place, perhaps a joint meeting with a limited agenda.

10.2.3 *The roles of mediator, lawyer and party in a mediation*

● *Deal-maker*

Conversely the mediator often will bear between the parties, or himself make suggestions for, offers and counter-offers, concessions, or 'packages' that represent party negotiations channelled through the mediator. In sensitive or difficult negotiations, the mediator may be much better placed to do this than the parties could in direct face-to-face negotiations.

● *Post-breakdown resource*

If a mediation fails to produce a settlement, the mediator remains available to broker or continue directly to participate in further discussions if these would be helpful.

10.3 THE ROLE OF THE LEGAL REPRESENTATIVE

There has been much more attention given recently to analysing the role of the lawyer who attends at a mediation to represent the client's interests. This will be looked at in this section, in an attempt to help lawyers establish clearer guidelines for themselves within the process. These will inevitably vary according to the nature of each dispute, the relative power relationship between each party and the composition of the team attending.

The fundamental role of any lawyer at any time is that of the skilled adviser. Classically, the lawyer is the well-informed champion of the client, advising on law and procedure, articulating the client's views to others and pursuing the client's best interests. Most lawyers are used to the requirements of such a role in litigation, but fewer have grasped the different, and subtler, application of that role in mediation. Let us look at some of these components.

10.3.1 Preparation

The amount of preparation needed to be effective at a mediation is still seriously underestimated by lawyers, if the observations of many experienced mediators are to be believed. Putting it another way, like most spheres of endeavour, the better prepared participant will almost always do better than the less well prepared. It is vital to have a session with the client to prepare in detail, going over the facts carefully, discussing and analysing the risk factors playing on the case honestly and openly. This session must also involve any or all of the following:

- a thorough investigation and understanding of the client's and the opposing party's position, motivation and imperatives, financial, technical and legal, so as to be able to deal with them in terms that they understand;

- thinking of as many concessions as possible which will be of value to the other side but which do not involve great cost to one's own client, such as regret, empathy, apology, or services of marginal cost to the client which are of much greater value to the opponent, in effect equivalent to money;

- deciding how best to demonstrate to the other party that the case being presented has substance, is being run competently, and needs to be respected as such and taken seriously;

- thinking through a series of stepped concessions in advance, costing honestly what each option will mean in terms of management time, public and internal relations, as well as money;

- testing each proposition against what the best or worst alternative is;

- assessing the risk factor for each possible outcome and valuing them realistically, in order to reach a composite approach to chances of success which can be set against what emerges as being on offer;

- taking the client through their part in presenting the best case both in joint sessions with the opposing team and in private with the mediator, rehearsing all the likely questions and issues that might emerge and how to respond to them;

- endeavouring to define the provisional 'bottom line' point below which negotiations within the mediation are simply not worth continuing because the chances of bettering the proffered outcome by continuing the litigation are clearly better;

- trying to define what factors would make a difference to the decision about bottom line and which would cause a change of approach.

10.3.1 *The roles of mediator, lawyer and party in a mediation*

These are what a sophisticated mediator will expect to be done at the mediation, and it is as well to do most of the thinking in advance.

That said, much of the impact of mediation is in the parties' revising previously held views in response to what they hear. The value of detailed preparation is to give the parties a clearly thought-out platform from which to negotiate.

10.3.2 Diplomacy with client and opponent

The lawyer is primarily responsible for selecting the team to attend the mediation. Everyone who attends should be necessary and have a clear role to play. If they do not, then they should not be there. Perhaps the most vital aspect of this is to be able to ensure that a person with sufficient authority to concede the worst case attends the mediation, however much either lawyer or client expects or merely hopes to improve upon that. It is impossible to predict what might emerge at a mediation to alter advance thinking. If parties are truly going to attend a mediation to listen, ready to change their mind in the face of persuasive argument, it is no good having to explain the niceties of this to someone more senior by telephone, often outside office hours, who has not been involved. Even if a more senior person needed to give that higher level of authority is reluctant to attend, it is essential that every effort be made to bring about a change of mind. There may be situations with a company, a trust or public corporation where authority can only be obtained by referral back to committee or Board. This must be flagged in advance with mediator and opponent. The mediator may be able to add weight to such a discussion in advance of the mediation.

10.3.3 Professionalism

Lawyers should never over-impose themselves on their client's case. Some clients will never allow that to happen, particularly the more sophisticated or commercial clients. The risk is greater with apparently less sophisticated clients with little previous experience of the law in action. It is easy to forget whose case it is with such clients. It is also easy to over-identify with the client in a determination to act the role of knight-errant. Loss of objectivity in the approach to advising a client can be extremely dangerous in skewing and depriving the client of their proper control. This is no less dangerous than the lawyer who runs a case for the lawyer's own financial benefit rather than the client's. Lawyers have no business (literally) to run a case to satisfy their own emotional needs.

10.3.4   Presentation skills

Key decisions have to be made about what may most effectively be expressed in the pre-mediation written submission as opposed to oral presentation at the mediation, and how to mobilise the client to best effect at the mediation. This is as much a question of presentation as content, and needs to be approached in that light. While there may be an element of advocacy in it, there may also be a need to ensure client participation in the presentation, to demonstrate credibility as a witness, or even to conceal lack thereof. This calls for considerable perception and sensitivity to the client's needs and capacities.

The role for advocacy is however limited. At the opening session, the presentation is to the opponent and not to the mediator, and it is in an informal and non-technical setting, with no rules of procedure or evidence to observe or circumvent. The process is much more like a negotiation than a trial. Thus counsel's negotiating and advisory skills are more relevant to mediations than advocacy skills, and hence counsel only rarely attend mediations. When they do, they need to be clear about their role.

10.3.5   Process skills

This can present problems for those who have not been to mediations before. Undoubtedly the client's case will benefit from being represented by someone with a good understanding of the dynamics of mediation, even if they have not been at one before. Role-play is a very effective teaching tool and recreates with surprising faithfulness what a mediation is like. It is poor client care to have to admit little or no prior experience or training in an area where the client is instructing a lawyer to look after their interests in a significant dispute. Mediation requires entirely new considerations, strategies and tactics to be taken into account and deployed. For instance, there is the question of how to harness the neutrality of the mediator to convey your case effectively to the other party in private sessions with them. How can the mediator be persuaded to bring back and share useful information about the opponent's thinking and negotiating stance for the benefit of your client? These skills require insight, forethought and practice.

10.3.6 Negotiation skills

A good understanding of the range of negotiation theory and technique is always going to single out the best lawyers at mediations. These are unlikely to be 'hard-nosed' or combative negotiators, though there may be a place for them sometimes. Co-operative or principled negotiation technique is often, if not always, more important and effective than confrontational stonewalling over a position, and is certainly less well understood and practised. It has to be founded on sound risk assessment. As the process continues, a flexible approach is essential, able to cope with the need to reappraise an initial risk assessment in the light of new information. A hard-line stance can simply have the effect of confirming to the other party an absence of good faith in seeking an outcome, which results in driving them away from the mediation. Undue negativity or aggression may simply waste the opportunity created by mediation to reach settlement without trial. A constructive problem-solving approach will at least ensure that every option is explored at the mediation, even if agreement cannot ultimately be reached.

10.3.7 Knowledge of law and procedure

It is sometimes assumed that sufficient knowledge will repose sufficiently in a single lawyer. It is asking quite a lot for one person to combine all the essential skills needed. On the one hand, the lawyer must understand the law in a given area, the commercial implications behind the topic and the pitfalls in trying to draft a new commercial relationship, plus sufficient knowledge of the procedural alternatives through litigation or arbitration. On the other, the lawyer needs sufficient knowledge and practical experience of mediation or whatever ADR process is being used. A team approach may on occasions be needed.

10.3.8 Understanding the commercial or personal options and realities

This is a vital aspect of a lawyer's job, linked with the need to retain a professional objectivity about the client's control of the claim. It is easy for both lawyers and clients to lose sight of the commercial or personal realities which hide behind the legal issues. The prospect of a solution which does not irreparably damage an existing commercial relationship, however strained by the dispute in issue, should not be forgotten.

10.3.9 Self-confidence, candour and courage

A mediator cannot necessarily be expected to solve all a lawyer's problems. One of the most frequently encountered reasons for non-settlement at mediation is that the lawyer has frankly found it impossible to get the client to accept the lawyer's risk assessment, or has been compelled to revise downwards the prospects of success to a level unpalatable to the client. This leads in turn to worries that the client may withdraw instructions, blame the lawyer or refuse to pay their bill in full in the event of 'failure' (according to the client's definition of 'failure'). Sometimes both lawyers may have difficult clients and tacitly or even expressly concede as much to each other. The temptation then is to advise the clients to go to mediation and hope that the mediator can somehow resolve the matter for them. It should never be assumed that this will succeed, though doubtless it happens.

Mediators do indeed use their independence as neutrals to reality-test with difficult parties. It is undoubtedly one of their most useful roles. But if such parties suddenly start to get an unacceptable message by this route that things look less good than had been hoped, at least from one perspective, they might well want someone to blame other than themselves. This could be the mediator or their opponent or even a malign fate, but they might just as probably turn on their legal adviser. There is a high risk that mediations will fail where either or both lawyers hope to mobilise the mediator to discipline a difficult client. There is no substitute for good and fearless legal advice from the outset, giving an honest appraisal of the risks of losing.

Mediators can and do help intransigent parties to change their minds. Their strength in being able to do so lies in their neutrality. But the client will respond badly to mixed messages from lawyer and mediator about prospects, probably by an angry retreat into an entrenched position. A lawyer who wants a mediator to perform this role must tell the mediator and then give full support to the undertaking, otherwise it will probably fail. The mediator can help the lawyer with trying to avoid loss of face if earlier advice has been unrealistically optimistic.

In the final analysis, wholly unreasonable parties may deserve an appointment with a trial judge with the authority ultimately to make a binding order to resolve it, and to make penal costs and interest orders against such parties. In cases like this, one or other party is almost certainly going to lose badly. The lawyer can only (and must) advise the client fearlessly of the risks and consequences of failure, placing responsibility for decision-making on the client.

On occasions, a lawyer has informally explored with the opposing lawyer a level at which settlement might be advised but without telling the client in advance or immediately afterwards. This must be dealt with openly by the lawyer to both client and mediator, as it will have raised expectations of the settlement range for the opposing team, and neither client nor opponent will understand the negotiation parameter expected by the opponent unless this is honestly disclosed.

10.4   THE ROLE OF THE PARTY

Although dealt with briefly here, this is the most important role of any involved in a dispute. For too long the parties have felt marginalised by the litigation and arbitration processes. Lord Woolf recognised it and this is a recurring theme throughout this book. By taking a problem to a technician – a lawyer – the person whose problem it is will, in the absence of great determination or sophistication, lose control of the solution process. Indeed, what usually happens is the solution is made subordinate to the process. Litigation has always been a process, and it remains so even in the CPR, however improved. It is circumscribed by several features:

- *the legal principles* it promulgates (based largely on retrospective precedent);

- *the remedies* it offers (again usually retrospective, to put the wronged party into the position they would have been in if the contract or the tortious duty had not been breached);

- *the procedures* it lays down to reflect those elements, which are technical and still not particularly accessible without the use of an expert.

The problem which gave rise to the claim was the party's before the lawyer was consulted and the outcome will be the party's after the final bill has been paid and the lawyer ceases to act. How involved can the party or client be in the process which leads from one to the other?

Proponents of ADR say that party involvement should be both encouraged and ensured by the process of exploration and settlement, though at all times with proper and full advice from a lawyer to assist proper assessment of prospects and options. Thus the lawyer, whether in-house and effectively integral to the client, or an external consultant, is vital to the process. But the party is the owner of the dispute and needs to preserve that final primacy.

10.4.1 Litigation and the removal of client control

It is perhaps too harsh to contrast the way that mediation deals differently with parties as contrasted with litigation or indeed much negotiation. Parties often attend commercial negotiations, sitting beside their lawyers as a deal is worked out. They are much less often at settlement discussions between lawyers of personal injury and clinical negligence claims, or employment disputes. Such cases are usually settled by telephoned negotiation or in writing, perhaps by acceptance of a Part 36 offer. Of course the client gives instructions to accept or reject, but it is the quality of the settlement event that gives rise to questions.

There is an increasing use of settlement conferences or joint meetings, perhaps with counsel present as well as solicitor and client. Even these are likely to be under the control of the competing lawyers and may not have an independent chair. As a result, counsel may go off and negotiate privately just as occurs at the door of the court. Again the control and input of the party may be reduced to a minimum, though probably to nowhere near as limited an extent as occurs in a trial.

The very layout of a court-room emphasises the way that parties are marginalised by the litigation process. Usually they will sit two or sometimes three rows back behind their lawyers. The general flow of communication on behalf of each party is from the advocate (facing away from the party) to the judge, who is usually an appreciable distance from the parties. Parties attend essentially as witnesses and have no control at all of the proceedings, which are highly technical. Communication between party and advocate is usually conducted by scribbled note during the hearing or out-of-court conversation, which will often be too late, or at least seem to be so.

Once the witness box is entered, the party normally may not discuss the case with their lawyers. Now that examination-in-chief has largely been replaced by reading witness statements, there is no real opportunity for a party to tell their story to the court, or in that sense to have a hearing at all in a personal sense. The party's case is presented for the client by the hired technician – the advocate – but only to the extent that it has not already been presented on paper. Indeed, the majority of testimony is going to be given in the hostile mode of cross-examination. Each party will thus spend the majority of their time compelled to defend their position without having any real opportunity to assert it free from challenge.

10.4.2 Mediation and the restoration of client control

Mediation restores control and centrality to each party, who will usually sit next to the mediator, and will be drawn into discussions in private session as a principal in the dispute. Parties should be encouraged and permitted to take this greater role if they want it (there will of course be those who do not). They should also be allowed to develop an increasing role through the course of a mediation if they choose. After all, inexperienced clients are allowed to learn as much about mediation and grow in confidence over their role as the process unfolds as inexperienced lawyers. Each party can strengthen the credibility of their case by active participation in joint and private sessions.

On a more negative note, a lawyer having difficulty with one layer of management in taking a reasonable line on the dispute may be able to involve a more senior layer. This might be done perhaps by reference to the need for adequate authority to settle, compelling the case to be taken seriously by the client at an earlier, safer and less expensive stage than trial. The client must clearly be prepared to engage in the dispute, and at least the forum offered by mediation makes it easier and in most cases quicker and more economical in management time terms for the party to do so. It is no more sensible for a client to dump a dispute on a lawyer than it is for the lawyer to snatch it away and exclude the client from the process of resolving it.

Teamwork is the key to success at mediation. Lawyers should, as experienced participants in the mediation and litigation processes, mobilise clients as effectively as possible and give them the central role that so often is not offered by the dispute resolution process. At the end of the day, having been thoroughly and wisely helped to look at all the legal, commercial, personal and financial issues that surround any dispute, clients can, and should be allowed to, make up their minds as to whether to settle on terms offered, taking into account all their interests and properly assessed risks as well as their legal rights and obligations. The skilled mediator is there to facilitate all those processes.

CONTENTS

Chapter 11

What happens at a typical mediation

11.1 DURATION

The duration chosen for a mediation has to be a matter of experience and intuition. What do the parties feel comfortable with in terms of time commitments and potential cost, set against the perceived need for a long or short enough period. Where the case can be quickly moved into settlement offers over a few central issues, a short time-scale can be proposed. If the case will demand that the mediator and parties work through a range of information and case investigation before a sensible stage of settlement discussion can occur, then a longer time-span will have to be set. Parties used solely to working with litigation will normally expect the mediation to take longer than it need, although mediators should not brush aside party expectations. At the same time, setting aside only a day or two for mediation can be a useful discipline on both the parties and the mediator. It will focus their objectives primarily on mediation as a settlement process rather than an investigation process and avoid concerns that mediation may be used as a deliberate time-wasting exercise.

Standard commercial cases can often be mediated within a day, albeit a day which can sometimes stretch well into the evening before settlement is achieved. Very high value, complex or multi-party cases may need two to three days set aside, and even more complex cases or cases with many parties may require between a week or several months (usually in a series of separate meetings rather than continuous mediation). In such cases it may be unrealistic or inadvisable to keep all parties together for the length of the case, but care should be taken with this as a sense of meeting together at some stage helps settlement momentum.

11.1 *What happens at a typical mediation*

The key objective for mediators, whatever the case duration set, will be to ensure that parties feel that the process continues to make or promise progress towards settlement. Open-ended time-scales should be avoided. Setting a deadline for the mediation to be completed helps discipline the parties into looking to make realistic decisions on settlement. ADR contract clauses, with mediation as a stage prior to arbitration or litigation proceedings, generally set time limits from initiation of the mediation. Parties can always agree to extend a deadline if they are satisfied progress can, or is likely to be achieved.

Two further models need mention. For simpler cases, the Central London County Court has pioneered the use of three-hour *time-limited* mediations, taking place on court premises between 4.30 and 7.30 pm. ADR providers are now increasingly offering time-limited mediations as an option. In order to be effective, these call for a high degree of skilled time management and careful but brisk focus on the issues by the mediator. However, if all parties accept responsibility for using the time as productively as possible, this short-form process can work well if the ground to be covered is not simply too extensive. Repeat users of mediation can take much of the process framework for granted, but a lay party new not only to mediation but to making a claim at all may well need time and space to adapt to its demands and possibilities.

At the other end of the scale is what has been termed *strategic mediation*. This was developed particularly with catastrophic personal injury cases in mind. Its thrust is to overcome some of the intense problems of communication which make such cases difficult, especially in the early stages. The idea is related to mediation schemes where a dispute resolution structure is made available to be used whenever disputes arise during, for instance, a lengthy civil engineering project like the Hong Kong Airport. A mediator will be appointed from a panel well versed in the general structure of the contract who is thus able to intervene effectively and speedily. In strategic mediation, the same idea is applied to a single personal injury case which is almost certain to be long-running. Typically, the mediator is appointed very early in the life of the claim and will assist the parties in sorting out both the issue of liability and, where liability is likely to be established, provision for rehabilitative treatment. Sympathy and regret can also be expressed at a time before positions have hardened. This early contact also means that a sensible working relationship, moderated by the mediator, can infuse the quality of all subsequent negotiations. The mediator, armed with full knowledge of the

200

dispute from the outset, remains available to mediate in a formal way with parties on any large issues which later prove difficult to settle. The fact that the parties have learned to work well together from the beginning will probably minimise the need for such later intervention.

A similar type of process has been called *pathfinder mediation*, where the mediator is in effect assisting the parties to design their own process for resolving their dispute. Mediation can be used to address purely procedural questions, ignoring substantive ones, at least at the outset. For instance, in one mediation the parties sought to address only the disagreement between them over the extent of disclosure of documents which should take place, and not the substantive claims and counterclaims. Rather than argue their respective cases at an interim hearing, they chose to bring the matter to mediation (in fact, once the mediation was under way they chose to address the substantive issues as well and were able to settle the matter in its entirety).

11.2 VENUE

Venue is perhaps more important a topic than might be imagined. A normal mediation is potentially going to last from six to twelve hours or more, during which time there will be a mix of hard work interspersed with periods when not much seems to be happening. There will almost certainly be times of tension and emotion. Each party and their team will spend a good deal of the day in their own room, at times working with the mediator, or reworking figures or arguments on their own, or waiting for the mediator to return with news of the next stage in the process. The venue must be geared to coping with a possible late finish. Another consideration is the documentation. If there are a number of parties each with quantities of documentation which they want at least to have available for reference at the mediation, the convenience of being able to drive to an out-of-town location with bulky documents parked close to the mediation suite is considerable.

Thus the more comfortable the surroundings are, the better participants will be able to cope with the varying pressures that a mediation imposes. Rooms with natural light, suitable furniture, perhaps with easy access to a garden area or the outside – all can ease and enhance the process. There are a number of purpose-designed mediation suites being made available now, and some mediation providers hold mediations at their offices. In recent years, parties have begun to use the offices of one of the parties' solicitors, and very often these meet the necessary comfort criteria, as well as minimising expense. If they do not offer the necessary comfort and out-of-hours servicing, serious consideration should be given to using, say, a hotel.

Mediators should inspect location arrangements before parties arrive to confirm that room layout is appropriate and to confirm or amend any requirements set out in preparations for the mediation. The following points should be remembered:

- Rooms should be of appropriate size for joint and private meetings (remembering that parties sometimes bring along additional unexpected participants).

- The layout of the main room should be suited to round-table negotiations rather than courtroom advocacy (and of appropriate size to avoid too much or too little distance between parties).

- There should be reasonably comfortable separate private rooms for each party (or coalition of parties).

- Soundproofing should ensure privacy for each party's discussions.

- Flip charts should be available in rooms and any audiovisual aids requested by the parties.

- Catering arrangements should be checked (buffet style refreshments, preferably in an open setting between rooms, can assist parties to make informal contacts between sessions).

- Telephone, fax facilities and other business services need to be available.

- Overnight arrangements for rooms to be locked or other document storage facilities must be made where mediation is to last longer than a day.

- Rooms should be available for discussions to continue late into the night.

11.3   DOCUMENTATION

The parties should have exchanged and copied to the mediator a brief case summary (and the objectives they seek, if felt appropriate) before the mediation, together with essential supporting documentation. These might include the relevant contract or leases, expert witness reports to be used to substantiate the case, schedules of losses claimed and counter-schedules etc. An agreed bundle should be produced if advisers are in active contact or some way towards litigation or arbitration proceedings. The mediation agreement will be signed at the beginning of the mediation, if not previously done. Many mediators use a simple notebook to take with them from meeting to meeting to emphasise the informality of discussions, though a ring binder with separate tabs may be more helpful with blank sheets of paper behind each tab. This can serve as a model for a lawyer's mediation file, adjusted for the different role. It might take the following shape:

- Seating chart with name and occupational details of each attender for easy reminder.

- Mediation contract and notes of any other agreed details on procedure.

- Personal memory-jogger list of key mediation tactics.

- Separate tabs for each party's statements and any essential documents.

- Chronology of significant dates and a list of issues.

- Damages data and calculations.

- Section for recording key points made in the opening joint meeting.

- Separate sections for each private meeting (the mediator must be careful not to leave pages open which reveal notes of private discussions with the other party).

- Section for offers, counter-offers or statements that the mediator has permission to reveal to the other party.

- Draft of a settlement agreement with blank schedule for details of terms.

- Address details of the ADR organisation administering the case, of parties' contact details, details of any other parties involved but not present (for example, insurance company, government department, etc).

A laptop computer and printer, with a form of settlement agreement in blank on disk which can be built up during the day, can be extremely time-saving at the end of a mediation.

11.4 ARRIVALS

The mediator should show the parties to their private rooms or make suitable arrangements for this to happen. Meeting the parties as early as possible gives the earliest opportunity for the mediator to begin the process of building rapport. Making the geography clear over where the main meeting room is, where the toilets and telephones are, and how to contact the mediator during the day, all help parties to settle into an often unfamiliar environment. In general it is helpful to allow parties a short time alone with their team for a final briefing. The mediator should call into each room to allow for informal introductions, to check if everyone will be ready to move into the opening meeting and to deal with any final queries on procedure which parties may have.

There are cases where it is particularly important that the opening joint session is handled sensitively. In a clinical negligence case, for instance, a patient and the allegedly negligent doctor may be facing each other for the first time since things went wrong; or in a fierce family company feud, where there is deep animosity between directors. If pre-mediation contacts have been unable to deal fully with these issues, it may well be wise for the mediator to use private sessions with each party at some length to prepare them for the opening joint meeting. Both party and representative need to be sure of the wisdom of what they are planning to say, and also to prepare to receive comments that may be very difficult to hear. Careful preparation which makes sure that each party is approaching the impending joint meeting in a sound and respectful way is vital for its success.

11.5 MEDIATOR'S OPENING AT THE JOINT MEETING

Most mediators have their own style and approach to their opening remarks. However, in every case mediators should be looking to establish their authority, win the parties' confidence, set an appropriate tone for discussions (in terms of formality or informality), and begin to create momentum. This is particularly important where the parties or their advisors have not previously met the mediator. First impressions can be vital in terms of the mediator's effectiveness during the mediation itself.

The length of the opening remarks should also be thought through beforehand. If they last too long, it may frustrate parties who are keen to get to grips with the issues, and may tend to over-formalise. If they are too short, it may lead to key points being omitted, depriving the parties of understanding or clarity about the process.

In general, mediators will normally deal with the following points:

- Seat the parties according to a pre-arranged seating plan, placed between their advisers and the mediator, to encourage them to contribute.

- Do formal introductions, during which the mediator fills in the seating chart, where seating has not been pre-planned.

- Present the mediator's background and qualifications, keeping this to a minimum, as the parties should have seen the mediator's CV beforehand.

- Outline the purpose of the mediation.

- Deal with the key legal points of the mediation agreement; authority to settle, confidentiality, without prejudice, etc (this can be done where appropriate by directing attention to the mediation agreement provisions) and arrange for it to be signed, if not already done.

- Outline the structure of the day, describing briefly the nature of opening statements and their duration, questions, private meetings, possibility of further joint meetings or of occasions where the mediator may want to meet only principals or advisers to assist in achieving progress towards a settlement.

- Deal with the effect of a settlement if reduced to writing and signed.

- Suggest and agree any other ground rules.

- Decide whether to adopt a more informal approach by use of first names or by removing jackets, best adopted where relationships are already relatively amicable: otherwise informality is perhaps best left to the caucus sessions, though this is a matter for a mediator's preference and judgment.

- Ask parties to state formally that they have full authority to settle, in order to emphasise again the purpose behind the meeting. This should normally have been confirmed, however, at a preparatory stage. Mediators should not generally labour this issue or it may spark off early destructive arguments. In some cases parties will only have authority up to certain limits and may have to refer back if the mediation moves them potentially beyond those limits. It is of great comfort to lay claimants to meet, usually for the first time, a person representing an insurer or a bank who tells the party face to face that they have come with authority to settle their case. The dispute and particularly the faceless opponent is suddenly humanised, and this in itself often makes settlement feel much more possible. Conversely, if an institutional party later claims not to have authority or only to have a limited authority, this can have a seriously demoralising and indeed inflammatory effect on the other party. They may legitimately feel that perhaps the opponent has not taken the amount of the claim with adequate seriousness, or that the right person could not be bothered to attend.

● Check each party's time constraints for the day: are they available if the mediation runs into the evening or not.

● If not previously done, explain any previous contacts with parties or advisors and allow adjournment for parties to consider if they wish to withdraw if unexpected conflicts of interest emerge at this opening phase (this should really be done at the time the mediator accepts the appointment).

● Deal with the estimated time-scale of the process.

● Check for any questions or problems.

● Then invite party A to start because . . . (they are making the claim or they called for the mediation or they are first alphabetically – mediators should have a reason for selecting the first party, to prevent arguments or uncertainty).

11.6 OPENING STATEMENTS BY EACH PARTY

The opening statement at a joint meeting is a crucial tool in the mediation process. Its context bears review. In many cases, this is the first time that all the parties and their advisers have sat around a table to discuss the issues since the dispute began. They may have been together in court corridors before procedural hearings, but usually then in separate huddles. For the first time too, the opposing parties and not just their lawyers are there to hear what the other party has to say about the dispute. They have declared that they have authority to settle the case. Now, therefore, is the opportunity for each party to explain both the strengths of their own case to the other party or their key negotiator personally, and why the opposing case might be less strong.

11.6.1 Conciseness

The opening statement should therefore be concise, yet firmly take advantage of the context in which it is made, as suggested above. The presentation should be made, not with the mediator in mind, but the other party. The mediator is not there to make an award or to judge the merits. It can sometimes be useful to appear to address the mediator, especially if very difficult things have to be said. If possible, however, the opening statement should be made to the other team, maintaining eye contact as much as possible with the other party or key negotiator, this being the person that really needs to be persuaded.

11.6.2 Courtesy

Conciseness and firmness should not be at the expense of courtesy and human sensitivity. It is a matter of judgment in each case as to what is the right tone to adopt. It is essential in preparing effectively to test out in advance what is proposed to be said to the opposing team by asking how it would feel to receive such a presentation. If a claimant has undergone a terrible experience which has led to the claim, it is vital to acknowledge and express sympathy with that even if compelled in the next sentence to say that in law there is arguably no liability for what occurred. The occasion is without prejudice, so it is possible to express regret, and sympathy, even an apology, without in any way compromising arguments on liability that may be mobilised, whether during the mediation or in any subsequent litigation if no settlement is achieved.

11.6.3 Cogency

There is a slightly different yet very important reason why an opening presentation needs also to be cogent and attractive to the mediator. In private sessions, the mediator will be testing out with each party the strengths and weaknesses of each case. A party whose opening presentation, coupled with the written sub-mission, provides clear material with which the mediator can test out the other side's case, can be sure that the mediator, clothed with the strength of neutrality, will be equipped to reality-test effectively in the privacy of the other team's room. The same must of course be expected in return.

11.6.4 Key points

Thus when planning an opening statement:

- Stress your alternatives to settlement and their credibility.

- Aim to highlight and emphasise only the key parts of your written submission: say something new or different to reflect the fact that this is a face-to-face occasion, and to acknowledge that the mediator and the other participants will have read your submission – even if they have not yet done so properly, they will be able to refer back to it during the day, but an oral presentation is deliverable only once.

- Identify any fair or objective standards by which you seek to have the strength of your case or any weakness in their case measured and approved.

- Respond to any new points made by the other side's written submission or oral statement.

- Involve other members of your team to corroborate key claims or assertions, to vent their sense of grievance or determination to secure a just outcome, or to establish their credibility as a potential witness.

- Acknowledge the other side's just grievances.

- While addressing yourself to the other party or key negotiator, do not ignore or demean the lawyers or their role, as this may antagonise them and jeopardise their commitment to the process and even compromise the mediator's ability to reality-test your case with them.

- Make concessions where possible, either for all time or (as is perfectly possible) for the purposes of the mediation only, reserving the right to withdraw that concession if the case does not settle.

- End on what it is hoped can be achieved by the mediation.

Some longer points should also be borne in mind.

1   Willingness to move

It is sometimes said that it is always necessary to come to a mediation prepared to move from your opening and public position to achieve settlement. *Being prepared to move* is almost certainly a wise approach. It by no means follows that a party *has to move* from their pre-stated position if no reason emerges to justify doing so, if such a possible course of action is flagged up clearly in advance. It is perfectly justifiable to come to a mediation and open it by saying something like: 'We have come to this mediation believing that our case is unanswerable and that you have no prospect of success. We believe in the mediation process [and have paid for it/paid our contribution towards its cost] as providing us with the earliest possible occasion on which we can tell you our view. We want to be sure that we are right, and want to give you the best possible opportunity to present your best arguments to suggest that we are wrong. We have come to listen carefully to those arguments, and will take them fully into account. We ask you to do the same with our arguments. If we are persuaded by you at the end of the day, we are open to moving [and the decision-maker with authority to do so is here]. If, however, we are not persuaded, we shall tell you and invite you to withdraw your claim/defence so as to save any additional unnecessary costs risks.'

Mediations do on occasion end effectively by withdrawal of the entire claim by one party, and the above illustrates a perfectly respectful way in which to frame that possibility. It should not be overplayed nor used as a tactic, as that might undermine the good faith approach that should characterise participation in mediation and you may have to deal with the same lawyer or party in a future mediation. This approach might especially be considered where proceedings have not been issued: thereafter, either side can apply for summary judgment under CPR Part 24 if they prefer.

2   The impact of opening statements on each side

Do not underestimate the importance of the opening statements in terms of making an impression on the other party or parties. It may well be the first time that a senior decision-maker on the other side has heard your case put in a succinct and cogent manner. Even more importantly, it will probably be the first time that the case has been put without being filtered through legal advisers, thereby perhaps losing much of its initial impact. The impression created by a short, cogent, articulate, polite and eminently reasonable presentation can have a significant effect on the settlement position which that decision-maker will ultimately adopt.

Equally, it is wise to listen carefully to the other side's presentation. It may well contain hints about their true aspirations, and in any event attentiveness will demonstrate a good faith approach to the mediation. Interruption will also have an impact on the whole atmosphere of co-operation which should imbue the mediation process.

3   Division of labour

Give considerable thought to how much of the presentation should be made by advisers, and how much by the parties themselves. It may be instinctive to assume that advisors will make them, and indeed that may be appropriate, particularly if, for example, complex legal arguments are to feature. However, the presentation phase of a mediation is the closest that the process comes to providing a 'day in court'. A party may well want the opportunity to address the other party directly, to convey the depth of feeling and the importance with which the dispute is regarded. Indeed, a vital factor to the success of the mediation may be to enable that party to express emotion properly, being able thereby to move on to discuss specific settlement proposals. That kind of party contribution is made easier by the informal environment of a mediation. At the very least, if advisers are to make the opening statement, then parties should be asked if they wish to add anything.

4   The length of opening statements

Consider in advance the length of time given over to opening statements. The intention is generally to provide a short succinct summary, and therefore brevity is usually regarded as important (indeed, if a lengthy presentational phase is accepted as being important, a mini-trial format might well be more appropriate: see Chapter 13). However, in complex mediation cases it may also be important to spend time conveying to the other side the exact nature of a detailed argument, and if the opening statement is too short, this may not be achieved. The mediator should have formed a sense of what will be appropriate from reading the case summaries and from initial pre-mediation discussions with each side. It can be useful to agree a specific timetable for opening statements, so that each side knows how to prepare its statement, and so that the issue does not become too contentious within the mediation. However, as with any mediation procedure, an agreed timetable will need to be flexible enough not to impose a rigid structure on the mediation, and much of the skill of handling these situations will rest with the mediator.

11.7   QUESTIONS, CLARIFICATION AND INFORMATION EXCHANGE

It entirely depends on the way the opening presentations have been made and received as to whether the mediator immediately breaks into private sessions, or whether the joint session continues for a short or an extended period. The following points may be helpful.

11.7.1   Points for advisers

- Encourage an early sense of adopting a constructive approach to the process and to negotiation, especially if you feel that previous contacts have not led to an effective relationship for negotiation.

- Avoid antagonistic or provocative questions or comments.

- Limit any questioning simply to seeking clarification of what you or your team genuinely do not understand, trying to use open questions and receiving the answers without comment unless they themselves require clarification.

- Use the opportunity if the atmosphere is right to seek and exchange information about areas of factual doubt, so that subsequent negotiations and discussions are founded on a full appreciation of what each party's assertions actually are, trying to minimise any misunderstandings.

- Stress willingness to search for settlement if it meets your client's understanding of the merits of the case (maybe later you will revisit settlement terms which reflect the client's personal or commercial interests: it is very rare for these to be openly debated at the joint meeting stage).

11.7.2 Points for mediators

- Ensure no interruptions from other parties (preferably by restating this ground rule just before the opening presentations, rather than by quelling later interruption) and stress that there will be plenty of opportunity for each party to put its case and to respond to comments.

- Ask silent team members at the end of each presentation if they wish to add anything at this stage (to encourage involvement in the settlement process).

- Keep this period short if the parties are clearly antagonistic or going over well-trodden ground or repeating themselves.

- Ask neutral questions for general clarification.

- Avoid questions in open session that might imply an early view of the case or predisposition to one side.

- Avoid questions that may require parties to touch on sensitive areas in front of the other parties – these can be left to the private sessions if they have not been raised by other parties already (eg do not ask if they wish to continue in a business relationship in a joint session).

- Some venting of emotions may be appropriate if there are strong feelings in the case and the parties have not had any real opportunity to have such a 'day in court' before; the mediator needs to judge when and how to move beyond such emotional contributions to further questions, information or caucus sessions.

- Thank the parties for their contributions.

- Explain the next stage and underline that:

  - private sessions are confidential: nothing said to the mediator will be conveyed to other parties without express authority;

  - nothing should be read into the time the mediator may be taking with each side as to whether support or criticism of their case is implied;

  - when the mediator is absent, this is an opportunity for each party to reflect further on the case or on any requests for further work the mediator may leave with them, or to make contact with their office or to relax;

■ try to provide, for the parties not in caucus, an estimate of the time you will take with the other party (and keep to it).

● Give rough estimates of the time before expecting to finish each private session and move to the next or other party, trying to stick to the estimate or send messages about any slippage as the mediation proceeds.

11.8 PRIVATE MEETINGS (OR CAUCUSES)

In recent years, the tendency in the UK has been to adopt the description 'private meetings' instead of the imported American term 'caucus', meaning a confidential meeting of a small political group. The word *caucus* is still used for this phase in US mediation practice, and as it is a convenient shorthand, and is also an alternative term which is in use in the UK, we mention it, but normally use the term 'private meeting'.

11.8.1 Their purpose

These meetings between the mediator and the individual parties are usually vital to progress in a commercial mediation. They are an opportunity for the mediator and each party and their advisers to explore frankly and in confidence the issues in the case and options for settlement. A mediator should always seek authority to convey to another party anything specific said during such private meetings.

In addition to ensuring an easier setting for open discussion, private sessions:

● give the mediator an effective forum for making progress and the opportunity to build good relationships with the parties;

● prevent a party becoming locked into positions and judgments stated in front of the opposing party;

● allow for deeper, sustained discussion on issues without arguments or interruptions or the necessity of posturing;

213

- give more time and space for offers or counter-offers to be thoroughly examined and analysed rather than requiring an immediate reaction that tends to be demanded in joint negotiations;

- make it easier for mediators to discuss a proposal's strengths and weaknesses without appearing to take sides;

- allow the parties to build up more trust in the mediator.

Generally the mediator will first meet privately with the claimant or the party who most recently declined to respond to an offer, or where the emotion is highest. Mediators should beware of simply becoming locked in to the private meeting mode of shuttling back and forth until agreement. In some mediation settings, such as family and neighbourhood disputes, private meetings are more rare. They work well in commercial mediations, but mediators should remember that there are other options.

Private meetings may, for example, be mixed with further joint meetings on particular areas of disagreement. This helps to build up relationships across the parties and to encourage the parties to feel that the mediation is a joint venture and a more fluid and dynamic process. The more time spent on private meetings with the mediator, the more the mediator will tend to be a shuttle negotiator. Finally, the more the settlement is likely to involve parties working together afterwards, the more the mediator should structure joint meetings to help this new phase get started on an appropriate note. The mediator may also encourage meetings between principals only (on commercial issues or to see if a figure can be struck), or legal advisors or experts to establish points of agreement or differences and their implications in terms of further information requirements, etc. The mediator may or may not choose to attend these meetings, depending on his judgment as to likely progress.

11.8.2 Issues to address in private meetings

Since the aim behind the process is to achieve agreement between the parties, the mediator should endeavour to leave each private meeting (with the possible exception of the first meeting with each side) with something new. It might be a change of offer or counter-offer to put to the other party, or some new issues or emphases that need to be explored, a new factual concession or waiver of a position for the purposes of the mediation only. If there is no real change by either party after two private sessions, the mediator should be beginning to consider ways of changing the dynamics of the meetings or identifying new information that needs to be researched.

In early private meetings, there should be an emphasis by the mediator on the use of open-ended questions and clarification of what parties would ideally like from a settlement. There will then often be a series of private meetings discussing the gap between the parties and searching for options to overcome their remaining differences. The pattern of private sessions is often similar to the core phases of the negotiating process, namely:

Discussion → *Bargaining or Problem-Solving* → *Closing the Deal;*

or

Exploration → *Negotiation* → *Settlement.*

11.8.3   Issues which the mediator should raise

The choice of issues to raise in private meetings will depend on the case and the mediator's judgment. It is a useful principle to follow that the mediator should allow the parties to lead with their agenda at the start of early private meetings. Subject to that, a mediator will generally wish to cover the following:

1   Ventilation of grievances and self-justification

Parties will often feel freer to 'sound off' in private session. This is an important phase of letting off steam where parties can 'have their day in court'. Mediators should acknowledge that they recognise parties have these strong feelings without necessarily sympathising or agreeing. Such ventilation should not be cut off or suppressed but should after an appropriate period be diverted into more positive issues.

2   Strengths and weaknesses on both sides

Where a settlement will be primarily geared to potential trial outcome, the mediator will need to address with each party the strengths and weaknesses of their claims, again avoiding any appearance of personal judgment or evaluation (unless explicitly part of his requested role). Thus, for example:

11.8.3 *What happens at a typical mediation*

- 'What do you feel are your strongest points?'
- 'Are there any areas where you think you might be vulnerable on the facts/principles/expert testimony/costs/ rules/real chances of recovery?'
- 'What about the other side? How do you see their case?'
- 'How do you think they see things?'

A good understanding of the issues helps the mediator challenge each side's claims using material from the other party as the basis of the challenge rather than the mediator's own views, so acting as a neutral devil's advocate. In this context, there may well be a temptation for legal advisers to want to focus exclusively on the legal arguments in a dispute, and to 'address' the mediator on those points. Certainly the legal issues in a case are generally important, and will inform the negotiating stance that a party is willing to take. However, legal arguments are usually most valuably dealt with, in caucus, by an open discussion of the strengths and weaknesses of a given argument, followed by discussions on the degree to which it should alter a party's current position. Legal advisers in particular need to remember the shift from advocate to negotiator which the majority of their role in mediation entails.

3 BATNA and WATNA

- 'What is your Best Alternative To a Negotiated Agreement (BATNA) if you fail to settle?'
- 'What is your Worst Alternative (WATNA)?'
- 'How confident are you? Where are you vulnerable?'
- 'What else would make a difference in terms of these alternatives?'

This area will generally involve a mediator testing the advice being given to the client on likely trial outcomes, and the costs and time elements associated with that, and in exploring the commercial context of the conflict.

4 What do you need? What do they need?

One of the mediator's goals, even where no future relationship is likely, merely a question of early settlement of damages, is to help parties to start thinking about the present and the future. What are their needs and wants? What lies behind these that might be met by other means than currently claimed? In other words, what are their true interests? What would they ideally like to see in an agreement at the end of today? Similarly, how do they see the other side's true interests? Is there a way to help them say 'yes' to a deal you would like?

5 What's been on the table?

The history of settlement negotiations should be explored to establish how close the parties have been in the past and the obstacles to settlement then. It may be that a previous offer is now acceptable under changed circumstances or can be made acceptable with sufficient adjustment/new elements.

6 What else could be relevant?

Explore all possible settlement options in terms of:

- figures (and how they could be amended, where they come from, how they can be justified to colleagues);
- timescale of payments;
- services;
- future business relationship possibilities;
- performance criteria/guarantees;
- apologies or other actions.

7 What other information/comfort would you need to settle this?

Keep searching for options.

8 What are you willing to offer?

This ensures that a specific settlement momentum can be established. Sometimes parties will be unwilling to be specific unless the mediator reassures them on the confidentiality of the statement. The mediator can say in confidence that something is needed to encourage the other party to show willingness to move also. The parties may be closer together than they think.

11.8.3 *What happens at a typical mediation*

9 Is there anything else?

This is always a valuable question for a mediator to ask to ensure that a team has revealed all that they want to reveal at that stage.

11.8.4 Disclosure of information

The instinct to conceal information from the other side is pervasive in disputes. Within mediation, there are two issues to address – disclosures to the other side and disclosures to the mediator.

1 Disclosures to the other side

If a mediation is to be effective in generating movement from entrenched positions, much of this will come from a fresh assessment of the respective merits, facts, risks and other circumstances of each party. Such an assessment will be prompted, though not delivered, by the mediator, acting in a 'devil's advocate' capacity. That in turn will often flow from fresh information brought to bear on the discussions. It follows, therefore, that the disclosure of information can be important in generating movement. Indeed, the failure to disclose may well only serve to make settlement impossible until a later date, and much of it will come out at trial in any event.

On the other hand, the possibility that the dispute may not settle in mediation, leading to the commencement or continuation of proceedings, will always act as a check on the willingness of parties to make disclosures to each other.

In mediation, a balance has to be achieved between these two competing priorities – sealed lips may prevent settlement, but an over-willing tongue may prejudice a position. This balance is something which parties and their advisers should discuss at length. Although there are no fixed rules, a useful guideline is to have to justify each non-disclosure, rather than each disclosure.

Much, though not all, of the problem is resolved by the 'without prejudice' nature of the proceedings. Thus offers and admissions made in the context of a mediation may not be produced or referred to in subsequent proceedings relating to the same dispute. However, the 'without prejudice' rule does have limitations (see Chapter 5).

The rest is a matter of judgment for the parties and their

advisers. In fact, such judgments, and the considerations on which they will be based, are exactly the same whether the parties are in direct negotiations or in mediation.

2 Disclosures to the mediator

The structure of mediation is designed to generate an environment in which frank and open debate is possible, so as to increase the likelihood of settlement. Recognising that such debate is unlikely to take place directly between parties who are instinctively protective of their positions, the private meeting becomes the primary tool for the mediator. As we have observed several times, all discussions between the party, their advisers and the mediator which take place in private meetings are confidential between them and may not be discussed with other parties without the disclosing party's consent. If the mediator feels that disclosure to another party would assist settlement, permission may be sought to make the disclosure, but if this is not forthcoming, the mediator remains bound not to disclose it. It is the parties themselves who control the outflow of information from them to the other side, irrespective of what is discussed in caucus with the mediator. This structure should, and does, encourage parties to be frank with the mediator. There is in fact little to be gained from hiding information from the mediator.

Some parties are prone to negotiate with the mediator, as well as with the other side. For example, they might only partially disclose their position on a given issue to the mediator, hoping by so doing to affect the way it is then presented to the other side. In practice, however, the net result is likely to be that the mediator's task is harder and settlement less likely or at least that the whole process will take considerably longer than necessary. Mediators need to be alive to this happening, but parties should be encouraged where possible to avoid it.

Parties will also often ask the mediator to leave the private meeting while they discuss a possible change of position or a revised offer without the mediator there. Quite frequently there is little necessity for this. It betrays a positional approach to negotiation and is symptomatic of feeling uncomfortable to share a sense of weakness with the mediator. Wise mediators will not object, however. Parties need at times to protect themselves against apparent loss of face by changing a previously asserted position. Indeed, mediators spend much of their time helping parties gently to accept or avoid loss of face in moving towards settlement.

11.8.5 At the end of the private meeting

It is a useful practice for mediators at the end of a caucus to summarise or clarify the points of information or offers they are able to reveal to the other side, anything else being confidential. It is also important to leave behind some questions for the party and their advisor to consider or work on until they see the mediator next. This can help generate further evaluation or movement as well as just filling the time. Otherwise make clear they have time to call the office or explain where they can find refreshments, and that the amount of time you spend as mediator with the other side has no special significance as to where the case is going.

In a multi-party case, this may also be a good time to suggest that some of the parties seek to work together towards agreement on some of the issues while the mediator caucuses with another.

11.8.6 Between private meetings

The mediator does not have to shuttle directly from one room to another. In a complex case or where a private session has been particularly tough, it may be wise to spend a little time reflecting on the case, reviewing the issues raised in the previous meeting or where to go on the next one. Representatives can use the time to review negotiating strategy with their clients, to do some recalculation of figures involved, or to research further information relevant to discussions with the mediator.

11.8.7 Further joint meetings

Whether these should be convened is a matter of judgment for the mediator as the custodian of the process. There is also a range of practice and preference among mediators. Some prefer to keep parties separate for the whole mediation, from the end of the opening until the final meeting, at which either the settlement agreement is signed or regret expressed that no deal was done. Conversely, some mediators see strength in keeping the parties together to work on the problems for as long as possible after the opening. This is so especially where there is almost certainly to be a continuing business or employment relationship which needs to be tested out and in effect modelled at the mediation to see how possible it is or whether redefinition is necessary.

A middle course is for the mediator to derive as much as

possible from the opening joint meeting and then from meeting confidentially with the parties, but to keep open the possibility of a further joint meeting or meetings. These have the incidental value of reassuring those who attend a later joint meeting that the other party is still there and still engaged in the mediation process. This can be lost sight of when there is only contact with the mediator in your own room. More substantive practical reasons for such meetings are:

- To avoid misunderstanding about issues which are likely to be key to the success of one party's case and which have either to be accepted or rejected by the other party for them to formulate their negotiating position. It is usually better for such key points to be conveyed party to party rather than risk that the strength of feeling behind the message, or even its precise contents, may not be faithfully conveyed.

- To remedy past failed communication between the parties by giving them a chance to say and hear what perhaps should have been said and heard long ago.

- To review the issues together and the stage reached by that point in the mediation (being careful not to breach confidentiality in that review) and to plan for the next stage of the process.

- To try to advance understanding and agreement over highly technical issues relating to the substance of the business itself, or to matters of law or expert opinion, which might best be addressed by joint meetings of the technical, legal or expert members of each team, with or without the mediator.

11.9 MOVING FROM FACILITATION TO EVALUATION, IF REQUIRED

As discussed in Chapter 1, this is a delicate area, but one that needs to be considered. A distinction must be drawn between the following uses of the word 'evaluation':

- Formal evaluation towards the end of a mediation in which settlement seems unlikely to be achieved at the mediation.

- The evaluation implicitly underpinning any reality-testing with parties (often based upon mediator expertise in the subject area in dispute) to help them assess the strengths and weaknesses of their case. It is not easy to avoid giving the impression of having formed an opinion when reality-testing, but wise mediators in effect ask for permission to reality-test vigorously, and would not attempt to start doing so until a degree of trust with each party has been established.

- A form of 'evaluation' quite often invoked by a mediator, by expressing views privately to each party as to whether a certain level of settlement is either realistic or likely to meet with favour. Where deadlock occurs, a mediator might be persuaded to give an objective assessment to both sides as to the terms on which both parties might give consideration to settling if they want a deal. This will not breach confidentiality, as it is a mutual exercise, but each side will learn whether there is room for movement. The reaction to such a proposal can be given privately, so that neither side actually hears the other's reaction, but if the proposal is acceptable, then a deal is done.

When approaching the possibility of evaluation towards the end of a mediation, a balance must be struck in relation to how the parties see the future. At one end, if the amount or the issues in dispute are of sufficient importance to justify a BATNA (best alternative to negotiated agreement) of going to court trial or arbitration, the parties are unlikely to invite the mediator to give even a non-binding view to resolve their differences. Again, if the process has brought the parties much closer, but with still an appreciable margin in dispute, the mediator may well be of much more value to them by continuing in role as a neutral mediator available to facilitate further discussions, once the parties have had time to reflect after the mediation.

Where the gap between the parties is such that they are content in effect to let the mediator suggest how to close it on what has been heard, then such an invitation can be issued. The reasons why this needs a health warning are:

- The mediator will inevitably be making a decision or settlement recommendation in the light of confidential information received in private meetings from each party: reasons for the outcome are therefore unable to be given, and this may ultimately prove more frustrating for the parties than closing the gap (or not) themselves.

- The parties may have chosen mediation as a means of *retaining* control over the outcome: to pass any degree of responsibility to another, even a trusted mediator, will derogate from that. It is thus important that parties are clear that this is what they really want to do.

Thus evaluations should only be given if all the parties request it, and only after the implications have been fully considered. It might be wise for a mediator to discuss these in a joint meeting, so that all can hear the advice and can also discuss and contribute to the way the mediator suggests that the evaluation should be done.

Evaluations can really only be made (and respected by the parties) if they are given either by a mediator valued as possessing sector expertise; or if in the form of a general view expressed in terms of commercial common sense from the viewpoint of a detached observer. They are always best given in private session with each party, and should be given consistently between each party, as they have the choice at a later stage to exchange them. Also, mediators might otherwise be tempted to tell both parties that they have a bad case in order to generate pressure to settle.

Advisers might want to consider inviting a mediator to give an evaluation if they are uncertain of the real strength of their case or perhaps have differences with their client over assessment of the strength of the case. They may, however, find that a mediator will resist accepting ultimate responsibility for undertaking what is really a task for the lawyer, however difficult: namely to form a clear a view of what advice to give to a client, and also to give the client bad news about the claim and adjust any unrealistic expectations.

There is further general discussion about these issues in the following section, and also in Chapter 3 in relation to med-arb, a process in which the parties sign up to a formal move from facilitation to arbitration from the outset.

11.10 NO AGREEMENT AT THE END OF THE MEDIATION

If a scheduled time for ending a mediation is approaching (at the end of the first or subsequent agreed days), the mediator must determine whether to continue working with the parties in the hope of reaching a settlement that day, whether to suggest a return to mediation at a future date, or whether to terminate the mediation. As well as the question of whether the days set aside for the mediation are coming to an end, there may be an issue of time limits in a contractual ADR procedure.

If a mediator has a strong sense that there is sufficient momentum to achieve an agreement, it is usually worth pressing on even late into the night. If undecided, it is still worth consulting with the parties (privately) if they wish to press on. Otherwise the mediator should encourage an adjournment. A week or two will help the parties reflect, unless it is obvious the gap between the parties gives no grounds for belief that a settlement is achievable. This last position should rarely be adopted and only when at least one party tends to agree with it. Mediation experience suggests solutions are very often achievable with sufficient patience and persistence. A final suggestion from the mediator on a new proposal can be tested privately with each side.

Where the mediation is being terminated without settlement, the mediator's role remains one of doing what can be done to leave room and an atmosphere for future settlement or cost-effective outcomes. After consulting privately, the mediator may reconvene a joint meeting, and thank all parties for the efforts they put into trying to achieve a settlement, reminding them of the advantages of settlement over litigation. The hope can be expressed that the process will have at least brought them closer, clarified the issues dividing them and enabled them to have a further meeting more easily or to reconvene in a further mediation. He can point out that most such cases end up settling within a few months after mediation. Indeed, if the case merits it, the mediator should have explored in the final private sessions whether the parties might consider another cost-effective dispute resolution procedure, with a view to clinching settlement. For example, if the parties are effectively arguing about a reduced gap between them on a few items, a 'pendulum' or final offer arbitration might be acceptable as the next stage. An alternative process is an arbitration which can award only between agreed limits ('hi-lo' arbitration) after summary presentations (or the mediator may have suggested in caucus a final 'splitting the difference' proposal as a last resort).

It is important here to distinguish the process from the substantive dispute. Where no agreement is reached on the latter, the mediator still has responsibility for the former. The closing stages of a mediation that has not (yet) settled can be valuably used to steer parties into a discussion of the way forward in terms of process. A framework can then be established which may well lead to agreement on the substantive issues, albeit weeks or months later. Parties will often be too focused on the substantive disputes to have a sense of what process options still exist.

As we have suggested, the mediator should not normally take on the role of arbitrator unless both parties are enthusiastic about this and clear on the potential procedural and legal pitfalls of 'med-arb' (see Chapter 3).

Where settlement is not reached, parties sometimes cannot even bear to meet again, though it is broadly a good idea for the mediator to encourage this out of respect for each other. By virtue of the absence of settlement, the parties are likely to meet again, if only at court.

11.11   DRAFTING A SETTLEMENT AGREEMENT

In over 80% of cases, the parties reach agreement through mediation, even despite the fact that an appreciable number of cases are court-referred. In the final private sessions, the details of this agreement will have been hammered out, so that the mediator should have a clear summary that has been confirmed with the parties. Alternatively, the last sessions may have involved either joint meetings, meetings to resolve commercial details between principals, or between legal or other professional advisers. The mediator should help confirm all the elements agreed in a final joint session and deal with any final uncertainties or demands. It can be a mistake at times to bring parties together prematurely when key items have not been agreed in private. It can also create problems to allow parties to leave after an oral agreement without ensuring they sign up to a formal agreement in writing. A signed memorandum (even if not legally binding) ensures greater commitment with less chance of rescinding.

The legal aspects of settlement agreements are considered in Chapter 12. The commitment value of writing and signatures still holds even where an agreement is expressed to be not binding in law. If parties are all legally represented it may be simplest to ask the advisers to work together in order to agree a draft, ensuring that the clients stay around to sign this. The waiting period is a good opportunity to end on a personal and amicable note, again reinforcing commitment to the implementation of the agreement.

CONTENTS

Chapter 12

Settlement at mediation and beyond

12.1 THE SETTLEMENT AGREEMENT

It is late. Hours of hard negotiation have eventually resulted in a mutually agreeable set of terms on which the dispute can be settled. The parties, the lawyers and the mediator are relieved and pleased. What remains to be done? We consider the answers to these questions.

12.1.1 Written or oral?

It is vital that the agreed terms should be reduced to writing and that the parties should indicate their consent to these terms. First of all, this ensures that the terms of agreement are commonly understood by all concerned. All who have attended a mediation or indeed a protracted negotiation will be well aware of the difficulties that arise in translating an apparently agreed oral position into an agreed written one!

Secondly, it gives the opportunity for further detail on the agreed points, and indeed further substantive points, to emerge. Although hearts may sink if they do, it is far better to have this happen during the mediation than a few days later.

Thirdly, some mediation agreements (including the CEDR one at Appendix A) provide that no agreement reached between the parties during the mediation will be binding unless and until it is reduced to writing and signed. This helps to create a freer atmosphere for debate and consideration of offers during the mediation, but obviously imposes a need for any binding settlement agreement to be in writing.

12.1.2 Binding or non-binding?

The settlement agreement, whether oral or written, can be made binding or non-binding in law. This is a matter for agreement between the parties. Most agreements are likely to be legally binding subject to normal contractual principles, in the absence of this point being explicit in the agreement itself. In most cases, particularly where the dispute is in litigation, the parties will opt for a binding agreement. An agreed and executed binding document will commit the parties to the outcome they have agreed in the mediation. Considerable momentum should have been generated during the mediation, and parties may have arrived at a different view of the dispute from that with which they began the mediation. It is important to harness that momentum in the form of a written commitment.

Inevitably that leaves mediation open to the charge that parties, worn out by the process, will commit to terms which in the cold light of day they would reject. If this is an overriding concern, then of course they are free to conclude some form of non-binding memorandum of understanding or 'gentleman's agreement'. They might agree to implement a cooling-off period during which the terms can on reflection be rejected. In practice, however, the agreement will reflect terms at which they have freely arrived, albeit in a tough negotiating environment. There is no reason why the agreement should not be binding. Furthermore, if those of their colleagues not present at the mediation find it hard to understand why such terms were accepted, that is more than likely a reflection of the fact that they were not present to hear the arguments, participate in the discussions with the mediator, and watch the positions emerge. It is not necessarily an indication that the terms agreed were unfavourable or wrong in any objective sense.

In some disputes, however, a non-binding agreement might more accurately reflect the agreed terms and the nature of the future relationship which the parties are trying to create. A cooling-off period may also be appropriate in consumer cases or where one party is not legally represented.

12.1.3 Detailed agreement or heads of terms?

The question of how much detail to put into a settlement agreement at the end of a mediation will often arise. Where the nature of the dispute is relatively simple, the drafting of a document incorporating all the relevant detail should not pose a problem. If, however, the dispute has been highly complex, the settlement agreement may itself need to be a lengthy document. In addition, the terms of settlement reached may contemplate a new contractual arrangement between the parties, such as a new distribution agreement, which may itself require detailed drafting. Further formalities may also be required to implement any agreement reached, for example, to transfer land from one party to another.

A balance needs to be achieved in the drafting process. Clearly detail is more likely to provide clarity and less scope for future argument. On the other hand, it may simply be unrealistic for the parties to be able to produce a highly detailed document during the mediation itself. If that is the case, heads of agreement which set out the main points will often be prepared. These themselves contemplate a further more detailed agreement being drafted over the coming weeks. The only note of caution which needs to be sounded is as to the degree to which such heads can be made binding, prior to the signing of the more detailed agreement. They will need to contain sufficient detail to avoid being unenforceable (as to which see section **12.2** below).

12.1.4   Commonly used terms of settlement

Much of the substance of a settlement agreement, whether a contract or a consent order, will be fairly standard 'boiler-plate' drafting including the identity and addresses of the parties, the recitals and even some of the substantive clauses. This, coupled with the fact that in many mediations the drafting of agreed terms will take place after many hours of arduous negotiations, leads some mediators to use standard form settlement agreements. An example of this is to be found in Appendix E.

Clearly the content of any settlement agreement will need to be agreed between the parties and much of the detail cannot be prejudged. However, as an outline structure, a standard form can be a valuable skeleton on which to hang the flesh of the agreement. This is particularly so where the substantive terms of the agreement can simply be inserted as an Appendix, or as one clause of the existing outline agreement.

It also serves as a checklist for the parties as to some of the clauses they may want to consider including. Thus, for example, the agreement at Appendix E includes:

- A warranty by each signatory of his/her authority to sign the agreement.

- A checklist, at clause 2, of issues which might need to be considered in relation to the substantive terms of agreement.

- Consideration of the effect that breaches of the settlement agreement will have on the remainder of its terms.

- Provision for dealing with disputes arising out of the settlement agreement (see also section **12.3** below).

- Provision for dealing with matters still in dispute, if the mediation has only resolved part of the dispute.

- Consideration of whether any elements of the mediation agreement remain in force following settlement, and how those should be addressed.

Parties and their advisers may conclude that many of these provisions are not in fact required in their particular case, but at least the points will have been raised and considered.

12.2 ENFORCEABILITY

Many parties, and their advisors, will want to be sure that an agreement reached in mediation is going to be enforceable, should the need arise. Sceptics who criticise the process for having no teeth forget that most mediated agreements are, in fact, binding and enforceable. In addition the terms of agreement reached in mediation are likely to be simpler and clearer for the purposes of enforcement, probably by summary judgment, than the original matters in dispute.

There are several traps, however. One is the problem of uncertainty of terms. If it is decided to use heads of agreement rather than to purport to set out all the details of the agreed terms in the settlement document, care must be taken not to omit any significant term which might lead a court to construe the 'agreement' as void for uncertainty. Another is to draft a settlement 'agreement' which is a mere agreement to agree, and thus not binding in contract law. A third is to draft the settlement agreement in terms making it a conditional contract which is only enforceable if a certain condition is met. That might even be a condition that a consent order is drawn up and filed. If there is no enforceable duty to conclude such an order, the contract may never become legally enforceable because that condition is never met. There is not normally any problem over consideration for a settlement agreement, because most involve the payment of money or the compromise of litigation, with the exchange of promises as to future conduct, representing valid executory consideration. If there is any doubt as to the validity of consideration to support a settlement contract, the parties can always opt to embody the terms in a formal deed, for which consideration is not necessary.

Assuming that the agreement itself is intended to be binding, the following options exist.

12.2.1   Contract

The settlement agreement can take effect between the parties as a contract and bind them under normal contractual principles. Thus there will need to be the usual contractual elements of an offer and acceptance, consideration and intention to create legal relations. In practice, these are very likely to feature in any event. Furthermore, any relevant contractual formalities, such as those governing the transfer of an interest in land, will need to be observed.

Assuming that the correct content and formalities exist, the agreement can be enforced in the same way as any other contract. The court will be able to look at its terms if and when invited to enforce it, as it always has been able to do. This is so even when the contract is negotiated through 'without prejudice' negotiations (albeit here within the mediation process) as was made clear in *Tomlin v Standard Telephones and Cables* [1969] 3 All ER 201 CA.

12.2.2   Consent or 'Tomlin' Order

If litigation proceedings have been commenced, terms of settlement reached between parties can be given the force of a court order by using a Consent or 'Tomlin' Order to impose a stay on the proceedings, except for the purposes of enforcing the terms of settlement. This applies whether the agreed terms have been arrived at through mediation or direct negotiation and is a relatively straightforward procedural formality to implement. A precedent of a Tomlin Order is set out in Appendix F.

The advantage of such an order is that, depending on the way it is phrased, its terms can be enforced through the court as if it were a judgment without the need for starting a fresh action. The enforcement of the kind of contract referred to in section **12.2.1** would require the issue of proceedings based on the alleged breach of the settlement contract. A Tomlin Order properly drawn can permit immediate application to enforce the settlement terms in the existing proceedings. Tomlin Orders also have the advantage of permitting the terms of the settlement to be kept off the face of the Order lodged with the court. It is perfectly permissible to refer in the Schedule to the Tomlin Order to terms set out in an identified document (ie the written settlement agreement signed at the mediation) the original of which is to be kept in safe custody by the mediator. Thus the order kept on the court file will not have on its face (and so preserved from possible public access) such terms as parties might prefer to remain entirely confidential.

12.2.3   Arbitration Consent Award

As with litigation, the arbitration process can be used to record terms of settlement reached between the parties before final hearing and the equivalent of a Tomlin Order – a Consent Award – is available. The agreed terms of settlement are drawn up and submitted to the arbitrator for approval. The Consent Award, in those terms, is then issued and published. Parties should remember that there are formalities for a Consent Award to be considered, details of which can be found in standard textbooks on the subject. A precedent form of Consent Award is set out in Appendix F.

Where arbitration proceedings have not been commenced, it is still possible to use the Arbitration Award to record a mediated settlement. This may be a useful technique where concern over enforcement exists. There is widespread international recognition of arbitration awards for enforcement purposes. The parties, having reached agreement in the mediation, appoint the mediator as arbitrator, purely for the purpose of recording the terms of settlement. Once appointed, the mediator (now arbitrator) can issue and publish a Consent Award encompassing the agreed terms of settlement.

12.3   THE MEDIATOR'S CONTINUING ROLE AFTER SETTLEMENT

Some settlement agreements can be performed almost immediately, for example, by the payment of cash, release of goods, signing of documents, etc. Others, however, by their very nature, will be performed or implemented over a period of time following agreement. Where this is the case, parties may well welcome the idea of the mediator (or ADR organisation) continuing to perform some overseeing role. A mediator who has performed effectively will be seen by the parties to be impartial, committed to resolution of the dispute and informed as to its detail, and thus ideally placed to contribute in an on-going way.

12.3.1 As a mediator

It is not uncommon for a settlement agreement arrived at in mediation to provide that any disputes arising out of the agreement will be referred, in the first instance, to mediation, perhaps with the same mediator. The fact that mediation is stipulated at all suggests that the parties have been relatively satisfied with the process thus far, and of course the use of the same mediator will be cheaper and more efficient, being already familiar with the issues. This approach is particularly effective where the agreement envisages the performance of various future events, and there is concern about whether and how that will occur.

12.3.2 As an adjudicator or arbitrator

If the settlement agreement involves, for example, the subsequent sale of assets, the parties may choose to appoint the mediator to adjudicate on the valuation of those assets. This appointment can be included as a term of the settlement agreement.

12.3.3 As an overseer

The future role of a mediator might be less formal than that of mediator or arbitrator. For example, if a partnership dispute is settled on terms which provide for the future management of the partnership to be conducted according to certain general principles, the parties might appoint the mediator as an 'overseer' of their conduct. This role, in essence, would be to assist the parties in the practical implementation of their agreed principles, and to be available to discuss and resolve with the parties any problems which might arise.

12.4 WHERE THE DISPUTE DOES NOT SETTLE AT MEDIATION

It is an interesting feature of mediation that in the small percentage of disputes that do not settle in the mediation itself, the parties nonetheless usually express themselves satisfied with the process. Furthermore, a high proportion of such disputes do then proceed to settlement in the immediate aftermath of the mediation. It is therefore often inappropriate to talk in terms of the mediation having failed, since manifestly it may well have played a pivotal role in generating settlement. Very often, the parties to a 'failed' mediation will comment that they now understand both their own and the other side's case more fully, and that the gap between their respective positions, although not closed, is significantly narrower than before. If nothing else, this may make a subsequent trial quicker and cheaper, because only some of the original issues may remain to be decided.

12.4.1   Partial settlement

Mediation may result in a partial settlement, where some but not all of the issues in dispute have been resolved. In this situation, it can be very valuable to draft a document which is not legally binding, but which sets out those matters that have been agreed, and the parties' positions in respect of those that have not. This has the effect both of encapsulating, and therefore in some way preserving, the progress that has been made, and at the same time reminding the parties that it is only the remaining issues which have so far prevented final agreement being reached.

If the issues are separable, it may even be possible to reach a binding agreement on some without resolution of the others.

12.4.2   Further mediation

Further mediation should not be ruled out. Some mediations have lasted up to five days or more, sometimes spread across several months. The adjournments provide important time for reflection, so that parties are not pushed too fast into settlement. Further information can be gathered, without which the decisions about settlement may not be capable of being made. The opportunity is given for reassessment of positions and perhaps the generation of further options for settlement.

Mediation should never be seen as a fixed, one-session process. One of its great strengths is its flexibility. Mediators, parties and advisers should be alive to the possibility of adjournments and reconvening where necessary. Thus, for example, the parties might send in a fresh negotiator or negotiating team, or add some additional experts to the old team. The presence of fresh minds (perhaps with wider settlement authority) may help break the log jam. The parties may even elect to appoint a new mediator, or an additional expert to advise the mediator.

It is often the case that a subsequent mediation session, perhaps with time for reflection in the interim, can bring a change of approach.

If they cannot be persuaded to meet, the parties may none-theless be prepared for the mediator to continue discussions with each of them in private. This could be done by visiting each of them in turn as a 'shuttle diplomat', or indeed by continuing the mediation more informally over the telephone, or via telephone conference calls or video conferencing.

12.4.3   Further direct negotiation

It may well be that the mediation has brought the parties to the point where they can manage to hold further direct talks without the assistance of the mediator. By coming to mediation in the first place they have indicated a willingness to talk. The mediation process may well have encouraged the perception that, although settlement has not (yet) been reached, further talks may make progress. It may even be that, at the end of the mediation, the parties will be prepared to sign a declaration of intent to have further talks and even to commit themselves to a date.

12.4.4   Using a different ADR process

The reason that many different ADR processes exist is that each can play a different role in generating settlement. What is applicable for one situation may not be for another. It may well be that, during a mediation, problems emerge which might best be dealt with through a different ADR process.

Typically, for example, one element of a dispute may prove hard to settle in a mediation because the parties had, and have maintained, a genuine good faith disagreement about a particular point of law, or technical issue. Depending on the view they take, they can come up with diametrically opposing views on the impli-cations, and the whole settlement is put in jeopardy. Even a highly effective and trusted mediator may be unable to break this impasse through mediation. One option would be for the parties to submit the particular issue to, for example, a judicial appraisal or neutral evaluation. This would provide a non-binding but authoritative view to the parties jointly on the issue in question. Armed with that, they may well be in a position to return to the mediation and progress beyond the earlier obstacle.

Similarly, a mediation might have settled five out of six issues dividing the parties. They might therefore agree to commit to settlement of those on condition that the sixth issue be referred to some form of short-form binding adjudication process, perhaps binding judicial appraisal or documents-only arbitration.

Combining processes such as these exemplifies the way in which ADR can, with a little imagination and flexibility, be used to provide a settlement forum designed to address the particular problems of a given situation.

12.4.5 Proceeding to trial

This always remains an option, whether or not proceedings have been issued by the time of the mediation. The question may arise as to whether the court is going to explore why mediation failed and try to make a costs order which reflects its interpretation of which party should take responsibility for the failure of the mediation. This is a very uncertain area for parties and mediation as a whole. The CPR certainly confer a general right on judges to make orders relating to indemnity costs and penal interest on both damages and costs which can penalise parties who behave unreasonably, whether they otherwise 'won or lost' the case. One party at a failed mediation might well be tempted to invite a judge to step behind the veil of confidentiality created by the mediation agreement and consider such orders in relation to alleged unreasonable conduct at a mediation.

How is this to be established? It is certainly clear that no mediation agreement will permit either party (or indeed the court) unilaterally to compel a mediator to attend to give evidence as to what transpired at a mediation. Even if both parties agreed to call the mediator, it must be doubtful whether a judge would compel a mediator to give evidence if (s)he chose not to do so, relying on the exemption written into the contract. There is a more important public policy interest at stake than sorting out costs arguments between two or more specific litigants. Who would be willing to mediate or indeed use mediation if its claimed confidentiality would not stand up to judicial investigation?

What of the parties themselves? By definition, this problem is only likely to be presented where a mediation has not resulted in settlement, and Party A has lost subsequent litigation of either an interim or a final nature to Party B, to whom Party A would normally be ordered to pay costs as well as whatever the court awarded Party B on the substantive issue. If Party B behaved unreasonably in refusing, as Party A would see it, to engage properly in the mediation process so as to run up substantial legal costs to and through trial which proper engagement might have averted, has Party A any remedy? If Party A raises the point with the judge deciding the costs issue, should the judge refuse to hear it?

Present thinking suggests that the issue should not be raised, and that the judge should indeed refuse to hear it, however unfair that might seem to Party A. Again the higher public interest involved in protecting mediation confidentiality must be preserved, so that mediation may remain an effective and safe tool for use in achieving pre-trial settlement. Exactly the same considerations apply to 'without prejudice' discussions. A judge cannot look at the course of any such discussions in order to determine reasonableness or otherwise of a party's conduct in litigation. It is, however, arguable that a judge can enquire whether a party was prepared to enter into 'without prejudice' discussions at all and make consequential costs orders. Indeed, that was part of the court's reasoning in *Ford v GKR Construction* [2000] 1 All ER 802, in which the insurers refused to discuss settlement when they disclosed video film to the claimant part of the way through the trial, and were not awarded costs despite securing a damages award of less than their Part 36 offer. It is noteworthy that the standard current Commercial Court ADR order permits enquiry as to why a mediation failed, but makes such enquiry 'subject to matters of privilege'. Thus there is a saving at the very least for communications preserved from disclosure by the 'without prejudice' rule, and probably stretching further to the contractually created assent to confidentiality.

But, broadly, if a party attends a mediation and engages in the process in good faith, failure to settle there should not of itself have adverse costs consequences, win or lose at later trial. Those who engage in bad faith may also find themselves protected, but they should nevertheless beware. Aggrieved parties and potentially frustrated judges can still comfort themselves with the proposition that it is extremely unlikely that unreasonable litigants or lawyers will manage to restrict themselves to demonstrating unreasonable conduct only while it is cloaked with the protection of mediation confidentiality. An unwise letter or step on the record will always be likely to convict such a party.

12.4.5 *Settlement at mediation and beyond*

Furthermore, with the ability to make Part 36 offers available to both claimants and defendants, this must be the way aggrieved parties seek to protect themselves against unreasonableness in mediation. The mediation process should at least have given some better idea to a party with a sense of grievance about an opponent's attitude and position as to where such an offer should be pitched.

Part D

Specialist processes and interests

CONTENTS

Chapter 13

The mini-trial (executive tribunal or executive appraisal)

13.1 PURPOSE AND FORMAT

The mini-trial has been described as a hybrid or 'blended' ADR procedure because it combines a more formal legal advocacy procedure with elements of information management, negotiation, neutral facilitation and case evaluation. It is a channel for a streamlined information exchange between parties with a view to subsequent negotiation between clients. In essence lawyers or other advisers for each party present a 'mini' version of their case to a panel consisting of a senior executive of their client and of the other party or parties. This provides an appropriate base from which the clients can get to grips with the problem and negotiate resolution, having been given a foretaste of what would occur at a trial of the action. The term 'mini-trial' was apparently coined by a New York Times journalist when reporting on an early information exchange procedure.

The procedure may take place without a neutral's involvement but will usually be more effective with a capable neutral to chair the presentation stage. The neutral will also be available to facilitate negotiations or to offer a case evaluation towards the end of the negotiations if there is still a gap between the parties. Strict rules of evidence and strict cross-examination procedures are normally not deployed in the procedure. Typically, the panel consists of senior executives from the companies involved who have not had previous direct involvement in the disputed matter. However, the procedure may vary in these and other respects as the parties choose, so that panel members may be the managers involved in the dispute or even a claimant in a complex personal injury case.

The scope for procedural variations in mini-trials helps to

241

13.1 *The mini-trial (executive tribunal or executive appraisal)*

indicate the essential objectives behind the mini-trial. It provides a forum for an exchange of views on case merits that is more formal than a mediation, but more streamlined than an arbitration or trial of the case. It allows advocates on each side to speak directly to the other side's client on the weaknesses of their case in law or fact (or ethics). And it puts clients in a position of greater detachment from their professional or in-house advisers by physically placing them in a panel or tribunal format where they can try to listen more objectively to an overview of the evidence before negotiating directly with the other side's client. The 'neutral' (as he or she is often described in this process) provides a vital mechanism to referee the joint meeting and subsequent negotiations, and sometimes also to referee and advise on the preparatory stages of the mini-trial.

The process can be described more simply in diagrammatic format.

TYPICAL NEGOTIATING STRUCTURE

L1		L2
D1 ... M1		M2 ... D2
W1		W2

L1 = lawyer for Party 1.
M1 = manager for Party 1 who has been 'running' the case.
W1 = witness (expert or factual) for Party 1.
D1 = director of Party 1 with some knowledge of the case but not previously directly involved.

MINI-TRIAL FORMAT: PRESENTATION STAGE

The senior representatives of each party, plus a neutral, constitute the 'tribunal'.

D1   N   D2

Witness area

W1   M1   L1   L2   M2   W2

N = Neutral.

MINI-TRIAL FORMAT: NEGOTIATION STAGE

The neutral and the senior representative of each party adjourn for private negotiations.

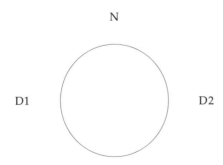

13.1 *The mini-trial (executive tribunal or executive appraisal)*

MINI-TRIAL FORMAT: MEDIATION OR EVALUATION STAGE

The neutral and the senior representatives of each party adjourn for joint mediation session, or evaluation.

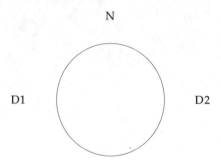

and (giving each side a chance for private caucuses with the neutral)

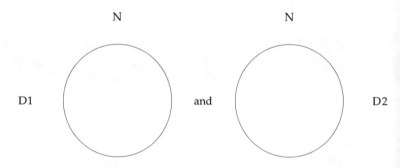

13.2 APPROPRIATE CASES FOR MINI-TRIAL PROCEDURES

There is a substantial overlap between mediation and the mini-trial (and indeed many mediations have most of the elements of a mini-trial other than the name and the seating arrangements). Since the mini-trial is typically more formal and more costly, it is normally used in cases where:

- there is a great deal at stake for the parties;
- the parties have significant differences in their interpretation or evaluation of the law and/or facts of the case;

- all parties would prefer if possible to reach an amicable resolution rather than go to trial or arbitration, for reasons of cost, publicity or corporate relations.

Such cases might include situations where, for example, a serious difference arises between joint venture partners, between companies over intellectual property rights, or between defendants over how to apportion liability contributions or indemnities. Ironically, however, there is no particular reason why disputes of that nature should not be dealt with in straightforward mediation, and indeed many have been. It seems, then, that the rationale for using a mini-trial format rather than mediation lies in:

- The psychological attraction of a more procedurally formal process. This might, for example, create a stronger feeling of having had a day in court than a mediation, through the use of a more formal presentation phase, witnesses, etc. This may appeal in particular to the lawyers involved, as the forum is slightly closer to a court-room, with which they are likely to be more familiar.

- The element of justification of this process, and therefore of any terms of settlement reached, to a third party, or other constituencies within each party. It is often the case in very high value or commercially sensitive cases that the parties will feel that the case somehow merits a correspondingly formal resolution process, albeit that they have chosen to avoid the court-room if possible. There is a sense in which the formality of a mini-trial will enable the parties to feel that the case has been fully heard and explored. They might feel that a mediation was somehow too informal to be appropriate for such a significant dispute. This might be particularly significant for those senior representatives of each party who attend and who will ultimately sanction (or otherwise) any settlement terms. They may well find the terms easier to sell to their respective boards, third party insurers, or whoever, if the process has been seen to be a relatively formal and thorough one.

- The presentational stage may well provide a better opportunity to assess the performance of key witnesses than would be available in mediation. Thus, if the contributions of such witnesses are critical to the outcome of the case, a mini-trial may create a better environment for testing those contributions.

● There may also be cases where lawyers or middle managers have reasons to resist putting the case before senior directors. These may in fact be appropriate for mini-trials, but contain political grounds for one side's resistance to the suggestion.

13.3 THE MAIN STAGES IN MINI-TRIAL PROCEDURE

13.3.1 Pre-hearing stage

1 Initiating agreement to use mini-trial procedure

As with other procedures, the parties have to reach the point of agreement that they will use the process. If not based on contract or court-referred, parties may choose to work from a simple contractual agreement, working out at a later date a more detailed protocol describing the mini-trial procedure.

2 Procedural details

The agreement or protocol on the mini-trial should normally cover the following issues:

● Identity of a neutral, and the neutral's fees and role, including if appropriate a role in helping parties agree details of mini-trial procedures and pre-hearing preparation or procedures. It is generally helpful for an experienced neutral or ADR organisation to assist in at least some preliminary discussions and for the neutral to meet the respective teams and panel representatives before the hearing.

● Setting down timescale and schedule of actions.

● Extent to which the parties will be negotiating their own rules or relying on the neutral or an ADR organisation's standard rules.

● Venue, dates for mini-trial, arrangements at venue, including hearing and private rooms, catering, office facilities etc.

● Extent of documentary disclosure (if required).

● Procedures at the mini-trial – length of presentations, replies, panel question and answer session, whether witnesses used, questioning by other counsel or by panel only, post-hearing negotiations, neutral role, grounds for withdrawal or continuation.

- Contents of any bundles of documents.

- Notice of witnesses (if used), advocates and other panel members due to attend.

- Panel members' authority to settle the case.

- Date for exchange of notice of exhibits, witness statements, and other documentary material.

- Costs of the process (usually each side bears its own costs and shares equally the other costs of the procedure).

- Notice of others who will attend mini-trial.

Given the range of activities involved, mini-trial pre-hearing procedures are likely to take at least two to three months.

3   The legal framework

The mini-trial agreement should also deal with the key legal questions discussed in relation to mediation agreements, for instance its effect on other proceedings, authority to settle, confidentiality between parties, neutral and ADR organisation, privilege, immunity, costs. Because of the similarity between the processes, a mediation agreement is a useful starting-point from which to draft a mini-trial agreement, certainly in so far as issues of confidentiality and 'without prejudice' are concerned.

CEDR's model Executive Tribunal agreement is to be found at Appendix G.

13.3.2   The mini-trial stage

Typically the presentation stage is abbreviated compared with a trial, taking up only a few hours or a half-day or day per party. The aim is to give each party time to deliver its presentation effectively to the panel and the panel time to consider it: for instance:

Day 1	09.00 – 12.00	Claimant's presentation.
	12.00 – 13.00	Defendant's reply.
	14.00 – 15.00	Question and answer session with panel.

13.3.2 The mini-trial (executive tribunal or executive appraisal)

Day 2	09.00 – 12.00	Defendant's presentation.
	12.00 – 13.00	Claimant's reply.
	14.00 – 15.00	Question and answer session.
Days 3 and 4		Panel negotiations.

Longer hearings may be encountered in multi-party or more complex cases, but care should be taken to avoid the procedure duplicating arbitration or trial because of lawyer expectations. The procedure is meant after all to be an abbreviated version, a 'mini-trial', in order to optimise executive time in dealing with the case and to resolve it on a reasonable and realistic basis. For this reason, too, it may be best to allow each party to present its case as it sees fit, subject only to clear rules on timetable, on use of witnesses and exhibits, and on whether cross-examination is to be allowed (not a good idea in most cases).

Presentations can be done with more fluidity than an opening or closing address in court, involving an extended display of one's best case, perhaps calling on two presenters and interspersed with some exhibits, references to key passages in documents, and short statements from important witnesses of fact or opinion. Rebuttals to such presentations should also be compact and able to highlight major weaknesses in the other's presentation.

Cross-examination may be best avoided, since it may heighten adversarial attitudes, but some scope should be given for opposing counsel to invite the panel to include some key questions in a panel question session following the presentation and reply phase.

There may also be value in building in time for short closing addresses to remind the panel of the major features of the case.

13.3.3 The negotiation/mediation stage

Negotiations can commence after an adjournment, possibly mid-morning on the third day through to day five or as set out in the protocol. The neutral's role in this part of the process is discussed more fully below. If negotiations succeed, the parties' advisers can be called in to draft or execute the agreement. If they fail, parties are free to reconvene by agreement, can allow a 'cooling-off' period to consider proposals or neutral recommendations, or can return to continuing litigation or arbitration procedures. Negotiations may commence without the neutral being present, or with the neutral being called on only if an opinion or mediation role would assist. However, there are advantages in the neutral at least spending a short period with the parties to obtain an initial sense of their positions.

13.4 MAKING MINI-TRIAL PROCEDURES EFFECTIVE: PARTICIPANT ROLES

It has been said that mini-trials are effective because everyone involved gets a chance to do what they are best at doing. *Lawyers* get an opportunity to present legal argument and analysis in a semi-formal setting and what is more to address themselves directly to the other parties. This latter point is a feature of mediation as well, and its value to the settlement process can be immense. In the normal course of litigation/ arbitration, parties are generally only confronted with the other side's case via their own lawyers and experts, until, that is, the case gets to trial. The element of raw exposure of each party to the other side's case, which most ADR processes provide, is often critical in generating settlement. *Factual and expert witnesses* get a chance to summarise their evidence in their own words without the stress and distortion of trial cross-examination. This is now only rarely available under the CPR in litigated trials, where evidence-in-chief ('telling your own story') has largely been superseded by written witness statements. *Managers* get the chance to take commercial decisions in the light of expert advice, a careful risk assessment, the commercial context and their feel for the situation and the people involved. *Neutrals* can nudge the process along with a detached yet considered contribution to discussions.

It is worth bearing this overall perspective in mind in deciding on procedure and on the way to allot and perform the various roles involved in the mini-trial.

13.4.1 Role of the lawyer

The lawyer's role in the mini-trial can be more easily described formally than in mediation, although lawyers should not make the mistake of assuming that mediation requires less preparation than a mini-trial. However, there is more overt advocacy and more of a forensic research element in the mini-trial. The stages a lawyer must review are:

- organising procedure, particularly with regard to information collection, presentation and exchange;

13.4.1 *The mini-trial (executive tribunal or executive appraisal)*

- selecting the neutral and agreeing on the neutral's role (if any) in organising pre-hearing procedures;

- counselling the client and witnesses on points of presentation before and during the hearing;

- presenting the client's case at the hearing;

- counselling the client where appropriate during the negotiation or mediation phase;

- drafting and/or executing a settlement agreement.

Key practice pointers for lawyers involved in a mini-trial are:

- Remember at all times the objective – to persuade the other party and the neutral of the credibility of your case, and to strengthen the confidence and skills, where appropriate, of your own client for the negotiation and evaluation stage.

- Be careful to avoid the trap of becoming over-rigid in negotiations on pre-hearing procedures. Your goal is not to prove you can win over your legal opponent, but to lay an effective foundation to achieve your objective. Neither clients nor a neutral are likely to be impressed with a lawyer scoring technical points, and such an approach is likely only to delay proceedings and add to costs.

- Similarly, consider whether your case might be assisted by consenting to the other side's choice of neutral – if you can win over *their* choice during the mini-trial, how will they fare when they have less control before a judge?

- Coach your own client to respond effectively to strong arguments likely to be put across by the other side or by the neutral; to have a structured negotiating plan; to be aware of the possibility of calling an adjournment in negotiations if further advice may be needed.

- Select and prepare witnesses so that their presentation is compact yet telling, and so that they are able to respond in a similar vein to questions from the panel.

- Remember the goal at the advocacy stage is not *merely* to win over the neutral. First and foremost, you need to help the other party adjust their expectations on the outcomes of the negotiation stage and alternatives to a reasonable settlement.

● In the same vein remember that an over-adversarial presentation can lead to resistance to your case from the other party
or neutral – you need to be part of their solution to this
dispute, not the biggest problem in it.

13.4.2 Role of the neutral

The neutral's role in the mini-trial may also be more wide-ranging
in a complex case than that of a mediator. Like the lawyer, the
neutral needs to review his or her role in the following stages.

1 Pre-hearing procedures

Where involved at this stage, the neutral should adopt as much as
feasible the role of facilitative mediator rather than adjudicator of
procedure. This will help avoid either party deciding that the
neutral is biased at an early stage. Such a development may undermine the neutral's credibility if a later evaluative stage becomes
necessary. On the other hand, where the parties have a high regard
for the neutral, they may be prepared to defer to that neutral's
greater experience. Even in such circumstances an effective neutral
should ensure the parties feel they have had a full airing of their
concerns.

2 The hearing

The neutral's role is very much to demonstrate capability as a fair
chair of proceedings and an insightful questioner, again to reassure
the panel members and their advisers of his or her fairness, credibility and experience. The neutral should in particular ensure that
he or she uses the various breaks in proceedings to develop a good
relationship with the executives on the panel, and to avoid indications of favouritism to either party.

3 Post-hearing negotiations

This is perhaps the most delicate stage of the procedure for a
neutral. Classical theory on the mini-trial suggests that the
executives should spend a period of time on their own in order to
attempt to negotiate a settlement before resorting again to the
neutral. However, the neutral should be alert throughout the

13.4.2 *The mini-trial (executive tribunal or executive appraisal)*

hearing phase to whether a more active role may be called for, and in particular:

- whether to spend a short period after the hearings reviewing with the panellists their initial reactions and helping summarise the key issues and evidence in a non-evaluative way;

- whether to step immediately into the role of facilitative mediator.

These approaches may be justified if the neutral senses that relations between the executives are initially so sensitive or rigid that a direct negotiation session may be fruitless or unproductive without the assistance above.

Whichever route is adopted, the neutral should remind the panellists of the timetable and of how and when to recall him if negotiations seem to be floundering. Determining the appropriate tactics is a matter of professional judgment based on the neutral's experience and sense of the type of case and type of parties or personalities involved. In particular, however, neutrals should be aware that if they intervene too early the parties may not have developed fully their negotiating sense of the situation; intervene too late and the parties may have frozen into resistance to movement even on the basis of the neutral's evaluation.

Again it is a matter of judgment as to how the neutral plays the role if negotiations have not produced a settlement. In general the neutral should first obtain a sense from each side of the extent and cause of progress or lack of it. If required, evaluation of the case should initially be given in private caucuses, but should be a review of strengths and weaknesses on each side that is consistent and detached between them. In some cases this may lead to discussion of a flexible settlement proposal; in more narrow cases a suggested monetary figure or bargaining range. The neutral should bear in mind at this stage that there may be some need for 'face-saving' to justify further movement by one or both parties. It may even be necessary to help the parties 'revisit' some of the witnesses or legal advisors to help matters forward, or to suggest a 'cooling-off' period followed by a further meeting to have a 'last shot' at settlement. An offer to take the executives to dinner for a final attempt may not go amiss!

The power of the mini-trial lies in the range of techniques and roles it draws into the more informal mediation process. It is an extremely valuable option in major corporate disputes and used perhaps less frequently than its potential impact merits.

CONTENTS

Chapter 14

Adjudication, expert determination and ADR in the construction industry

14.1 DISPUTE RESOLUTION IN THE CONSTRUCTION INDUSTRY

The construction field has always been known for acrimonious litigation, with its characteristic mix of complex contractual relationships, huge sums of money at stake, highly complex projects and remorseless time pressure. It has also had a reputation as a tough and aggressive world in which the weakest and even at times some of the strongest will go to the wall. Yet the Technology and Construction Court (the TCC) and its predecessor, the Official Referee's Court, have constantly been in the vanguard of procedural reform and have lent several key procedural concepts, such as case management, early trial fixture and 'without prejudice' meetings of experts to the CPR as useful tools for more general use. We look at how ADR has developed in this field over the last ten years and at two of the processes which have taken on particular importance in the field, namely adjudication and expert determination.

14.1.1 The need for ADR in construction disputes

In his Lionel Cohen lecture entitled *Judicial Processes and Alternative Dispute Resolution* delivered in Jerusalem in May 1996, Lord Mustill characterised construction disputes as involving 'prolongation and aggression'. These, he said, feed on each other to make dispute resolution in the construction industry 'conspicuously exhausting of time, energy, money and spirit'. He went on to try to define cases in which ADR might well be tried. These were:

255

- where the bitterness of the dispute outweighed its real significance and the parties needed to be led gently back to a sense of proportion;

- where a genuine dispute existed in good faith, but it had been exacerbated by obstinacy or resentment, and where a judicial process might well make matters worse;

- where there is no obviously right answer to a dispute in which all the parties were at fault to some degree and must be made to see it;

- conversely, where the dispute is too complicated to be assimilated by busy decision-makers, and where the participation of a neutral, whether interventionist or facilitative, might restore to decision-makers control of the dispute and its outcome, and a reliable basis upon which to make decisions;

- where the dispute arose within the course of a continuing relationship, which ought if possible to be kept in being, but which would be fractured by orthodox litigation.

Commenting on Lord Mustill's list in his review of the effect of the CPR, the first judge in charge of the TCC, Sir John Dyson, continued:

'The merest glance at Lord Mustill's list shows that many typical TCC cases are suitable candidates for ADR. I particularly have in mind his third and fourth categories. I accept, of course, that some cases are not well suited to ADR. For example where the issue which lies at the heart of a dispute is a difficult question of construction of contract, or some other point of law: or perhaps where the key question is one of a technical nature, as to which the parties' experts have taken irreconcilably differing positions. But it seems to me that most TCC cases are potential candidates for ADR. After all, about 90% of all proceedings started in the TCC do settle. What underlies the new procedure in relation to ADR is the desire to achieve settlements earlier than would otherwise be the case, and, in some cases, achieve settlement when it would not be achieved at all.'

14.1.2 The construction pre-action protocol

A pre-action protocol for construction and engineering disputes has been published by the TCC in conjunction with the relevant practitioners' associations, TecSA (solicitors) and TecBAR (barristers), as a benchmark of good practice, against which doubtless the TCC judges will measure litigation conduct when weighing costs decisions. This requires:

- exchange of letters of claim and defendant's response before proceedings are issued:

- a pre-action meeting the aim of which is to agree (among other things) whether and if so how issues might be resolved without recourse to litigation; those attending the meeting should include any insurer or legal representative of any insurer involved;

- consideration by the parties as to whether some form of ADR would be more suitable than litigation in respect of each agreed issue or the dispute as a whole and, if so, endeavouring to agree which ADR process to adopt.

14.1.3   The TecSA ADR protocol and model mediation rules

TecSA (the TCC Solicitors' Association) has also produced its own ADR protocol for members. This encourages the use of ADR among its members, requiring members to consider mediation or early neutral evaluation as soon as possible after receiving instructions, and to advise clients and report within seven days in relation to any proposal made for immediate or future ADR.

Interestingly, the TecSA ADR protocol also acknowledges that the court may take into account suitability for ADR when later assessing reasonableness and proportionality of costs, and any open (but not 'without prejudice') correspondence on the subject. It also establishes that the costs of considering ADR, even if ultimately not utilised, should be recoverable on assessment, subject to reasonableness and proportionality.

TecSA's own model mediation rules are likely to underline and encourage use of a power set out in the CEDR model rules but rarely used, namely of asking the mediator to produce a non-binding recommendation on terms of settlement if mediation does not produce full agreement. This reflects the ICE Conciliation Procedure, which provides that where mediation does not produce an agreed outcome, the conciliator recommends a solution to the dispute, being an opinion as to how the parties can best dispose of the dispute. The opinion need not necessarily be based on the terms and construction of the contract, nor on principles of law and equity.

14.1.3   *Dispute resolution in the construction industry*

The TecSA model (similar to the CEDR wording) is slightly different, in that the recommendation:

> '. . . will not attempt to anticipate what a court might order or determine are the legal rights and obligations of the parties, but will set out what the Mediator suggests are appropriate settlement terms in all the circumstances.'

Thus, despite the superficially unfavourable environment for ADR in the construction industry, and after much heated debate and doubt among judges and practitioners in this field, ADR in a variety of forms, be it adjudication, early neutral evaluation or mediation, has taken a strong hold and is developing rapidly.

14.1.4   The main forms of ADR in use in construction cases

What perhaps can be said to characterise construction disputes and to distinguish them in a significant way from other types of dispute is the fact that problems will arise at unpredictable but frequent intervals during the course of what can be a protracted contract period. Throughout the contract, maintenance of work-flow on critical paths set against demanding timetables is vital. A serious dispute which brings the contract works to a complete halt because of deadlock over what might be a relatively small component of the contract works will have disproportionately serious consequences unless at least a working solution can be found quickly.

For this reason a range of ADR processes may well be required for such disputes. Some need to be adapted for providing interim solutions to problems so as to protect the critical path, and some perhaps more adapted for providing final solutions at the conclusion of a contract when time pressure is no longer so great. However, with the flexibility and speed with which any ADR process can be set up, the real determinant of which process to use may be the needs of the parties and the situation, and the preferred relationship between the disputants and the neutral.

While *mediation* might be said to be best suited as a process to provide finality, there is no reason why it could not be deployed during the course of a contract. This might be because the parties prefer an outcome facilitated rather than determined by a neutral, and such a process matches the demands of time pressure.

There has, however, always been a tendency in construction disputes towards seeking third party decisions. Two ADR processes which provide decisions of slightly different kinds, but which are quite different from arbitral awards have become of special attractiveness: *adjudication*, which can provide provisional decisions, and *expert determination*, which will provide contractually binding final decisions on a defined issue.

It should be emphasised that these two ADR processes are not exclusively confined to use in the construction industry, though this may be where they are most commonly used. Expert determination in particular has a wider application in valuation disputes of a wide variety of kinds, and that section of this chapter should be read in this light.

There is insufficient space in this book to consider the processes of adjudication and expert determination in detail, but a brief description and analysis may be of assistance.

14.2 ADJUDICATION

14.2.1 Definition

We referred in Chapter 2 to adjudicative processes, and in Chapter 3 briefly to adjudication, to describe conceptually a range of processes in which some form of a decision or adjudication on the outcome of a case by a third party takes place. This should not be confused with adjudication as dealt with in this chapter, which is a very specific type of adjudicative process.

Adjudication in this context is a process that bestrides ADR and litigation or arbitration. It has been described as a procedure whereby a summary inter-decision-making power in respect of disputes is vested in a third party individual (the adjudicator). The appointed adjudicator is usually not involved in the day-to-day performance or administration of the contract, and is neither an arbitrator nor connected with the state. The feature emphasised by ADR commentators, when differentiating adjudication from other ADR processes, such as mediation, executive tribunal and even early neutral evaluation, is that the latter are essentially consensual, whereas the function of the adjudicator is to reach a decision having considered submissions from both sides.

Unlike litigation and arbitration, adjudication is not subject to the CPR or the Arbitration Acts, except in relation to the construction industry (see below). Nor is the adjudicator afforded any immunity from suit in carrying out those contractually imposed tasks.

14.2.2 General features

1 Speed

Most adjudication procedures contemplate a very short timetable with the appointment of the adjudicator taking place within 7–14 days of implementation of the procedure, and submissions being delivered within the same period. The adjudicator is required then to produce a decision shortly thereafter.

2 Documents only

Because of the constraints of the timetable, submissions will often be by documents only, with little or no scope for oral submissions to be made. The documents produced in support will be those upon which each party relies, there being no time or allowance for any sort of formal mutual disclosure.

3 Inquisitorial procedure

The adjudicator is commonly allowed to investigate areas deemed appropriate, and in technical disputes this may involve a visit to, or an inspection of, the matter in dispute.

4 Qualification of the adjudicator

Normally it is contemplated that the adjudicator will be an expert in the field of dispute, hence the provision for an investigation and if necessary an inspection. Expertise avoids the necessity of briefing the adjudicator fully on the technical subject-matter. It may also be helpful if the adjudicator has some knowledge of court or arbitration procedures in order for him to conduct the process in a judicial manner. The adjudicator is therefore likely to come from a background of litigation or arbitration practice.

5 Enforceability of the adjudicator's decision

In *Drake & Scull v McLaughlin & Harvey* [1992] BLR 102, an Official Referee enforced an adjudicator's decision by granting a mandatory injunction requiring the defendant to pay monies to a trustee-stakeholder. It is uncertain whether the injunction would have been granted if the adjudicator had ordered that the money be paid direct to the claimant.

The question of enforceability was a hotly debated subject in the construction industry, following the introduction of the Housing Grants, Construction and Regeneration Act 1996 (the HGCRA). However, the judges of the Technology and Construction Court made it clear early on that they would fully back a successful party in enforcing a decision of an adjudicator, though not usually by granting mandatory injunctions. In *Macob Civil Engineering Ltd v Morrison Construction Ltd* [1999] CLC 739, Dyson J indicated that the appropriate course was normally to issue proceedings for monies found by the adjudicator to be due and apply for summary judgment. In *Outwing Construction Ltd v H Randell & Son Ltd* [1999] BLR 156, another TCC case, the judge allowed a claimant to seek payment ordered by an adjudicator with considerably shortened procedural time limits.

6 Challenging the adjudication

Adjudicators are not encouraged to give reasons, as this would lay their decisions open to attack. The underlying principle behind the adjudication concept is to produce what has sometimes been described as 'rough and ready justice' upon an interim basis, with a view to defusing the argument, easing the claimant's cashflow and allowing the parties to proceed with their contract. Adjudication rules normally provide that the decision is binding upon the parties subject to the right to take the matter to litigation or arbitration upon the giving of notice within a specified period after the adjudicator's decision. It is this feature that primarily distinguishes adjudication from normal arbitration. Furthermore, the procedure is not conducted on a 'without prejudice' basis, so that both submissions made to the adjudicator and the decision itself can be referred to in later proceedings, though in construction disputes under the HGCRA the matter is reheard afresh.

7 Immunity

As stated above, adjudicators have no immunity. They are subject to normal professional standards and can be liable in negligence. This underlines why adjudicators are wise not to give reasons. Any party to a dispute contemplating an action for negligence against an adjudicator will of course have to take into consideration the information that was supplied to the adjudicator and upon which the decision was based, coupled with the time frame within which the decision was reached.

8 Identifying an adjudicator in the contract

As with arbitration clauses, it may not be appropriate to identify or nominate a particular adjudicator in the relevant contract clause. This is not only because the parties will not know the expertise required of the adjudicator until a particular dispute arises, but also because of the element of speed. The adjudicator needs to be readily available, and probably not already committed on any other adjudication at the time.

14.2.3 Statutory adjudication in the construction industry

Provision for adjudication was increasingly made in building contracts, but there is now a statutory right to adjudication created by the HGCRA 1996.

1 The statutory right to adjudication

This Act provides that a party to a construction contract has the right to refer a dispute to adjudication under a procedure laid down by the Act. Curiously, there is no definition of adjudication as such, but s 108 sets out the features of a compliant adjudication procedure including (among other things):

- requiring the adjudicator to reach a decision within 28 days;
- imposing a duty on the adjudicator to act impartially;
- enabling the adjudicator to take the initiative in ascertaining the facts and the law;
- providing that the decision is binding until finally determined by legal proceedings, arbitration or agreement.

2 The statutory scheme and contractual alternatives

While the HGCRA created the right to adjudication, secondary legislation set out in the Scheme for Construction Contracts (England & Wales) Regulations 1998 provided a statutory adjudication scheme as from 6 March 1998. This operates as a default mechanism. Parties are allowed to devise their own contractual schemes, which will be effective if they comply with s 108 of the Act. If they do not comply, or the contract is silent, the statutory scheme applies. Following the introduction of this legislation, many construction bodies introduced their own schemes, as did ADR providers like CEDR. A copy of the CEDR scheme is to be found in Appendix H.

The CEDR Rules contain a mediation option, by which the parties are allowed to refer the dispute to mediation at any time before the adjudicator's decision. Pending the outcome of such a mediation, the adjudication is suspended, as of course mediation frequently produces a final and contractually binding agreement, obviating the need for an adjudicator's provisionally binding decision. Unlike the CEDR expert determination agreement, the CEDR Adjudication Rules provide that the adjudicator shall not act as the mediator.

3   Take-up of adjudication in construction disputes

Initially, take-up was slow. However, once the TCC judges had made it clear that they were quite prepared not only to back the general objectives of adjudication, but also to support adjudicators' decisions and to encourage enforcement, take-up increased significantly. This in turn has had a significant impact upon disputes in the construction industry, such that:

- the number of cases referred to litigation and arbitration has dropped appreciably;

- whilst often not wholly satisfied with the adjudicator's decision, parties nevertheless accept it without exercising the right to refer to litigation or arbitration;

- often the decision (or sometimes even the prospect of adjudication) encourages the parties to resolve their disputes directly.

Thus adjudication appears to be achieving what was originally intended (though doubted in advance by many commentators), namely a significant reduction in the number of disputes in the construction industry with their associated costs.

14.2.4   Usage of adjudication outside the construction industry

Use of adjudication has continued to increase, being found in such private sector areas as property valuation, finance, and in the public sectors of immigration, social security and in the Prison Rules.

14.3 EXPERT DETERMINATION

Often the dispute between parties is one of valuation or of a purely technical nature. Following legislative restriction on rights of appeal, coupled with a wish to avoid formal arbitration, parties often opt for a dispute to be determined by an independent third party acting as an *expert* rather than in a judicial or arbitral capacity. Whilst there are many parallels with adjudication, nevertheless expert determination demonstrates significant differences. It is a well-used process both within and outside the construction industry, as we shall see.

14.3.1 Acting as an expert

It is important that the clause providing for the dispute to be determined by an expert specifically records that the person nominated is acting 'as expert'. Firstly, this helps to ensure that the procedure is not governed by the Arbitration Acts. Secondly, assuming this to be the case, there is no right of appeal, thereby giving the parties finality. However, merely using the term 'expert' will not suffice if in reality the person concerned is in fact acting as an arbitrator. It will be a matter of construction as to what was intended.

14.3.2 Procedure

Again, there are parallels with adjudication. The parties are likely to make their submissions by way of documents only. It is not subject to due process (unless the parties agree otherwise). The expert is normally clothed with the power to investigate, ie to act inquisitorially by virtue of acting in a specific expert capacity, and may even conduct investigations without reference to the parties. The expert must, however, be mindful of the overriding duty to act fairly as between the parties, especially as it is likely that the decision reached will be final.

14.3.3 Appeal

There is no statutory right of appeal. The only circumstances in which a decision can be challenged is where the expert has asked himself the wrong question or decided the wrong issue. Because there is no immunity either, the expert can, like an adjudicator, be vulnerable to a claim for negligence for any failure in performance of a professional duty.

14.3.4 Identity of the expert

As in adjudication, it may be preferable not to name the expert in the contract. However, unlike adjudication, it is helpful to identify the particular expertise needed; for example, a surveyor in respect of rent reviews, an accountant for share valuations and an IT expert for computer disputes. There is nothing to stop a lawyer being appointed as an expert in respect of a legal dispute. In practice, such an appointment is more likely to be made where a dispute arises after the contract has been agreed, as most lawyers (and indeed their clients) would like to think that the document they have drafted is clear.

14.3.5 Finality

By way of contrast to adjudication, it is intended that the expert's determination is final and binding on the parties, and the contract terms providing for this means of dispute resolution will make this clear. Thus there is usually no provision for the parties to have a time limit following the determination within which to reject the finding and take the matter to arbitration or litigation.

14.3.6 The CEDR model expert determination agreement

To complement its family of model agreements for the main ADR processes, CEDR has published a model expert determination agreement, to be found in Appendix I. In accordance with CEDR's philosophy, the agreement allows for a stay for mediation. The agreement allows the expert to act as the mediator in those circumstances. Perhaps more controversially, in the event that the mediation does not produce a settlement, it then permits the expert to resume the previous role of expert. This could pose some difficulties unless the parties have foreseen and provided for such an eventuality beforehand. For instance, how is the expert to treat information given in private mediation sessions with each party? To what extent should parties divulge confidential information and opinions when the possibility exists that the mediator may revert to an independent expert determination role? Will the expert be able to exclude from consideration any such private communications?

Whilst such matters should not be fatal to such a role change, it is vital that the parties, their lawyers and indeed the expert/ mediator fully appreciate all the dynamics, sensitivities and risks before embarking upon such a course. If such matters are only fully appreciated halfway through the process, resulting either in the resignation of the expert or the realisation by one party that it has unduly compromised its public position by private disclosure, there may be a danger of wasted time, energy and cost.

14.3.7 Usage of expert determination outside the construction industry

It needs emphasising that expert determination in particular has much wider application than in the construction industry. It can be deployed in a wide variety of ways where contractually binding valuation by an expert is required, such as:

- share valuation (in which cases there need not actually be a dispute);
- development value in land;
- rent review;
- sale and purchase of businesses;
- transfer and valuation of pension rights;
- information technology disputes.

CONTENTS

Chapter 15

Commercial ADR development: new opportunities

In this chapter, we look at ADR development opportunities, both from the point of view of practice development generally for professionals as participants in ADR processes and also with regard to some of the sectors in which ADR is beginning to emerge.

There is a huge range of ADR expertise and experience within the legal profession. Many firms of lawyers now approach ADR in a systematic way, seeing it as a means of delivering a better process and better outcomes to clients. Other firms have hardly encountered ADR. While there may seem to be a clear marketing choice to be made, we suggest that there is really no choice over ADR now, in the light both of the CPR's impact on the legal system and in the light of client demand. ADR has unavoidable implications for any legal practice that deals with resolution of disputes, which means virtually every practice, bearing in mind that dispute resolution is a much wider concept than litigation. ADR has therefore to be built into the thinking, planning and marketing of every practice, because both courts and clients will demand it. Thus we set out and explore some of the considerations for those who have yet to make that choice, or who have made the choice without really knowing where to take it.

15.1 HOW DOES ADR ENHANCE A CLIENT'S PERCEPTION OF A LAWYER?

15.1.1 Good results

The client comes to the litigation professional with a problem and wants a solution. The effectiveness of the lawyer's service is

269

measured by a number of factors, not just simply whether he 'wins' or 'loses', but also:

- the time and cost required to obtain the result;
- the nature of the process through which the result is obtained;
- the relevance of the result to his own commercial or personal situation;
- whether any pre-existing commercial or personal relationships survive the process;
- how the client feels about being in dispute during and most importantly at the end of the process.

Indeed, it is probable that the client judges the value of the lawyer's service to him by a broader range of criteria than lawyers themselves use to judge their own service.

ADR will frequently obtain for a client a better result than might otherwise have been achieved, particularly where 'better' includes reference to the wider commercial or personal priorities of the client. Since the practice of law is essentially demand-led, it must make sense to be offering services that the clients want (or would want, if they were informed about them).

15.1.2 Reputation

Reputation is critical to any professional, and certainly to those engaged in disputes. Different professionals covet and pursue different reputations, but few would shy away from a reputation for getting good results. There is little doubt that a number of lawyers and other professionals have already emerged with a reputation for using ADR to resolve problems quickly and effectively. This is even more significant for those seeking 'repeat business' clients – those, such as insurance companies or banks, for example, who have a regular throughput of litigation. Clearly, the benefits accruing to the client are multiplied for each piece of litigation which is successfully and quickly resolved. For repeat litigants, the benefits of ADR, and hence the reputation and kudos falling on those of their advisers who offer it, can be very considerable.

Furthermore, there will always be a significant tranche of cases which are considered uneconomical to litigate, but which would be considered appropriate for ADR, thus bringing new work to those who can offer ADR.

15.1.3 ADR reflects well on non-ADR work

There can be little doubt that an informed commitment to ADR can send a powerful message to clients. This applies not only where ADR is used, but also where it is not. A client whose lawyer uses ADR properly will know that where the lawyer is not doing so, it is because ADR is not appropriate or possible, rather than because the lawyer is not informed or willing. It is much easier to convince a client of the necessity of continuing with the litigation process if the ADR option has been intelligently canvassed and validly rejected.

15.1.4 Competitive edge

The current professional climate is extremely competitive, with strong downward pressure on fees from an increasingly sophisti-cated client base well accustomed to shopping around for advisers, and negotiating strongly on fees. Thus the arguments about individual reputation transfer easily to firm reputation. For a firm seeking a competitive edge over their competitors, ADR offers a wide range of possibilities, ranging from general prominence in a 'beauty parade' to specific litigation tenders based on significant numbers of cases going to ADR, and costed accordingly. It is fair to say that even now relatively few law firms in the UK have begun fully to exploit the true potential of ADR in a systematic and sophisticated way.

15.1.5 The converse – potential liability for ignoring ADR

Essentially, many of the arguments compelling the use of ADR are the reverse of the positive ones, and none more so than those of reputation and the competitive edge. A reputation for not using processes which other lawyers or other professionals can use to good effect is never likely to attract business.

If the above points are sound, then *not* to acquire and market ADR skills and experience will put client relations and practice development at risk. Good reputation and competitive edge are key to success in this highly competitive market-place. Taken with judicial willingness to penalise those who behave unreasonably, which is clearly going to include unreasonable attitudes to engage-ment in ADR, the need is reinforced.

Given the value which ADR can deliver to a client, it is not hard to argue that the failure to alert a client to the existence of ADR is, at best, falling short of best practice. The more widespread its use becomes, the more likely such a failure is to become an act of professional negligence, although the question has not yet been tested in the English courts. Naturally, it might be difficult to prove causation and loss in such circumstances, but the mere fact that the conduct itself may come close to, or even be, negligent gives an indication of the significance which ADR has achieved within the legal process. In any case, and more cynically, it is always useful if a lawyer can say to a client who, following lengthy litigation, complains about the cost or result – 'I did tell you about ADR but you rejected it'.

There are of course times in the life of any case when the time is not ripe for its use, as we have seen in Chapter 7. Negotiation may supply all that the client wants without the added formality and expense of the ADR process. But when the time is right and particularly where negotiations are deadlocked or ADR may well deliver a better outcome than trial, it has a proven track record of delivering faster and better outcomes. Opposition to it on principle is now a hazardous course. Equally, ADR cannot any longer be ignored with safety. Lawyers are indeed using it systematically to improve outcomes for clients, and those that can deliver imaginative, effective and commercial outcomes are going to fare better than those who do not.

15.2 DEVELOPING AN ADR CAPABILITY

15.2.1 Solicitors in private practice

Once a decision is taken to endorse ADR, and develop a capability for it, practical questions arise as to how to put that into effect. The following points, at least, may merit some consideration.

1 Decision and policy

Any serious use of ADR needs to stem from a conscious decision to use it, rather than from a drift into it. Not only is this a more intellectually and professionally credible position, it is also likely to result in a more coherent approach to ADR and greater success in using it. It is also generally critical that those in more junior positions within an organisation are aware of the firm or company's decision and policy on ADR. If they are to be expected to grapple with new practices, they will need the comfort of knowing that their efforts are sanctioned by their superiors. If not, there will always be a tendency to adopt the safe option and continue with traditional methods.

2 Training

As with any new area of practice, good training is important. ADR presents legal and tactical questions for the professional, about which clients will require advice. It also presents lawyers in particular with the challenge of effective representation of the client within ADR. As we suggested in Chapter 11, this can differ markedly from representation in the traditional adversarial forums. Furthermore, the negotiating structure of, for example, a mediation is probably different from anything most lawyers have previously experienced. In order to understand fully how the process will operate and develop and so derive the maximum benefit for the client, lawyers should acquaint themselves with the subtleties of the process through an appropriate training programme.

3 Budget

It is not possible to launch any new product without a budget, covering for example planning, development and marketing costs. The same applies to ADR. However, the start-up costs of ADR are in reality fairly limited, covering perhaps some training and marketing. In fact, given the benefit that ADR is capable of delivering over the medium to long term, the minimal start-up costs can make it an attractive proposition. This is mainly because it operates within the context of an existing litigation and arbitration practice, on to which it can be grafted with relative ease.

4 Publicity and marketing

Professionals today are more conscious than ever of the importance of publicity and marketing. In many ways, ADR fits very easily into that arena because the essential message is a very positive one. It is, in short, a relatively easy product to sell, particularly to those accustomed to buying litigation services. It therefore makes sense to give such a product good exposure, whether in firm brochures, seminars with clients, newsletters, or however else the firm's marketing is conducted.

5 ADR units

Some firms originally established ADR units within the firm, consisting of practitioners who have some knowledge, training, and experience of ADR, able to offer specialist advice to colleagues within the firm and their respective clients. This can range from advice on ADR clauses through to the preparation and conduct of a mediation. While there is probably still an argument for concentrating particular expertise in a few people, the tendency now is for all litigators to develop a working knowledge of ADR, and for firms to deploy practitioners either according to the traditional divisions into contentious and non-contentious departments, or by reference to sector-based or client-defined groups which transcend the old divisions. ADR belongs very comfortably in mixed skill groups of that kind.

6 ADR schemes, tenders, and beauty parades

Following the competitive edge argument, ADR can clearly play a role in tenders for new work, or 'beauty parades'. The financial implications of the consistent and strategic use of ADR can be very significant, and that is not likely to be lost on any client who regularly buys litigation services. It may well be that the client requires some considerable guidance in working out, with their legal advisers, how best ADR can be integrated into their existing dispute-handling process. That in itself can be advice that the lawyer can give, and can also create a context in which to develop a good working relationship with the client as well as a sense that the lawyer is interested in reducing the client's exposure to litigation, rather than simply dealing with the results of it. With increasing sophistication among clients, however, lawyers must get used to the client being the driver of development and usage of ADR systems.

7 Making ADR systems work

It takes an immense amount of commitment and effort to translate a desire to systematise ADR into the practice of a law firm, and this should not be under-estimated. Staff in any organisation will tend to continue to conduct and resolve disputes in the traditional way until it becomes virtually a necessity not to do so, because of client pressure or management determination. If it is difficult to get criticised for pursuing the familiar path, human nature suggests that it will remain the first choice, by reason of its comfortable familiarity. Conversion of cases from an intention to mediate into actually mediated cases is surprisingly difficult until a system for doing so is in place. There always seems to be a little more information needed, when in truth very often that information might even be best obtained at the mediation itself, or it is not really essential to settlement. The lesson is that active management of the changes which an ADR policy requires is absolutely vital to its successful implementation

15.2.2 In-house lawyers and claims managers

In-house advisers are particularly well placed to promote ADR and ensure its proper use. They have been in the forefront of its development in the US in both corporations and insurance carriers. Not only do they not have the fear of lost fee income (even if their performance is measured in some other way), they have by contrast an incentive to control costs for their employers. In-house lawyer litigation and claim management will include ensuring that external lawyers are required on a regular basis to quote predicted costs and outcomes if they recommend litigation, and assessment of ADR potential at regular stages of litigation. In particular, external lawyers should be required to specify the risks of using ADR if they advise against it.

In addition to litigation management, in-house lawyers may be able to consider the strategic potential for adding value to their employer's business – by contract procedures, joint venture agreements, corporate policy statements on relations with suppliers and customers, ADR schemes for customer disputes or disputes between internal operating units of the company. As with their external colleagues, in-house lawyers should seek to ensure that they fully understand the practicalities of ADR by involvement in training. They can then test its use, albeit initially in cases which are not too sensitive for company politics, if there is limited knowledge of ADR amongst managers. Education programmes for managers will also assist corporate readiness to use ADR.

15.2.3 The role of non-contentious lawyers

Commercial disputes emerge, sometimes quite slowly, out of a previously negotiated or established legal relationship, such as a contract or a statutory scheme. There is often a grey area near the outset of a dispute between a commercial negotiation and a fully-fledged claim. Of course, vast numbers of potential disputes are settled at that stage, with or without the intervention of lawyers. But for those that do not, considerable thought needs to be given to the transition process, and particularly to the way in which it is handled within the law firm. Even a change of solicitor, as a case is handed from, for example, the commercial department to the litigation department, can send a powerful message (intentionally or otherwise) to the other side and to the client. A point of no return has been passed, meaning to the opponent that war is perhaps about to be declared, and to the client that the original contract has broken down (wherever fault for that may lie) and that peaceful resolution is no longer possible.

ADR can be a powerful tool in this transitional phase. Indeed, the mere offer of ADR (perhaps as a final attempt at resolution before the issue of proceedings) can help to preserve a negotiating environment that may be lost as soon as a claim form is issued. It follows that the non-contentious lawyer, perhaps well accustomed to handling negotiations up to a certain point prior to handing the case to a litigator, has as much need of fluency in and knowledge of ADR as the litigator. Indeed, the ADR processes themselves, supremely mediation, are in many respects more instinctive and habitual for a commercial lawyer than for a litigator.

Moreover, the distinctions between contentious and non-contentious work are beginning to blur and even break down. Some firms have departments created around subject-matter or dedicated to a particular client's whole needs, rather than around procedural functions, such as litigation or commercial contract drafting. Lawyers from both backgrounds work together on problem-solving in a cross-cultural way that is likely to make much more sense to clients. It means that both can contribute their particular skills and experience to the mediation process. Where a mediation might lead to a re-negotiated future commercial relationship, the skills of the non-contentious commercial lawyer are as important in terms of anticipating future problems as those of the litigator, who may reality-test the client well in terms of the litigation alternative, but be less fully equipped to help over issues of practical commercial import.

Mediation is more akin to a commercial negotiation, with lawyer and client working together as a team, than settlement events and hearings within the litigation/arbitration process, in which the lawyer usually takes the lead within a set procedure or negotiates without the client. Litigators may need to beware that turf wars take on a new aspect, with commercial lawyers seeing no need for litigators except in the narrow role of advising the client about the procedural litigation alternative to settlement.

Even more importantly, perhaps, it is non-contentious lawyers who control the drafting of commercial agreements, and hence the opportunity to include a contractual commitment to ADR use. Without doubt, this is an area where the draftsman can significantly affect the future relationship between the parties. That, on one analysis, could be said to be legal drafting at its best. A fuller discussion of ADR clauses appears in Chapter 6, but their importance cannot be overstated.

15.3 PROFESSIONAL DEVELOPMENT OPPORTUNITIES AS A MEDIATOR

So far we have assessed the relevance and value of ADR to professionals (particularly to lawyers) in the context of acting for their own clients, where they represent one party to a dispute. There is, however, also a role for professionals as mediators.

Mediation is not yet established as a discrete profession in the UK or in many other common law jurisdictions. While the number of accredited mediators has steadily grown, and new mediation providers have begun to spring up, mediation is still normally a satellite activity for all but a few professionals. Over the medium to long term, however, that is very likely to change. Many of those already acting as mediators are lawyers, both solicitors and barristers, and also ex-judges. An appreciable number are surveyors, academics, architects, accountants, management and training consultants, doctors, and so on.

The mental shift from adversarial representative to mediator is not always an easy one for lawyers, and indeed not one which all lawyers can, or would want to, make. But for those who do, it has proved an extremely satisfying and challenging role. The likelihood is that, as the field develops, an increasing number of lawyers will see a role for themselves as mediators. In the nature of the work, it can easily be an extension to an existing legal or any other kind of professional practice, rather than there being any need to become a full-time mediator.

Furthermore, it is certainly the case that the best understanding of the subtleties and potential of ADR stems from immersion in it, both as representative of a party and as mediator. Many lawyers have already sought to train as mediators not because they expect to generate much income from it, but because it enhances and informs their ability to represent their own clients in the process.

However, the delivery of ADR services from within the context of a law firm can raise its own particular problems. In particular, the sensitive nature of the mediator's position requires scrupulous attention to be paid to any possible conflicts of interest. In any one mediation, the mediator may well receive confidential information from at least two parties, which in itself may impact upon his firm's ability to act for or against either of those parties in the future. In addition, indications from the United States suggest that there is something of a conflict between a law firm offering its services as a representative of a party, and doing so as mediator. It may be, in the long term, that the reality of a mediator's position is that the services have to be delivered from an essentially independent base, and not one which is also engaged in partisan representation.

We have already seen that the role of the barrister in mediation is essentially advisory, as forensic advocacy has no real place in the mediation process, though there is perhaps more scope for at least modified skills of that nature in mini-trials. Barristers and indeed retired judges are turning to mediation as another way of finding a role in ADR. Some chambers are setting up mediation services, and several judges have become very distinguished mediators, following a pattern firmly established in other parts of the common law world. Problems of conflict of interest are less pervasive when dealing with individual lawyers rather than law firms. Their instinctive skills in terms of taking responsibility for formulating an opinion and advising on the strength of it mean that coping with the facilitative end of the ADR spectrum needs a considerable shift in mind-set, but this is well within the capabilities of many barristers and judges. It also fits them well for offering early neutral evaluation in disputes. As Professor Genn notes in her review of the Central London County Court mediation scheme, barristers proved very effective, especially in cases where the parties appeared comfortable with a more directive approach. If that is what the parties both needed and wanted, that of course is acceptable.

Because they approach acting as a mediator from a different perspective, maybe from a background of acting as expert witnesses in litigation or in non-contentious problem-solving in business and commerce, non-lawyer mediators have already made a distinctive contribution to the sound development of ADR. Although one school of thought in the UK has been that mediators ought to be lawyers, this is certainly not our view. The legal approach is only one model of how to resolve disputes, and up to the advent of the CPR at least it was not necessarily the most attractive or the most popular among clients and non-lawyers. ADR offers a fusion of skills and experience and a flexibility of options in which business and professional people, lay clients and lawyers alike, can create an exciting synthesis of ways to sort out the difficulties and problems which inevitably arise in a complex world.

CONTENTS

Chapter 16

ADR and injury claims: dealing with power imbalance and emotion

16.1 INTRODUCTION

Why should a book dealing primarily with commercial dispute resolution include a chapter on ADR in the field of personal injury and clinical negligence? ADR is now firmly established in England and Wales for use in commercial disputes of all kinds, with signs of parallel development in Scotland and Northern Ireland. Its use in the UK in personal injury and clinical negligence claims has developed at a slower pace, though growth is undoubtedly discernible.

We make no apology for including consideration of these two related fields, for which we use the generic joint description of *injury claims* for convenience. There can be no doubt of their rapidly increasing significance, if for no other reason than that in the UK they comprise the largest single sector of litigated cases, as is probably the position in every other common law jurisdiction. However, in all other common law jurisdictions, such claims also form the majority of all cases dealt with by ADR. While this is far from being the situation so far in the UK, we can see no structural reason, as we discuss below, why it should ultimately be any different here.

It is important to remember that for one prime participant in such claims at least, namely the insurer or public body which backs the defendant's case, the issues are indeed essentially commercial. In other words, the fundamental question for them is 'how much must we pay, if anything, to this claimant?' There will be other strategic issues for them to consider, like market image in claims handling, but the basic question, 'and what will the associated process cost us?', remains a financial one. When this 'commercial' agenda on the defendant side is juxtaposed alongside the claimant's agenda, which inevitably involves a considerable emotional content, we can see that there are the seeds of major conflict. There are lessons to be learned from dealing with such problems of mismatch of agenda between parties that have application across the spectrum of dispute resolution. It should also be remembered that defendants themselves – perhaps another driver, a treating clinician, an employer or even a complete stranger – may well have significant feelings about being sued. These can be aggravated by loss of control over defending the claim to their insurer or funder.

A related feature of injury claims is the fact that, for the very reason that they almost always involve claims between individuals and corporate or public organisations, they involve a potentially difficult imbalance of power. This characteristic is again something which has implications for all commercial claims, and not just in injury claims. One of the dynamic features of ADR theory and practice is the way in which there is cross-fertilisation of experience between various sectors, with opportunity to learn lessons from the widely differing ways in which disputes and disputants begin to re-define what they want in terms of process and outcome.

We examine now some of the specific features of injury claims and what ADR processes can do to assist.

16.2   INDIVIDUAL AND COMMERCIAL CLAIMS

In looking at these issues, we naturally compare and contrast what is typical of broadly *commercial* disputes (between commercial and professional parties) as against what is typical of what we call *individual* disputes (involving claims between individuals and corporate parties or funders). In individual disputes, an individual may be the claimant, as in injury or indemnity claims against professionals (where the defendant's case is usually handled by an insurer) or in claims brought by an employee against an employer, ultimately to be heard either in the employment tribunal or the courts; or he might be the defendant, as in a claim by a bank under a guarantee, or where an employer alleges breach of contract against an employee, sub-contractor or consultant.

16.2.1   Imbalance of power

At the risk of generalising, there is broadly a much greater degree of power inequality between the parties in individual disputes. Commercial businesses will of course be of different sizes, and often there will be an imbalance of power between large manufacturer and small supplier or between franchisor and franchisee, about which a mediator needs to take great care. But both parties are in business, and have traded freely into that kind of relationship. There is usually a degree of choice over the contractual terms which framed the relationship in the first place, or at least a choice as to whether to engage in a business relationship at all. The power imbalance is going to be potentially much more marked in disputes where an individual is in dispute with an organisation, perhaps by suing another motorist or professional firm whose defence is backed by an insurer, or maybe an employer, a public body such as an NHS Trust, or when being sued by a bank.

1 Funding

Very often the power imbalance crystallises over funding. A claimant who has limited ability to fund a claim is clearly disadvantaged when facing a defendant with limitless litigation resources. Starving out a less well funded opponent has been a well-recognised strategy, at least in litigation in the past. Unsurprisingly, the sense of grievance is if anything intensified for the individual by such an approach. It is also unsurprising that there has been a growth in support organisations for individual parties, to ensure that they can have access to the best advice and representation by specialist lawyers and experts as a counterweight to such power imbalance. Unions have for many years campaigned for employees in the working environment, and organisations such as the Association of Personal Injury Lawyers (APIL) and Action for the Victims of Medical Accidents (AVMA) have created new resources in and for claimant lawyers and experts. With the spread of conditional fee agreements to fund claims, insurers and the NHS will face a substantial penalty mark-up on costs where they fight and lose. Where insurers fight and win, their own industry will repay back their costs through claimant litigation protection insurance. Funding power has not always remained with the commercial organisations. A publicly funded claimant against whom no effective order for costs can be made, win or lose, is in a surprisingly powerful position, for instance.

2 Imbalance of litigation experience

There is a further power imbalance inherent in the litigation process, at least so far as the parties themselves are concerned.

16.2.1 *ADR and injury claims: power imbalance and emotion*

Individuals are very often first-timers when it comes to litigation, and indeed participation at a trial, if a case, as rarely happens, reaches that far. Corporate parties are often repeat players in the litigation game, with a vast reservoir of shared experience within their organisations. Individuals can be forgiven for feeling that they are pitted against an enormous faceless organisation. They can very easily be allowed to develop the sense that their opponent has little interest in paying attention to their self-perceived just grievances, strengthening the polarisation of the parties. If trial with its formality and technicality ever does take place, this will seem like a very hostile and frightening environment to all but the most experienced participants in the litigation process.

3 Procedural protections

Legislative and procedural steps too have been taken to address this power imbalance. One of the concerns of the CPR, enshrined in the overriding objective, is to give an equal opportunity to litigants to assert or defend their rights, placing them so far as possible on an equal footing. We can thus expect penal costs sanctions against those who try to use aggressive tactics against weaker parties, as has already been demonstrated in the approach of the courts to costs orders in such commercial cases as *Mars v Teknowledge* [1999] 2 Costs LR 44 and *Taylor v Ishida (Europe) Ltd* [1999] 22 IPD 22114, and also in the injury claim *Ford v GKR Construction* [2000] 1 All ER 802.

The human rights legislation (discussed briefly at section **5.6** above) regards 'equality of arms' as a fundamental part of a fair trial under art 6 of the Convention.

Does ADR make a contribution to the levelling out of power imbalances which is seen as necessary, especially in individual claims? We examine this issue below.

16.2.2 Emotional issues

What can be can safely said about both individual and commercial disputes is that almost without exception there will be feelings and emotions underlying and driving the individuals involved in them, whatever the nature of the dispute. They might be expected to take different forms, thus needing different approaches within a mediation. A manager in a business will have a number of pressures bearing down during a dispute. Was the original deal a mistake or misjudgment? Will the outcome impact on career development? There will be anger that something went wrong or that the other party may have forfeited trust or a previous reputation for competence. In construction disputes there are the ever-present pressures of time and money, with the need to produce a finished engineered product by the contractual date, whatever the intervening problems may have been. There is thus much scope for anger, frustration, and fear of the future in terms of personal reputation and financial or job security in commercial disputes.

In individual disputes, individual parties understandably see themselves as having been personally wronged. Sometimes this is by another individual (perhaps the other driver or the doctor), sometimes by a big organisation, such as a lender or an employer company or an employee for whom it is vicariously liable. But even with a claim against another individual, this usually turns into a dispute with an insurer. Again intense emotions are likely to be felt by the individual. Anger and a sense of being let down by another's negligence (whether driver, fellow employee, surgeon or beneficiary of a guarantee), coupled perhaps with parallel anger at any suggestion that the claimant was partly or wholly to blame through contributory negligence, financial imprudence or an excess of trust in a business partner. There can be intense frustration and anxiety over possibly permanent physical disability and fear for the future in financial terms. There will almost always be fear of the claim process itself, its unknown costs and uncertain outcome. Even if similar emotions arise in commercial disputes for those personally involved, the quality of impact upon a party is bound to be more intense on individuals, who may have suffered serious physical pain or racial or sexual discrimination, or who perhaps immediately face the loss of a home or bankruptcy.

A major problem which often arises is that the emotional and even the business agenda for each side is entirely different in individual claims. Individual claimants or defendants have all the feelings described above, whereas the commercial opponent's motivation is usually to minimise financial exposure, albeit in a way that is consistent with a suitable public image and reputation for fair dealing. For a claimant to feel that the defendant's approach is 'all about money' is likely to be additionally upsetting. It probably demeans claimant feelings to observe that individuals representing commercial corporations (whether in-house claims or legal staff or external lawyers) will have their own personal motivations, such as concerns over their own reputation by getting a good deal (or not), the implications for future employment and the public image of themselves and their employer. Claimants will probably have a different range of reactions in understanding and in wanting in any way to deal with the emotional agenda of the actual defendant motorist or the allegedly negligent professional.

So the lesson to be learned is that there will always be emotion pervading dispute resolution, albeit of varying intensity. We look at the ways in which mediation is a forum especially well adapted to dealing effectively both with its expression and its resolution. Few assumptions can be made from the nature of the dispute as to how strong or significant it is in each case and for each participant in the process. Those preparing for a mediation, whether as mediator, party or legal representative, who are insensitive to such dynamics can expect a difficult time. The only safe assumption is that emotion will undoubtedly underpin much of what goes on in a claim and any process undertaken to resolve it.

16.3 THE SPECIAL CHARACTERISTICS OF PERSONAL INJURY CLAIMS

As noted above, personal injury claims form the single largest category of proceedings issued in the courts, and yet ADR for such disputes has been slow to take off in the UK. There are signs of change, particularly as insurers develop experience of its application in dealing with difficult claims and begin to explore the advantages of ADR in producing economies in their claims costs budgets. Of course structural differences exist between most US jurisdictions and the English system, which are said to explain the differences in development – jury decision on liability and damages, contingency fees and an absence of a right to receive costs as well as damages. But these differences are not universal where ADR is the primary process in resolving personal injury claims. In Canada, Australia and New Zealand, ADR is a key resolution method for personal injury claims, and these are legal systems with essentially UK, rather than US, characteristics in these respects.

So why has ADR use grown more slowly in these fields in the UK? We explore some possible answers to this question.

16.3.1 Polarisation of claimant lawyers and insurers and their lawyers

It is noteworthy that personal injury and clinical negligence were the first two areas of practice which were seen as meriting (or needing) their respective pre-action protocols attached to the CPR. This may be a measure of sector size and importance. It may also speak of characteristic pre-action difficulties in a field traditionally dominated by a polarised legal profession where many solicitors and some barristers usually act either only for claimants or only for defendants. Commercial lawyers may act for manufacturers in one case, distributors in another, retailers in a third case; a company in one case, shareholders in another, creditors in the next. Except where involved in repeat litigation for an institution, there is less of a claimant or defendant specialisation in commercial fields than there is in injury claims generally. The polarisation among injury claim lawyers and insurers has been quite profound in past years. Union solicitors in particular, but also others acting for claimants, have at times seemed on a crusade against defendants and their insurers, seeking new ways of pushing back the boundaries of liability and new heads of claim. However, the CPR have begun at last to work a remarkable change of approach in the attitudes of these old adversaries.

16.3.2 Financial defensiveness

Cynics might suggest that ADR development in this field has been slowed by innate conservatism or defensiveness among lawyers who have a vested interest in keeping work levels up in this area of practice. This was certainly the pattern in the US 20 years ago, where adoption of ADR methods was primarily driven by the twin forces of client pressure on lawyers from the insurance industry and the judiciary with its overloaded court dockets. Such pressures are undoubtedly beginning to emerge in the UK. Furthermore, the threefold UK phenomena of the growth of non-lawyer direct claims handling organisations, removal of public funding from most personal injury claims, and the widespread merger of insurers with consequent shrinkage of insurers' legal panels, have certainly added even more problems to an already challenging environment for lawyers in the personal injury market.

16.3.3 The retrospective nature of purely monetary claims

Another suggested reason is the fact that injury claims are seen as being purely monetary, with little need or scope for attending to future relationships. Court remedies themselves are only for the payment of money, however adequate or inadequate an expression this can be as a means of valuing an injury and putting a claimant into the same position (in theory) as if the tort had not happened. The assessment of liability is a retrospective exercise. Who was to blame? Was a duty owed? Was it broken? The future is only relevant when it comes to assessing future disability and loss. But again it is payment of money that is the only available remedy, even if not the only need. The argument runs that where money alone is at stake, it only requires negotiation, offers to settle hedged with costs sanctions for the loser, or trial to reach a conclusion. Thus ADR and mediation have little to offer, it is said.

As is shown below, it is the very breadth of possible outcomes attainable through mediation that gives it an edge over what the courts can offer.

16.3.4 Continuing relationships between the parties

The suggested absence of any continuing relationship between the parties in injury claims is contrasted to commercial cases, where there may often be a genuine opportunity for parties to deal further in the future as an alternative to breakdown of the business relationship. At one level, claimants are likely to have the most casual and inconsequential of personal links with a defendant in any type of injury claim. This is much less so in commercial claims, which almost always arise from a contractual relationship freely entered into, and the same is true of professional indemnity, banking and employment disputes. The bank, the solicitor, the architect, the employer were all in a sense chosen by the claimant. Even the patient may have chosen the hospital and the consultant, and consented to the operation or treatment which went wrong. What could be more random than the relationship between two motorists involved in a car crash, or a visitor to a building injured by falling masonry or a fire, or a sub-contractor's employee injured by a main contractor's defective equipment? Instead of a relationship of choice, the relationship between the parties is created by what gave rise to the claim. Even if a tenuous relationship did exist, as for instance, in the case of the sub-contractor, it is immediately distanced by the fact that defence of the claim is undertaken by an insurer with whom no relationship whatsoever exists.

The last consideration for such a claimant in such circumstances is the preservation and continuation, perhaps in modified form, of a relationship with the defendant. Does this conceptual difference weaken the usefulness of ADR in personal injury claims in practice?

Mediation works very effectively in resolving commercial disputes, both where money damages would be the only outcome to litigation and where disputes do not involve the possibility of continuing business relationships. The usefulness of ADR may rest therefore in the nature and timing of the settlement event, rather than the nature of the claim, and we return to this below.

16.3.5 Power imbalance as inhibiting growth

More honourably, slower growth might be said to be linked to the perceived imbalance of power between parties which we have already discussed. If it were true that ADR preserved or exacerbated power imbalance between individuals and commercial organisations, it would be unworthy of use. However, such an imbalance exists between exactly the same parties in such cases in every jurisdiction where ADR is nevertheless a primary means of resolving claims, and we shall see that ADR can be highly effective in countering such imbalances.

16.3.6 The future of personal injury litigation and ADR

With litigation in general in such a state of flux since the introduction of the CPR and the revolution in litigation funding, it may take a little longer for the level of ADR activity in this field to become clear. While the British insurance industry is preoccupied with internal and international reorganisation, new ways of tackling claims cost control will be briefly postponed. The effect of the CPR is emerging, but all the implications will not be worked out fully for many years after their implementation. If and when the same twin forces for change – the litigation funders and the judiciary – are fully mobilised in the UK, adoption of ADR as the primary dispute resolution process of choice is quite likely to be established, perhaps almost to the level that no trial will be likely to occur without some attempt at ADR being expected by the court, leaving the unsuccessful litigant exposed perhaps to tougher costs outcomes as the price of not trying in good faith to explore settlement. The preservation of court discretion over costs would provide ample protection in cases of good faith disagreement.

16.4 THE SPECIAL CHARACTERISTICS OF CLINICAL NEGLIGENCE CLAIMS

These merit some comment distinct from personal injury claims because of a number of particular distinguishing characteristics. In

Access to Justice, discussed more fully in Chapter 4, Lord Woolf himself singled out such cases as needing special attention. A similar diagnosis was made in the report published in June 2000 of the Civil Justice Reform Group in Northern Ireland under the chairmanship of Lord Chief Justice Campbell. Both reports identified clinical negligence cases as especially suited to mediation as a settlement process. This too was presumably the reason for setting up the NHS Pilot Mediation scheme at a time when hardly any cases had been mediated in the UK. Why are such claims special, and why have they been thought to be particularly amenable to resolution by mediation?

16.4.1 Bilateral public funding

Perhaps their clearest characteristic is that clinical negligence claims always involve claims by individuals against professionals, usually in effect against a health provider like an NHS Trust in NHS hospital claims or an insurer for claims arising out of private or primary medicine. Legal Services Commission funding (replacing Legal Aid) remains in place for such claimants who are financially eligible, at least for the time being. Thus, in claims against NHS Hospitals, both sides of the claim will often be financed from public funds. The NHS is under constant pressure over its costs and anything which might relieve pressure on its budgets is to be welcomed. Insurance products have been developed to fund such litigation through CFAs or by direct litigation costs insurance, sometimes with loan finance attached, though with currently high premium levels.

16.4.2 The intensity of emotional content

There are non-monetary considerations too, though. Claims are very often highly emotive, especially when involving a birth trauma with consequent brain damage. Clinical negligence, like clinical intervention, will by definition affect fundamental things like health and capacity to enjoy life. Usually there has been a health reason for initial clinical intervention, whether illness, accident, correction of some undesired physical feature by plastic surgery, or normally positive, if occasionally hazardous, events like childbirth. These all have profound significance to individuals in any event, and for a trusted professional dealing with them to be said to have made an error is likely to increase the emotional dimension enormously. Claimants are suddenly confronted with the stark choice between making a fuss or putting what happened down to bad luck. It is hard to believe and then to cope with the possibility that a doctor has let you down.

This cuts both ways. For someone in a caring profession to be accused, whether justly or unjustly, of negligence can have a profoundly upsetting effect, with immeasurable consequences on that person's general levels of performance while under accusation, and even afterwards. We may expect a normally competent doctor to put such considerations out of mind when treating other patients, but it is asking a lot for such a process of sublimation to be easily achieved without some cost. Only a relatively few doctors will take refuge in arrogance and denial.

16.4.3 Technical problems on liability and causation

The fact that there is a pre-existing medical determinant in the first place for needing the allegedly negligent treatment highlights another major difficulty in clinical negligence claims. Establishing negligence is only the first hurdle to overcome. Often a greater problem is establishing causation of damage once negligence has been shown. The claimant must prove that the negligence has caused worse damage than would have resulted anyway from the condition treated. This can be a painful and difficult concept to explain to claimants and one over which the parties are heavily dependent upon highly technical expert opinion. If a judicial decision on such differences of opinion is needed, then mediation will not provide it. It will, however, provide a forum for debate as to what the chances are of one or other view prevailing at trial, with settlement possible as a consequence, once each party has assessed its perception of litigation risk.

Sheer technicality is often cited as a reason why mediation might be inappropriate for clinical negligence claims. With the need to apply the test in *Bolam v Friern Barnet Hospital Management Committee* [1957] 2 All ER 118, as modified by *Bolitho v City and Hackney Health Authority* [1997] 4 All ER 771, to establish whether there has been a departure from commonly held standards, expert evidence has become the norm in trials. Expert evidence is also required to establish causation. Very often, clinical negligence claims are for very large sums on behalf of claimants under a permanent lack of legal capacity, such as obstetric and anaesthetic accidents. Can these be mediated?

16.4.3 *ADR and injury claims: power imbalance and emotion*

The proper question is 'can this claim be settled? If it can properly be settled it can be mediated, even if a provisional outcome needs ratification by the court. Very difficult commercial claims are successfully mediated all the time, which may involve extremely complex legal and evidential issues. There is nothing more inherently difficult about clinical negligence cases. If a court decision *must* be sought (a rarity), then that can be done. If a reasonable settlement can be reached through mediation, a lot of time, expense and probably pain and strain can be avoided. There is the additional safeguard of court approval for cases involving patients and children.

16.4.4 Continuing relationships between patients and healthcare providers

Another key feature of clinical negligence cases is that there may well be an unavoidable continuing relationship between the parties. Any patient who has claimed against an NHS Trust will remain a consumer of the NHS in general, and quite probably of the particular NHS Trust. The unsettling effect of even a perceived negligence claim on a patient's view of health service professionals is profound, requiring careful attention. What the NHS can offer as a result of its position is a very wide range of outcomes, in terms of delivering kind as well as cash. Attention can accordingly be given to how the patient/hospital relationship can continue in the future, or what alternatives exist.

16.4.5 Claims and the NHS complaints procedure

An additionally complicating factor in the area of clinical disputes is the existence of an extensive complaints procedure through which many, though not all, claimants go first. Despite recent review and reform consequent upon the Wilson Report, the NHS complaints procedure is still not seen as an effective screening process and is yet again under review. Broadly, the complaints procedure can deal with non-monetary outcomes but not compensation, whereas litigation ignores the non-monetary outcomes and awards only monetary compensation. There is some blurring of these distinctions in practice, but there is a widely held view that the structure is still not right. Mediation can of course provide both monetary and non-monetary outcomes, as we see below.

16.5 SOLUTIONS OFFERED BY ADR IN INJURY CLAIMS

We look now at what ADR has been shown to bring to the resolution of injury claims so far, what lessons might be learned for the future of such claims, and how they may translated into other fields of dispute resolution.

16.5.1 Mediation as the best ADR process for injury claims

It seems to be a universally accepted proposition that, of all the various ADR processes, mediation is the one which best meets the needs of parties to injury claims. It might be possible to visualise cases or parties who might elect to use early neutral evaluation to deal with an issue of liability or causation or the recoverability of a certain head of damage: smaller cases in particular might benefit from summary adjudicative decision, a technique which is of course on offer relatively cheaply through the court system's small claims track. The truth is that the courts are not so inaccessible or expensive as to seem utterly beyond reach for parties who need decisions on matters of principle, certainly when funding is no problem. They may thus be disinclined to use other forms of binding ADR. It is those for whom funding may be a problem, and those who want a better or swifter outcome than the courts can and do provide that ADR is of attraction.

It is important to consider what consumers of the litigation system think about it. We already know what Lord Woolf thought about the old system. Perhaps the most telling feature of the research undertaken by Linda Mulcahy on the NHS Pilot Mediation Scheme (discussed at section 4.5 above) amply bears this out. The general enthusiasm for mediation expressed by participants in the pilot cases is starkly set against her research into satisfaction levels among claimants who went through the traditional litigation process, of whom a staggering 70% were totally or very dissatisfied with the outcome they achieved, even if they obtained monetary compensation. It would not be entirely surprising to find similar views about the injury claims field more generally. Bearing in mind that a civil litigation system exists to be of service to its consumers, this stands as a particularly telling indictment.

We therefore deal in the rest of this chapter specifically with mediation as the prime ADR process in this field.

16.5.2 The 'guaranteed day in court'

This is a key feature in injury claim mediation, and usually proves to be of great attraction to individual parties who may have feared or resented the marginalisation so typical of traditional claims processes. A 'day in court' comes as an integral part of the process, with all those present who need to hear what is said on each side and with the authority to come to a considered conclusion about the claim. Very often the mere chance to express feelings about what has happened will be of immense value to a claimant. At its simplest, there is the opportunity to tell the claimant's account of what happened (rarely available in court now) and the way it has affected the claimant's life. With examination-in-chief virtually a thing of the past in post-CPR trials, there is not even the opportunity for a party to tell their story in person: the witness box is largely a place in which to be isolated, undermined, attacked or doubted. No one goes into the witness box very often on behalf of a defendant to express regret or to make admissions.

Being able to discharge any pent-up feelings in the mediation environment without a sense of embarrassment or merely being given a glass of water is usually highly beneficial. Even more so is to receive a sympathetic hearing for such an expression of feeling, and a sensitive and understanding response from the defendant or those representing the defendant. Apologies really can mean a great deal in the safety of a mediation, where to apologise sincerely is not in any way an admission of legal liability, but can still be genuinely tendered and well received.

In litigation not only is the day in court no longer guaranteed, it is almost certain not to take place. This is perhaps even more so now that the CPR make court trial at once less attuned to individual litigants and a much more uncertain place in terms of the costs outcome. Cases will be settled by correspondence, or after a meeting with the claimant's own solicitor, but with no one present on behalf of the defendant to hear the claimant or to explain the reasoning behind the offer made. Very often the offer has been made under Part 36, so that the chief reason for accepting it or not is the threat of costs sanctions if a wrong decision is made. Acceptance is thus compelled on the claimant as a means of avoiding further risk, and this itself sends the old messages of defendant aggression and confrontation to the claimant, with no opportunity for a properly principled closure as a result. In fact, settlements negotiated by solicitors almost always exclude the client from the process. A figure is given, advice given and a decision sought with little attention given to any other needs that the client may have.

All such things are possible if the key players in a dispute gather to deal with it in an 'off-the-record' environment, with adequate time to deal with the issues and the chance to explain honestly why a claim is or is not right or likely to meet with success. There is a real opportunity to deal with emotion in an honest and open way which is far more likely to lead to resolution than frustration.

16.5.3   Adjusting power imbalances between party and party and between party and lawyer

We have talked much of the imbalance between parties in injury claims. Mediation tackles this problem by the simple expedient of reducing the dimensions of the settlement event to human scale. Probably the most important dynamic of such mediations is when the claimant for the first time encounters a small team of maybe two or three people sitting across a table who 'are' the opposition. No longer is it a faceless insurer or NHS Trust but a team of identified people with whom the process invites the claimant to relate at a personal level. The settlement event takes place in a hotel or a fairly ordinary office rather than a court. People wear ordinary clothes and may remove them if warm. Normal language is used. The process is conducted in a way which makes it accessible to anyone.

The dynamic goes further, however, because of the presence and role of the mediator. The occasion is not an undisciplined or unstructured confrontation without controls, but one in which a neutral person takes responsibility for the process and ensures a sense of security about appropriate participation by all there. This distinguishes mediations from joint settlement meetings, which are not chaired by an independent neutral. It is very hard to give due prominence to a lay party in such a meeting, and to prevent the lawyers (usually senior barristers) from dominating such meetings. Good mediators will always give proper status to the parties themselves, both in the joint meeting and also in the private sessions, checking their understanding and affording them every opportunity to express what they think and how they feel. At a mediation, a lay party ought to feel confident that any attempt to exercise undue power by an opponent will be deflected and moderated by the mediator. This is discussed further in relation to mediator intervention at section **10.2.2** above.

Power imbalance can also affect the lawyer/client relationship.

16.5.3 *ADR and injury claims: power imbalance and emotion*

A lawyer who takes on the client's case can easily forget whose case it really is. A mediator can assist with this problem, by gently returning the focus on the client's wishes, interests and needs, though always subject to the lawyer's very proper advisory role. At the end of the day, however, the claimant's personal agenda may not coincide with the lawyer's advice as to what might be possible if the case fights on. Fighting may be something itself that the client is keen to avoid or fears will be too risky or expensive. Once properly advised, the client needs to feel able to decide.

16.5.4 Control conferred on each party

Another way of putting the same point over protecting parties from power imbalance is to note the degree to which mediation confers control on each party over both the outcome and the route by which it is reached. There is nothing to prevent a party from choosing to settle or choosing to continue with litigation when all available options have been laid out at a mediation. The essence of control is for each party to be able to determine their own destiny in relation to settlement or otherwise and not to have dumped responsibility on a third party judge. But even so, if that is what seems the best option at the conclusion of the process, each party has a free choice.

The time available for decision-making is also important. The court door just before the trial judge is due to sit is a poor place to be obliged to make significant decisions. With enough time for debate, discussion, reflection and decision at a mediation, parties can reach a sensible conclusion without undue constraint and on the basis of measured advice.

Another illustration of how mediation can confer control in a way that litigation cannot is in the involvement of others besides the immediate parties. In injury claim mediation, it is usual now for the claimant's partner (spouse, friend or family member) to attend with the claimant and take a full part in the process. This does proper honour to the importance of the claimant's family at the heart of the settlement event. So often a spouse or partner or parent has lived and breathed the claim and has been one of the principal people affected adversely by the accident. It is right for these people so closely affected, and usually even more marginalised by the litigation process, to have a 'day in court' and a degree of input and even control over the outcome.

The composition of each team can be flexibly addressed. With the claimant will be the claimant's partner and lawyer. The defendant's team may comprise lawyer, insurer (with sufficient authority to pay the whole claim as framed by the claimant, if necessary) and a representative from the defendant insured. Lay and expert witnesses rarely attend: usually it is possible to take a view on their evidence in reaching a settlement, but there may be cases where their attendance is desirable or crucial. While barristers do sometimes attend to strengthen the advisory capacity of a team, it is highly desirable for counsel to be at a mediation which is dealing with damages payable to a person under incapacity, such as a child or brain-damaged claimant. Counsel will then have taken part in the discussions which led to provisional settlement and be able to speak authoritatively to the court when the time comes to seek approval of the court for its terms.

A settlement negotiated through a mediation with full involvement of all the protagonists creates certainty and finality in an uncertain situation. Certainly this can be of real appeal to claimants.

16.5.5   Inter-party encounter

There is a world of difference between each party (meaning in this case the actual claimant and defendant and not just those funding them) giving evidence in a court and meeting across a table at a mediation. It is possible for each party to ignore the other during a court trial, but not so when facing each other a short distance away in an ordinary room. Very often the mediation is the first time that, for instance, a patient has met the allegedly negligent doctor since the clinical accident which led to the claim. Such occasions can be very tense, but also very fruitful. Problems have arisen so often as a result of breakdown in communication. Positions have been taken up and become entrenched before any attempt has been made to arrange for a proper explanation between the protagonists in a claim. By then it is often far too difficult and the loss of face potentially involved is too great. Defendants may be fearful of admitting anything which might damage the defence of the claim, and hence refuse to communicate at all.

Mediation has been very frequently able to restore fractured relations by enabling conversation to start once more within a controlled and safe environment. This is of repeated and considerable benefit to claimants. There is a considerable benefit also for defendants personally, especially professionals accused of less than competent practice, but perhaps also drivers or employers who have caused a major injury. The chance to be able at last to deal in a direct and human way with such an allegation, perhaps to explain why decisions were made and to express regret that the outcome was as it was, and eventually to see the claim brought to a conclusion on suitable terms with the open acceptance of an accuser claimant offers immense release for those involved.

Perhaps it is not too unrealistic to add that the opportunity for a claimant to 'forgive' a defendant and for the defendant to accept such 'forgiveness' is potentially of profound and lasting power to both sides. Mediators often aspire to create 'win–win' outcomes: those mediations which attain this level have usually managed to do so by freeing all parties from the burden of the dispute and bringing them to a measure of reconciliation.

16.5.6　Imaginative outcomes

As we have noted, injury claim trials can really only provide claimants with a monetary remedy. There may be some prospect of satisfaction at having 'a day in court', especially if there was unpleasant cross-examination of the defendant, and also a sense of 'justice having been done'. But money is the only material compensation.

Besides its potential for supplying parties' needs by the nature of the engagement in the process itself, mediation can supply a much wider slate of outcomes than litigation. Especially in clinical negligence cases, NHS Trusts can supply future healthcare services as well as damages, as part of the usually inevitable continuing relationship between patient and trust. Mediations have supplied such other benefits as:

- apology and a reassurance that procedural changes have been made to minimise the risk of a similar future mishap;

- reassurance about prognosis and the availability of future treatment;

- an assurance about future re-employment to the claimant's partner after the claimant's death;

- satisfying explanations over what happened, accepted as justifying a modification of the allegations of negligence;

- information as to the whereabouts of the burial-place of a foetus.

In ordinary personal injury claims, there is scope for all kinds of imaginative negotiated outcomes. Structured settlements and tax-effective periodical payment of damages are highly consistent with the search for mutually beneficial outcomes which typifies mediation. In employers' liability claims, steps can be taken to explore consensually whether there is an alternative to job loss as a result of the accident, thus minimising any claim for future lost earnings while maximising the claimant's prospects and sense of worth. It also helps to make sure that the requirements of the employment protection and disability discrimination legislation are not infringed.

16.5.7 Savings in time and costs

Although these are regarded as available generally through the use of ADR, it is appropriate to say a little about this topic in specific relation to injury claims. Sceptics and reluctant participants in ADR in the UK have said that the cost of ADR is an unnecessary addition to existing legal costs, when lawyers can perfectly well negotiate settlements without the need of a third party.

Were such a proposition to be made in any jurisdiction where ADR usage is more developed, the large insurance carriers and the self-insuring defendants would simply not accept it. It is surely a matter for clients and funders to decide where the best course may lie to achieve economy, and not their lawyers, who inevitably would say that. The Legal Services Commission, before-the-event and after-the-event litigation insurers and the defendant insurers who pick up the vast majority of the legal costs bill are the ones to determine such an issue.

The other issue is that of giving the client, whether claimant or defendant, what each truly needs. If each is repeatedly marginalised, whether by the litigation process itself or the way negotiations are conducted and concluded without client involvement, there is scope for serious client dissatisfaction.

One has to ask why the CPR and the pre-action protocols became necessary at all if everything was so wonderful before Lord Woolf looked at the civil justice system.

There are undoubtedly proven costs savings to be made by deploying ADR. Outcomes can be accelerated by use of mediation in injury claims. Claims can be settled before proceedings are issued because of front-loading of investigation under the protocols. In more complex cases which have to be issued, mediation can be deployed long before trial. The lessons learned by the USA, Canada, Australia and New Zealand will be bound to be learned in the UK in time. Lawyers have a choice to anticipate that or to take the consequences of ignoring it.

16.6 CONCLUSIONS

The English experience in practice to date is that ADR, and in particular mediation, works extremely well and satisfyingly in injury claim cases. There is a much higher settlement rate than for commercial cases, well into the 90% bracket, and both claimants and defendants express considerable satisfaction with what mediation achieves for them. Claimants achieve a proper sense of just closure, they are heard and are given some acknowledgment of what they have suffered. Mediation is very apt for delivering these ancillary needs. Defendant funders are finding that mediation delivers not only better outcomes to claimants with no loss of opportunity to achieve proper discounts for litigation risk and contributory negligence where debatable, but also major savings in time and cost. Defendants themselves can also find closure to the process of being under accusation.

Time and again mediators have seen that the processes and outcomes of mediation help to create a solution to long-running and seemingly intractable claims, often starting with very large gaps (often hundreds of thousands of pounds) between the parties in terms of damages.

The experience of ADR providers, where the greatest pool of practical experience in mediation resides, matches and supports the conclusions of Professor Hazel Genn in her evaluation of the Central London County Court pilot mediation scheme on personal injury mediation (discussed in more detail at section **4.5** above). Despite the low take-up of mediation of such cases in the period studied, her conclusion was that 'personal injury cases are amenable to mediation even where liability and quantum are in issue'. Mediations have dealt effectively with claims involving issues of all types, and across a wide range of value in dispute.

The shape of the whole injury claims field is, as we have seen, undergoing transformation through the revolution in funding. This area is the most significant one from which public funding has been almost completely withdrawn, having probably been the largest single area for the grant of Legal Aid. What effect the wholesale use of conditional fee agreements (CFAs) is going to have on the way this market sector looks in a few years time is very difficult to predict. It is safe to say, however, that it will be dominated by insurance finance. Before-the-event and after-the-event insurers will help claims to get started, with solicitors funding the cost of their own work in progress and bearing their own costs in cases lost under CFAs. Defendant insurers will be invited to pick up the bill for the rest. If insurers decide to develop use of mediation systematically, it will rapidly become the primary dispute resolution process of choice.

The special features of clinical negligence cases have also in our experience been very successfully dealt with by the mediation process, matching the research findings in the Mulcahy report. Communication between patient and doctor is often restored, reassurance given about the course of past and future treatment, regret and explanation delivered in detail by clinicians without necessarily any formal admission of negligence or causation having to be made. They often involve painful exchanges, but also quite strikingly amicable resolutions.

Injury claims are palpably benefiting from resolution through mediation. Wherever mediation is a cost-effective alternative (which is in the large majority of cases, when measuring the cost of mediation against the difference in valuation by each party, and set against the potential cost savings), it can deliver startlingly effective results.

Appendices

CONTENTS

Appendix A

CEDR model mediation procedure and agreement with guidance notes

A.1 MODEL MEDIATION PROCEDURE

Mediation agreement

1. The parties ('the Parties') to the dispute in question ('the Dispute'), the Mediator and the Centre for Dispute Resolution ('CEDR') will enter into an agreement ('the Mediation Agreement') based on the CEDR Model Mediation Agreement in relation to the conduct of the Mediation. This procedure ('the Model Procedure') will be incorporated into, form part of, and may be varied by, the Mediation Agreement.

The Mediator

2. CEDR will, subject to the agreement of the Parties or any court order, nominate an independent third party(ies) ('the Mediator'). The Mediator, after consultation with the Parties where appropriate, will:

   - attend any meetings with any or all of the Parties preceding the mediation, if requested or if the Mediator decides this is appropriate and the Parties agree;

   - read before the Mediation each Case Summary and all the Documents sent to him/her (see paragraph 7 below);

   - chair, and determine the procedure for, the Mediation;

   - assist the parties in drawing up any written settlement agreement;

- abide by the terms of the Model Procedure, the Mediation Agreement and CEDR's Code of Conduct.

3. The Mediator (and any member of the Mediator's firm or company) will not act for any of the Parties individually in connection with the Dispute in any capacity either during the currency of this agreement or at any time thereafter. The Parties accept that in relation to the Dispute neither the Mediator nor CEDR is an agent of, or acting in any capacity for, any of the Parties. The Parties and the Mediator accept that the Mediator (unless an employee of CEDR) is acting as an independent contractor and not as an agent or employee of CEDR.

CEDR

4. CEDR, in conjunction with the Mediator, will make the necessary arrangements for the Mediation including, as necessary:

- nominating, and obtaining the agreement of the Parties to, the Mediator;

- drawing up the Mediation Agreement;

- organising a suitable venue and dates;

- organising exchange of the Case Summaries and Documents;

- meeting with any or all of the Parties (and the Mediator if appointed), either together or separately, to discuss any matters or concerns relating to the Mediation;

- general administration in relation to the Mediation.

5. If there is any issue about the conduct of the Mediation (including as to the nomination of the Mediator) upon which the Parties cannot agree within a reasonable time, CEDR will, at the request of any Party, decide the issue for the Parties, having consulted with them.

Participants

6. Each Party will state in the Mediation Agreement the names of:

- the person(s) who will be the lead negotiator(s) for that Party, who must have full authority to settle the Dispute;

- any other person(s) (such as professional advisers or colleagues) who will also be present at, and/or participating in, the Mediation on that Party's behalf.

The person signing the Mediation Agreement on behalf of each Party will be deemed to be agreeing, on behalf of both the Party he/she represents and all persons present on that Party's behalf at the Mediation, to be bound by the provisions of this Model Procedure.

Exchange of information

7. Each Party will send to CEDR at least two weeks before the Mediation, or such other date as may be agreed between the Parties and CEDR, sufficient copies of:

- a concise summary ('the Case Summary') of its case in the Dispute; and

- all the documents to which the Summary refers and any others to which it may want to refer in the Mediation ('the Documents'),

which CEDR will send simultaneously to the other Party(ies) and the Mediator.

In addition, each Party may send to the Mediator (through CEDR) and/or bring to the Mediation further documentation which it wishes to disclose in confidence to the Mediator but not to any other Party, clearly stating in writing that such documentation is confidential to the Mediator and CEDR.

8. The Parties should try to agree:

- the maximum number of pages of each Case Summary; and

- a joint set of Documents or the maximum length of each set of Documents.

The Mediation

9. The Mediation will take place at the arranged place and time stated in the Mediation Agreement.

10. The Mediator will chair, and determine the procedure at, the Mediation.

11. No recording or transcript of the Mediation will be made.

12. If the Parties are unable to reach a settlement in the negotiations at the Mediation, and only if all the Parties so request and the Mediator agrees, the Mediator will produce for the Parties a non-binding recommendation on terms of settlement. This will not attempt to anticipate what a court might order but will set out what the Mediator suggests are appropriate settlement terms in all of the circumstances.

Settlement agreement

13. Any settlement reached in the Mediation will not be legally binding until it has been reduced to writing and signed by, or on behalf of, the Parties.

Termination

14. Any of the Parties may withdraw from the Mediation at any time and shall immediately inform the Mediator and the other representatives in writing. The Mediation will terminate when:

    - a Party withdraws from the Mediation; or

    - a written settlement agreement is concluded; or

    - the Mediator decides that continuing the Mediation is unlikely to result in a settlement; or

    - the Mediator decides he should retire for any of the reasons in the Code of Conduct.

Stay of proceedings

15. Any litigation or arbitration in relation to the Dispute may be commenced or continued notwithstanding the Mediation unless the Parties agree otherwise or a court so orders.

Confidentiality etc

16. Every person involved in the Mediation will keep confidential and not use for any collateral or ulterior purpose:

   - the fact that the Mediation is to take place or has taken place, other than to inform a court dealing with any litigation relating to the Dispute of that fact; and

   - all information (whether given orally, in writing or otherwise) arising out of, or in connection with, the Mediation including the fact of any settlement and its terms.

17. All information (whether oral or in the form of documents, tapes, computer discs etc) arising out of, or in connection with, the Mediation will be without prejudice, privileged and not admissible as evidence or disclosable in any current or subsequent litigation or other proceedings whatsoever. This does not apply to any information, which would in any event have been admissible or disclosable in any such proceedings.

18. Paras 16 and 17 shall not apply insofar as any such information is necessary to implement and enforce any settlement agreement arising out of the Mediation.

19. None of the Parties to the Mediation Agreement will call the Mediator or CEDR (or any employee, consultant, officer or representative of CEDR) as a witness, consultant, arbitrator or expert in any litigation or other proceedings whatsoever. The Mediator and CEDR will not voluntarily act in any such capacity without the written agreement of all the Parties.

Fees, expenses and costs

20. CEDR's fees (which include the Mediator's fees) and the other expenses of the Mediation will be borne equally by the Parties. Payment of these fees and expenses will be made to CEDR in accordance with its fee schedule and terms and conditions of business.

21. Each Party will bear its own costs and expenses of its participation in the Mediation.

Exclusion of liability

> 22. Neither the Mediator nor CEDR shall be liable to the Parties for any act or omission in connection with the services provided by them in, or in relation to, the Mediation, unless the act or omission is shown to have been in bad faith.

A.2 GUIDANCE NOTES

The paragraph numbers and headings in these notes refer to the paragraphs and headings in the Model Procedure.

The same terms ('the Parties' etc) are used in the Model Procedure and the Model Agreement.

Introduction

The essence of mediation is that it:

- involves a neutral third party to facilitate negotiations;
- is quick and inexpensive, without prejudice and confidential;
- enables the Parties to devise solutions which are not possible in an adjudicative process, such as litigation or arbitration, and may be to the benefit of both parties, particularly if there is a continuing business relationship;
- involves representatives of the Parties who have sufficient authority to settle. In some cases, there may be an advantage in the representatives being people who have not been directly involved in the events leading up to the dispute and in the dispute itself.

The procedure for the mediation is flexible and this model procedure can be adapted (with or without the assistance of CEDR) to suit the Parties.

A mediation can be used:

- in both domestic and international disputes;
- whether or not litigation or arbitration has been commenced; and
- in two-party and multi-party disputes.

Rules or rigid procedures in the context of a consensual and adaptable process, which is the essence of ADR, are generally inappropriate. The Model Procedure and the Model Agreement and this guidance note should be sufficient to enable parties to conduct a mediation.

In some cases the agreement to conduct a mediation will be as a result of an 'ADR clause' (such as one of the CEDR Model ADR clauses) to that effect in a commercial agreement between the Parties, or a court order. Where that is the case the Model Procedure and Mediation Agreement may need to be adapted accordingly.

The Model Agreement, which has been kept short and simple, incorporates the Model Procedure (see paragraph 1).

The Mediation Agreement can vary the Model Procedure; the variations can be set out in the body of the Mediation

Agreement or the Mediation Agreement can state that variations made in manuscript (or otherwise) on the Model Procedure are to be incorporated.

Mediation Agreement – paragraph 1

If CEDR is asked to do so by a Party wishing to initiate a mediation, it will approach the other Party(ies) to a Dispute to seek to persuade it/them to participate.

Alternatively, the party who has taken the initiative in proposing the mediation may wish to send a draft agreement based on the Model Agreement to the other Party(ies).

Representatives of the Parties (and the Mediator if he/she has been nominated) and CEDR may meet to discuss and finalise the terms of the Mediation Agreement.

The Mediator – paragraphs 2–3

The success of the Mediation will, to a considerable extent, depend on the skill of the Mediator. CEDR believes it is very important for the Mediator to have had specific training and experience. CEDR will propose mediators suitable for the particular matter.

In some cases it may be useful to have more than one mediator, or to have an independent expert who can advise the Mediator on technical issues. All should sign the Mediation Agreement, which should be amended as appropriate.

It is CEDR's practice, as part of its mediator training and accreditation programme, to have an assistant mediator ('the Assistant

Mediator') attend most mediations. The Assistant Mediator signs the Mediation Agreement and falls within the definition 'the Mediator' in the Model Procedure and the Model Agreement.

It is advisable, but not essential, to involve the Mediator in any preliminary meeting between the Parties.

The Code of Conduct covers such points as the Mediator's duty of confidentiality, impartiality and avoiding conflicts of interest.

CEDR – paragraphs 4–5

The Model Procedure envisages the involvement of CEDR because in most cases this is likely to benefit the Parties and generally to facilitate the setting up and conduct of the Mediation. The Model Procedure, however, can be amended if CEDR is not to be involved.

Participants – paragraph 6

The lead negotiator(s) must be sufficiently senior and have the full authority of their respective Parties to settle the Dispute, without having to refer to anybody else. If there is any restriction on that authority, this should be discussed with CEDR and/or the Mediator before the Mediation.

Professional advisers, particularly lawyers, can, and usually do, attend the Mediation. The lead role in the Mediation is usually taken by the Representatives, because the commercial or other interests of the Parties will often take the negotiations beyond strict legal issues. The advisers, however, can play an important role in the exchange of information, in supporting their clients (particularly individuals) in the negotiations, advising their clients on the legal implications of a settlement and in drawing up the settlement agreement.

Exchange of information – paragraphs 7–8

Documentation which a Party wants the Mediator to keep confidential from the other Party(ies) (eg a counsel's opinion, an expert report not yet exchanged) must be clearly marked as such. It can be disclosed confidentially to the Mediator by the Party before or during the Mediation. It will not be disclosed by the Mediator or CEDR without the express consent of the Party.

One of the advantages of ADR is that it can avoid the excessive discovery process (including witness statements) which often blights litigation and arbitration. The Documents should be kept to the minimum necessary to understand the Party's case and to give the Mediator a good grasp of the issues. The Summaries should be similarly brief.

The Mediation – paragraphs 9–12

The intention of paragraph 12 is that the Mediator will cease to play an entirely facilitative role only if the negotiations in the Mediation are deadlocked. Giving a settlement recommendation may be perceived by a Party as undermining the Mediator's neutrality and for this reason the Mediator may not agree to this course of action. Any recommendation will be without prejudice and will not be binding.

Settlement agreement – paragraph 13

If no agreement is reached, it is nonetheless open to the Parties to adjourn the Mediation to another time and place. Experience shows that even where no agreement is reached during the Mediation itself, the Parties will often reach a settlement shortly after, as a result of the progress made during that Mediation.

Stay of proceedings – paragraph 15

Although a stay may engender a better climate for settlement, it is not essential that any proceedings relating to the Dispute be stayed. If they are stayed, it is the responsibility of the Parties and their legal advisers to consider and, if necessary, deal with the effect of any stay on limitation periods. Suggested wording for a stay, which can be incorporated into the Mediation Agreement, is: *No litigation or arbitration in relation to the Dispute is to be commenced [Any existing litigation or arbitration in relation to the Dispute is to be stayed] from the date of this agreement until the termination of the Mediation.*

Confidentiality – paragraphs 16–19

The CEDR Code of Conduct provides that the Mediator is not to disclose to any other Party any information given to him by a Party

313

in confidence without the express consent of that Party.

In para 16, the proviso as to informing the court is to assist the court in deciding what, if any, steps should be taken by the Parties in relation to mediation.

Documents which would in any event be disclosable will not become privileged by reason of having been referred to in the Mediation and will therefore still be disclosable. The position on this may depend on the relevant jurisdiction and it is the responsibility of the Parties and their legal advisers to consider and, if necessary, deal with this.

Fees, expenses and costs – paragraphs 20–21

The usual arrangement is for the Parties to share equally the fees and expenses of the procedure, but other arrangements are possible. A Party to a Dispute, which is reluctant to participate in mediation, may be persuaded to participate if the other Party(ies) agree to bear that Party's expenses.

International disputes – language and governing law/jurisdiction

The Model Agreement can be easily adapted for international cross-border disputes by the addition in the Mediation Agreement of wording along the following lines.

Language
The language of the Mediation will be [English] ... Any Party producing documents or participating in the Mediation in any other language will provide the necessary translations and interpretation facilities.

Governing law and jurisdiction
The Mediation Agreement shall be governed by, construed and take effect in accordance with, [English] law.

The courts of [England] shall have exclusive jurisdiction to settle any claim, dispute or matter of difference which may arise out of or in connection with the Mediation.

Where the law is not English or the jurisdiction not England, the Mediation Agreement may need to be amended to ensure the structure, rights and obligations necessary for a mediation are applicable.

A.3 MODEL MEDIATION AGREEMENT

Date . . . .

Parties

. . . .
('Party A')

. . . .
('Party B')

. . . .
('Party C') etc
    (jointly 'the Parties')   *Add full names and addresses*

. . . .
('the Mediator')

. . . .
('the Assistant Mediator') (and/or any advisor to the Mediator)
    (jointly and individually 'the Mediator')

Centre for Dispute Resolution, Princes House, 95 Gresham Street, London EC2V 7NA ('CEDR')

Dispute ('the Dispute')

Add brief description of the Dispute.

Participation in the Mediation

1. The Parties will attempt to settle the Dispute by mediation ('the Mediation'). The CEDR Model Mediation Procedure ('the Model Procedure') [as varied by this agreement] will determine the conduct of the Mediation and is incorporated into, and forms part of, this agreement. The definitions in the Model Procedure are used in this agreement.

The Mediator

2. The Mediator[s] will be . . . .

   [The Assistant Mediator will be . . . .]

   [The Mediator's adviser will be . . . .]

The Lead Negotiators

3. The lead negotiator(s) for each of the Parties at the Mediation will be:

   Party A: . . . .

   Party B: . . . .

   [Party C: etc . . . .]

   (jointly 'the Lead Negotiators')

   Add full names and corporate title

   Each of the Lead Negotiators will have full authority to settle on behalf of its Party – see Model Procedure paragraph 6 and notes thereto.

   A Party will immediately notify the other Party(ies), CEDR and the Mediator of any change to the above.

4. The person signing the Mediation Agreement on behalf of each Party, will be deemed to be agreeing, on behalf of both the Party he/she represents and all persons present on that Party's behalf at the Mediation, to be bound by the provisions of the Model Procedure.

Other participants

5. The following, in addition to the Lead Negotiators, will be present on behalf of each of the Parties at the Mediation:

   Party A: . . . .

   Party B: . . . .

   [Party C: . . . .]

   A Party will immediately notify the other Party(ies), CEDR and the Mediator of any change to the above.

Place and time

6. The Mediation will take place

   at: . . . .

   on: . . . .

   starting at: . . . . o'clock

Confidentiality

7. The person signing this agreement on behalf of each Party is deemed to be agreeing to the confidentiality provisions of the Model Procedure (paragraphs 16–19) on behalf of the Party he/she represents and all other persons present on that Party's behalf at the Mediation.

Model Procedure amendments

8. Set out amendments (if any) to the Model Procedure – see introduction to Model Procedure guidance notes.

    If any litigation or arbitration is to be stayed, paragraph 15 of the Model Procedure should be excluded/deleted and wording along the following lines should be added in the agreement:

    No litigation or arbitration in relation to the Dispute is to be commenced [Any existing litigation or arbitration in relation to the Dispute is to be stayed] from the date of this agreement until the termination of the Mediation.

Law and jurisdiction

9. This agreement shall be governed by, construed and take effect in accordance with, English law. The courts of England shall have exclusive jurisdiction to settle any claim, dispute or matter of difference which may arise out of or in connection with the mediation.

Human Rights

10. The referral of the Dispute to mediation does not affect any rights that may exist under Article 6 of the European Convention on Human Rights. If the Dispute is not settled by the Mediation, the Parties' rights to a fair trial remain unaffected.

Signed

On behalf of Party A . . . .

On behalf of Party B [Party C] . . . .

The Mediator . . . .

On behalf of CEDR . . . .

CONTENTS

Appendix B

CEDR model ADR contract clauses

B.1 WHY AND HOW

Including in a contract a clause which requires the parties to attempt to settle any dispute arising out of the contract by some form of ADR should increase the chances of settling any such dispute before, or notwithstanding that, the parties resort to court proceedings or arbitration.

In the context of the 1999 Civil Procedure Rules, such a clause may give the parties the chance to pre-empt an order from the court requiring ADR and enable them to conduct any ADR on their own pre-agreed terms.

This document contains a 'menu' of ADR contract clauses, with particular focus on mediation, which can be used individually or linked into 'multi-step' dispute resolution provisions. The clauses are only model clauses and will need to be selected for, and adapted to, the circumstances and legal requirements of the particular contract.

B.2 FAST TRACK DRAFTING GUIDE

Type of ADR clause required	Wording	Comment
Negotiation	See paragraph 1	Typical first stage of multi-step dispute resolution clause
Mediation – 'boilerplate'/core wording	If any dispute arises out of this agreement the parties will attempt to settle it by mediation in accordance with the Centre for Dispute Resolution (CEDR) Model Mediation Procedure.	See paragraph 2 For optional additional wording see paras 3–4 – if part of multi-step dispute resolution clause see wording at end of para 2
Mediation – dealing with disagreements on the mediation agreement	See paragraph 5	
Mediation – with the option of interim court remedies	See paragraph 7.4	For mediation in parallel with court proceedings/arbitration, see paras 7.1 and 7.2
Mediation – obligatory: restriction on terminating the mediation	See paragraph 8	Overrides usual voluntary nature of mediation/cl 14 of Model Procedure
Arbitration fallback	See paragraph 11	Typical third stage of multi-step dispute resolution clause

Wording such as 'the parties' and 'this agreement' may need to be adapted to the definitions in the contract. Square brackets indicate wording on which a decision needs to be taken, eg as to how long a period should be specified, or as to whether to include the particular wording at all.

B.3   CEDR MODEL ADR CONTRACT CLAUSES

Negotiation

1. If any dispute arises out of this agreement the parties will attempt to settle it by negotiation. [A party may not commence any ADR/court proceedings/an arbitration until [21] days after it has made a written offer to the other party(ies) to negotiate a settlement to the dispute.]

It is unlikely that this provision (even if it includes the second sentence) is legally enforceable (see comments in para 2). It is also unlikely that it is effective in practice if one of the parties has no interest in settling the dispute. The argument for including it is that it provides a credible reason for one party approaching another in circumstances where otherwise that party might be concerned (rightly or wrongly) that such an approach would be interpreted as a sign of weakness.

The purpose of the wording in square brackets is to try and make negotiations obligatory in the sense that it operates as a temporary stay on ADR and court proceedings /arbitration.

A refinement on this is to specify who is to conduct the negotiations, the most usual requirements being that they:

- *are of a certain seniority within the organisation; and*

- *have not previously been closely involved in the relevant matter/ previous negotiations on the relevant dispute.*

The rationale for these requirements is that those involved in the negotiations should have sufficient authority to settle and are able to be more objective and dispassionate than those who are close to the dispute. Wording along the following lines can be included:

Each of the parties is to be represented by a person who is a [director] or of equivalent executive authority with authority to settle the dispute and has had no direct day-to-day involvement in the relevant matter [and has not been directly involved in any previous negotiations in relation to the relevant dispute].

Mediation: 'boilerplate'/core wording

2. If any dispute arises out of this agreement, the parties will attempt to settle it by mediation in accordance with the Centre for Dispute Resolution (CEDR) Model Mediation Procedure ('the Model Procedure').

This clause by itself should be sufficient to give the parties the opportunity to attempt to settle any dispute by mediation/an executive tribunal (see para 10). The Model Procedure provides clear guidelines on the conduct of the mediation and requires the parties to enter into an agreement based on the Model Mediation Agreement in relation to its conduct. This will deal with points such as the nature of the dispute, the identity of the mediator and where and when the mediation is to take place. There may, however, be advantages in including at least some of the optional/additional wording (particularly para 3).

It may be argued that such a clause is an agreement to negotiate in good faith and lacks the necessary certainty to be enforceable. The counter-argument is that an ADR/mediation clause, if it is sufficiently certain and clear as to the process to be used, is enforceable. The reference in the clause to a model procedure should give it that necessary certainty. Additional certainty would be given by the inclusion of the wording in para 6 below.

This issue may be of little practical relevance. Most model ADR procedures/rules (see eg CEDR Model Mediation Procedure, para 14) enable a party to terminate a mediation at any time. The concept of mediation being a consensual process can, however, be overridden, either by agreement (see para 8 below) or by court order.

The reason for including an ADR clause is essentially the same for including a negotiation clause (see para 1 above). The advantage, however, of an ADR clause is that:

- *it prompts the parties to consider a process which, unlike negotiation, would not necessarily occur to them;*

- *it introduces a specific process, which gives the parties a framework for exploring settlement;*

- *ADR has other advantages over a typical negotiation (see guidance note to Model Procedure).*

If para 1 (negotiation) has been included, this wording needs to be revised so as to read: If the parties are unable to settle any dispute by negotiation [within [21] days] the parties will . . .

Optional/additional wording

Triggering/initiating the mediation

3. To initiate a mediation a party [by its Managing Director/ . . .] must give notice in writing ('ADR notice') to the other party(ies) to the dispute [addressed to its/their respective Managing

Director/ . . .] requesting a mediation in accordance with clause 2. [A copy of the request should be sent to CEDR.]

This wording/clause is not essential but is recommended. It sets out what is to be done to initiate the mediation provided for in the core wording. As such, it should make it more straightforward for the parties to get the mediation off the ground. In some cases, that may mean the difference between a mediation and no mediation.

The main agreement may have a provision as to how notices are to be served. If not (or even possibly notwithstanding) there may be an advantage in the ADR notice coming from, and being addressed to, a relatively senior executive.

Copying the notice to CEDR will enable CEDR to start administering the process as quickly as possible, and to provide early advice to the parties where appropriate.

Amendments to Model Procedure

4. The procedure in the Model Procedure will be amended to take account of :

- any relevant provisions in this agreement;
- any other agreement which the parties may enter into in relation to the conduct of the mediation ('Mediation Agreement').

This wording provides for the Model Procedure to be adapted to:

- *any specific wording in the ADR contract clause(s) (see eg para 7.1); and*
- *whatever is agreed in the Mediation Agreement.*

Apart from making the position clear, from a legal viewpoint this wording adds further certainty about the process (see commentary on para 2).

Disagreement on Mediation Agreement

5. If there is any point on the conduct of the mediation (including as to the nomination of the mediator) upon which the parties cannot agree within [14] days from the date of the [ADR notice], CEDR will, at the request of any party, decide that point for the parties, having consulted with them.

This wording almost mirrors paragraph 5 of the Model Procedure. It provides for a specific time from which CEDR can take decisions and its inclusion in the contract may reinforce the point that mediation is not to be used as a delaying tactic. (The Model Procedure, however, does not stop a party commencing or continuing court proceedings/an arbitration.)

This wording should help to speed up the commencement of the mediation by enabling an independent body (eg CEDR) to decide points upon which the parties cannot agree. It may also, by providing a mechanism to reduce the uncertainty as to the process, add weight to the argument that the ADR clause is enforceable (see commentary on para 2).

Timing of mediation

6. The mediation will start not later than [28] days after the date of the ADR notice.

This wording is specifically addressed to the concern that any mediation should provide a quick solution. Without the wording in para 5 above, it would in practice be difficult to enforce. The wording in para 5 may, however, by itself be sufficient in that a party could refuse to agree to a late date for the mediation and CEDR is unlikely to decide on a date which involves delay.

The best reason for including such wording may be simply that it evidences an intention that any mediation should happen quickly.

Juxtaposition with litigation or arbitration

Court proceedings in parallel

7.1 The commencement of a mediation will not prevent the parties commencing or continuing court proceedings/an arbitration.

Strictly this wording is not necessary as nothing in the mediation wording (para 2) prevents court proceedings. Furthermore, paragraph 15 of the Model Procedure states 'Any litigation or arbitration ... may be commenced or continued ... unless the parties agree otherwise'. The inclusion of this wording in the contract clause may, however, allay the concerns of a party who wishes to retain the ability to resort to court proceedings.

Mediation in parallel

7.2 Any party which commences court proceedings/an arbitration must institute a mediation /serve an ADR notice on the other party(ies) to the court proceedings/arbitration within [21] days.

This wording, which can be used with or without the wording in para 7.1, is to provide for the situation where the parties wish to retain the ability to go to court but want to add force to the agreement to mediate by requiring the plaintiff party to take steps to institute the mediation within a specified time.

The defendant party can in any event initiate the mediation (eg by serving an ADR notice) at any time.

Unless wording along the lines of para 7.3 (stay of litigation/ arbitration) is included, the court proceedings can continue in parallel. If, however, a stay is provided for, then the plaintiff party will still have time to seek interim relief before serving the ADR notice.

Mediation before litigation

7.3 No party may commence any court proceedings/arbitration in relation to any dispute arising out of this agreement until they have attempted to settle it by mediation and that mediation has terminated.

The rationale for this wording is that an ADR contract clause is intended to curtail court proceedings etc, and that for them to be run in parallel is not conducive to an attempt to settle. The prospects of settlement may be higher before the lines of battle have been drawn by the hostile step of commencing court proceedings/arbitration.

This wording is the 'agreement otherwise' in paragraph 15 of the Model Procedure (see commentary on para 7.1 above). If a party commences court proceedings/arbitration before attempting mediation it would be open to the other party(ies) to seek a stay pending the mediation.

If a party is concerned that the mediation is being used as a tactic to delay the commencement of court proceedings, it can (unless para 8 wording has been included) withdraw from the mediation and thereby terminate it (see para 14 of Model Procedure).

Stay of litigation after interim legal remedies

7.4 Any party which commences court proceedings must institute a mediation/serve an ADR notice on the other party(ies) within [3] days or as soon as an order for interim relief has been made, whichever is later. The parties will take no further steps in the court proceedings until the mediation has terminated.

This clause provides for recourse to court proceedings only in so far as is necessary to obtain interim legal remedies, eg an interim injunction.

If this wording is not included in the contract clause, the parties can still agree to this course of action when a dispute is referred to mediation.

Specific terms may need to be included in this clause or at the time of the stay about the effect of such a stay on time limits in the litigation/ arbitration.

Obligatory mediation – restriction on termination

8. Neither party may terminate the mediation until each party has made its opening presentation and the mediator has met each party separately for at least [one hour]. Therefore paragraph 14 of the Model Procedure will apply.

Paragraph 14 of the Model Procedure states that 'Any of the Parties may terminate the [ADR] at any time . . .' It would therefore be open to a party to negative the intent of the core wording by withdrawing from the mediation as soon as it starts (see para 2 above). Experience shows, however, that a skilful neutral/mediator may be able to increase the possibilities of a settlement if he/she is given the opportunity. The purpose of this wording is to give that opportunity, albeit to a limited extent, whilst not seriously undermining the intent of paragraph 14.

International contracts

9. The mediation will take place in [city/country of neither/none of the parties] and the language of the mediation will be . . . [see Model Procedure guidance notes]. The Mediation Agreement referred to in the Model Procedure shall be governed by, and construed and take effect in accordance with [English] law. The courts of [England] shall have exclusive jurisdiction to settle any claim, dispute or matter of difference which may arise out of, or in connection with, the mediation.

The model clauses above should be suitable for international contracts (ie contracts between parties in different jurisdictions) but consideration should be given to including provisions relating to the location and language of the mediation, as well as the governing law and jurisdiction applicable to the mediation agreement, along the lines of this paragraph.

Executive tribunal

10. *An executive tribunal (sometimes called a 'mini-trial') is essentially a mediation with a more structured opening presentation addressed to a panel comprising a senior executive from each party and a neutral.*

Appropriate contract clauses can easily be adapted from the wording for mediation clauses. In most cases this will simply involve substituting 'executive tribunal' for 'mediation'. There may also be consequential amendments to the cross-references to the paragraph numbers in the Model Executive Tribunal Procedure.

Arbitration

11. If the parties have not settled the dispute by the mediation within [42] days from when the mediation was instituted/the date of the ADR notice, the dispute shall [be referred to, and finally resolved by, arbitration under the Rules of the London Court of International Arbitration/Chartered Institute of Arbitrators/ [*relevant arbitral body*] which Rules are deemed to be incorporated by reference to this clause.]

If the parties to the agreement want the ultimate method of resolving a dispute to be arbitration rather than litigation/court proceedings, wording along these lines should be included. If no wording along the lines of para 7.1 or 7.3 has been included, then strictly a straight arbitration clause, without the reference to mediation, would suffice.

The arbitration reference wording used should be the model/recommended wording of the arbitral body to which the reference is to be made (or whose rules are to be used).

If the 'core' ADR/mediation clause does not include provision for service of an ADR notice (see para 3 above), the wording should be amended to refer to the 'initiation of the mediation' (although there is scope for dispute as to when initiation occurs, which is one reason why the wording in para 3 is recommended).

Litigation

12. *If the parties to the agreement want the ultimate method of resolving any dispute to be court proceedings, rather then arbitration, there is no need for any additional wording to provide for this (although choice of law and jurisdiction clauses may need to be included).*

CONTENTS

Appendix C

CEDR code of conduct for mediators

C.1   CODE OF CONDUCT FOR MEDIATORS AND OTHER THIRD PARTY NEUTRALS

Introduction

1. This Code applies to a person who acts as a neutral third party ('the Mediator') in an ADR procedure (such as mediation or executive tribunal – 'Mediation') under the auspices of CEDR.

Impartiality and conflict of interest

2. The Mediator will at all times act, and endeavour to be seen to act, fairly and with complete impartiality towards the parties in the Mediation without any bias in favour of any party or any discrimination against any party.

3. Any matter of which the Mediator is aware which could be regarded as involving a conflict of interest (whether apparent, potential or actual) in the Mediation will be disclosed to the parties. This disclosure will be made in writing to all the parties as soon as the Mediator becomes aware of it, whether the matter occurs prior to, or during, the Mediation. In these circumstances the Mediator will not act (or continue to act) in the Mediation unless all the parties specifically acknowledge the disclosure and agree in writing to the Mediator acting or continuing to act as Mediator.

4. Information of the type which the Mediator should disclose includes:

- having acted in any capacity for any of the parties (other than as Mediator in other ADR procedures);

- the Mediator's firm (if applicable) having acted in any capacity for any of the parties;

- having any financial or other interest (whether direct or indirect) in any of the parties or in the subject matter or outcome of the Mediation;

- having any confidential information about any of the parties or in the subject matter of the Mediation.

5. The Mediator (and any members of the Mediator's firm or company) will not act for any of the parties individually in connection with the dispute which is the subject of the Mediation while acting as the Mediator or at any time thereafter, without the written consent of all the other Parties.

Confidentiality

6. Subject to paragraph 8 below, the Mediator will keep confidential and not use for any collateral or ulterior purpose:

- the fact that a mediation is to take place or has taken place; and

- all information (whether given orally, in writing or otherwise) produced for, or arising in relation to, the Mediation including the settlement agreement (if any) arising out of it.

7. Subject to paragraph 8 below, if the Mediator is given information by any party which is implicitly confidential or is expressly stated to be confidential (and which is not already public) the Mediator shall maintain the confidentiality of that information from all other parties, except to the extent that disclosure has been specifically authorised.

8. The duty of confidentiality in paragraphs 6 and 7 above will not apply if , and to the extent that:

- all parties consent to disclosure;

- the Mediator is required under the general law to make disclosure;

- the Mediator reasonably considers that there is serious

risk of significant harm to the life or safety of any person if the information in question is not disclosed; or

- the Mediator wishes to seek guidance in confidence from any senior officer of CEDR on any ethical or other serious question arising out of the Mediation.

Commitment and availability

9. Before accepting an appointment, the Mediator must be satisfied that he/she has time available to ensure that the Mediation can proceed in an expeditious manner.

Fees

10. CEDR will inform the parties before the Mediation begins of the fees and expenses which will be charged for the Mediation or, if not accurately known at that stage, of the basis of charging and will not make any additional charges other than in exceptional circumstances.

Parties' agreement

11. The Mediator will act in accordance with the agreement (whether written or oral) made between the parties in relation to the Mediation ('the Mediation Agreement') (except where to do so would cause a breach of this Code) and will use his/her best endeavours to ensure that the Mediation proceeds in accordance with the terms of the Mediation Agreement.

Insurance

12. The Mediator will take out professional indemnity insurance in an adequate amount with a responsible insurer.

Withdrawal of Mediator

13. The Mediator will withdraw from the Mediation if he/she:
    - is requested to do so by any of the parties (unless the parties have agreed to a procedure involving binding ADR);

- is in breach of this Code; or

- is required by the parties to do something which would be in material breach of this Code.

14. The Mediator may withdraw from the Mediation at his/her own discretion if:

    - any of the parties is acting in breach of the Mediation Agreement;

    - any of the parties is, in the Mediator's opinion, acting in an unconscionable or criminal manner;

    - the Mediator decides that continuing the mediation is unlikely to result in a settlement; or

    - any of the parties alleges that the Mediator is in material breach of this code.

CONTENTS

Appendix D

CEDR's advice to parties on pre-mediation submissions

D.1 DOCUMENTATION REQUIRED FOR THE MEDIATION CASE SUMMARIES AND BUNDLE OF DOCUMENTS

1. Case Summary

The case summary is intended only as a brief document to allow the other party(ies) and the Mediator(s) to come to grips with the main issues in the dispute. It serves as a brief explanation of what the dispute is about and should aim to provide:

- a perspective of the dispute to the other party(ies);
- the mediator with the necessary background to the dispute in order to facilitate a discussion;
- clarification of parties' respective positions and their involvement in the mediation process.

The case summary should be no longer than 10 sides of A4 paper.

2. Content of Case Summary

The Case Summary should comprise the following components.

2.1 Dramatis personae

An identification of all the protagonists involved in the dispute including:

- explanation of business/personal relationships;
- details of decision makers.

2.2   The Dispute

A description of the dispute in narrative form that should include:

- *chronology of events* – a clear picture through time of the order of events relating to the dispute;

- *matters not at issue between the parties* – identification of main facts and/or issues relating to the dispute which are not at issue, eg events that led to crisis, background of parties, details of accident etc;

- *matters at issue between parties* – this should be the heart of the case summary. The identification of the key issues that are in dispute will assist in narrowing the spectrum of controversy and thereby focus the parties' energy on resolving them;

- *details of any attempts to settle or offers to date;*

- *cross-reference to key supporting documents contained in bundle* (see 4 below).

2.3   Conclusion

An opportunity to reiterate key interests and indicate expectations of the process whilst recognising the legitimacy of those of the other party(ies) involved in the dispute. It is also worth considering the best alternatives to a negotiated settlement in the event a resolution is not reached during the mediation, eg *consider resolution of dispute through courts (time, likely outcome, costs).*

3.   Other considerations

The parties may also wish to consider the following for inclusion in their case summaries or for discussion at/general preparation for the mediation:

- Identification of key interests whilst acknowledging those of other parties can assist in establishing a spirit of co-operation.

- Similarly, provision of/reference to independent criteria, precedents or principles may assist in setting objective standards of fairness or benchmark against which parties can measure and legitimise their own claims (eg independent valuation, industry standards, expert witness).

- Parties should also consider the comparative importance of issues and endeavour to balance factors of different nature: eg apology (expression of regret) vs liability (admission of responsibility), compensation (finality of payment) vs continuity (on-going relationship to resolve problems/explore new opportunities).

4. Bundle of documents

With an emphasis on keeping documents to a minimum, the bundle should consist of key supporting papers which clarify the matters in issue between the parties. The bundle is not meant to be a complete file of the case. The purpose is to clarify matters for the mediator and establish objective standards of fairness for the negotiations.

Often parties decide to submit an agreed combined bundle of documents and CEDR encourages this.

5. Other issues

It is important to understand that if a document is not in the bundle submitted to CEDR, it *can* still be relied upon by a party at the mediation. The party simply brings the document along to the mediation and draws upon it should the need arise.

The parties are free to submit confidential papers to the Mediator(s) if they wish to disclose information to him/her on a confidential basis. Such papers should be separate from the general case summary and clearly labelled 'for the Mediator's(s') eyes only'

All documents should be sent to CEDR and we will ensure that simultaneous exchange occurs. Parties should ensure that they send CEDR sufficient copies of the concise summaries and bundle of documents to exchange between the parties and the Mediator(s).

CONTENTS

Appendix E

Specimen settlement agreements

E.1 SETTLEMENT AGREEMENT 1

*(This document is intended to serve as a **standard form model only** to help mediators and parties to reduce to writing settlement terms agreed in mediation. In all cases it should be adapted with care to the specific requirements of the situation, and parties should rely on their own legal or other advice in relation to its terms and effect)*

THIS AGREEMENT is between

(1)   [   ] of [   ] ('   ');

(2)   [   ] of [   ] ('   ');

(together 'the Parties'):

DATED [   ]

RECITALS

Whereas:

The Parties were in dispute regarding various matters:

(2) The Parties have reached agreement as to the terms of settlement of those matters by way of mediation under the auspices of the Centre for Dispute Resolution, Princes House, Gresham Street, LONDON EC2V 7NA ('CEDR') pursuant to an agreement between them, CEDR and [   ] ('the Mediator'), dated [   ] ('the Mediation Agreement').

(3) The terms of such agreement are set out below and the Parties intend this document to constitute a binding contract between them in respect of such terms.

[(4) The parties have reached agreement as to the terms of settlement of some, but not all, of the matters in dispute between them. The terms of such agreement are set out below and the Parties intend this document to constitute a binding contract between them in respect of such matters. In respect of the remaining matters upon which no settlement terms have been agreed, the Parties wish to reserve all their rights to take such action as they may think fit.]

[(5) The following facts are agreed as the basis of the following agreement and are to be treated as terms of the agreement:]

(Recital 5 enables material facts on which the settlement agreement is based to be set out as part of the agreement. This means that if any such fact later proves to be wrong, the remedy will be based on breach of this contract term in the settlement agreement, and will not have to be based on an allegation of misrepresentation which might involve breach of mediation confidentiality)

OPERATIVE TERMS

1 Warranty of authority

Comment

Although each Party and signatory should attend the Mediation with appropriate authority to bind themselves and their principals, a warranty to that effect may be useful to focus their minds and give force to their assertions.

Sample clause

1.1 Each Party warrants and undertakes to the other(s) that it has full right, power and entitlement to enter into this agreement without further reference to any other person(s).

1.2 Each signatory warrants and undertakes to the Parties that he has full right power and entitlement to execute this agreement on behalf of the Party whom he represents.

2   Terms of Settlement

Comment

2.1 Substantive terms of the Settlement (it may well be helpful, for ease of reference, to include these in an Appendix to this Agreement).

2.2 Consider whether any timetable is necessary for the performance of the Agreement, and whether it will take immediate effect.

2.3 Consider how the Agreement will be enforced and how performance will be monitored or assessed (NB CEDR and/or the Mediator can play a very valuable role in this area).

2.4 Consider whether there are any contractual formalities which will be required to give effect to the Agreement (eg ensure consideration passes between the Parties (it almost always will in practice); if land is involved how will a valid transfer be effected, etc).

2.5 If the Agreement is to be contingent on certain things:

— *What are they?*

— *Is there a timetable for performance?*

— *How will performance be assessed?*

— *What will happen if the contingent events do not happen, or happen late?*

3   Future breaches

Comment

The Mediation Agreement sometimes provides that failure to give effect to any of the terms of this Agreement will entitle the other Party(ies) to be released from it. Consider whether this is actually what the Parties want, and if so whether it should apply to a breach of any of the terms of this Agreement or only of the more significant ones (ie whether a technical breach of a minor term should provide a pretext for rescinding this Agreement).

4   Future disputes

Comment

This Agreement provides a useful opportunity to decide how any future disputes arising out of this Agreement will be dealt with.

Sample clause

4.1 If any dispute or disagreement arises in relation to any matter which is the subject of this Agreement, the parties will attempt in good faith to resolve it promptly through negotiation between senior executives of the Parties having authority to settle it. If the matter is not resolved, the Parties will refer it to mediation under the auspices of CEDR [and will appoint [the Mediator] as mediator.]

5 Existing proceedings

Comment

In most cases the agreement reached will be in full and final settlement of all claims arising in relation to the matters in dispute and will involve the withdrawal of all court or similar proceedings by all Parties. This should be expressly stated in this Agreement. (Care should be taken where the Mediation has resulted in the settlement of some but not all of the matters in dispute, to ensure that those in each category are clearly identified.) Consider also the position as to costs in existing litigation.

Sample clause

5.1 This Agreement is entered into in full and final settlement of all claims [and counterclaims] arising in relation to any and all disputes the subject of the Mediation Agreement. Any and all court or similar proceedings issued in respect of such matters shall be withdrawn forthwith [and each Party shall bear its own legal costs incurred in those proceedings].

6 Matters not resolved by mediation

Comment

Where some matters are not resolved in the Mediation, it may be useful to list them (for clarity) and to state expressly that the Parties are free to pursue these matters as they see fit, or alternatively to provide for some other agreed means of dealing with them.

Sample clause

6.1 The Parties acknowledge that they have not been able to agree terms of settlement in relation to the matters set out in [Appendix [B]] below and that each reserves its rights in relation thereto.

7 The Mediation Agreement

Comment

Remember that the Parties are still governed by the Mediation Agreement. It may be helpful expressly to terminate the Mediation, and confirm that the Mediation Agreement remains in force following termination of the Mediation.

Sample clause

7.1 The Mediation is hereby terminated except as provided by Clause 7.2 below.

7.2 Notwithstanding Clause 7.1 above, the Mediation Agreement shall continue to bind the Parties, in particular as regards Clauses 7, 8 and 9 and the relevant provisions of the Model Mediation Procedure which the Mediation Agreement incorporates.

8 Future agreements

Comment

Where an agreement envisages the execution of further agreements in order to give effect to it, consider whether or not it will be binding on the Parties (an agreement to agree not being enforceable, as a matter of law). If the Parties envisaged, say, the execution of a distribution agreement between them as part of the terms of settlement, consider whether it is possible to agree at least the salient features of such an agreement, so that there is less chance of the settlement subsequently breaking down over such terms.

9 Conflicting agreements

Comment

For clarity, it may be useful to stipulate that this Agreement overrides any existing agreements which have conflicting provisions.

343

Sample clause

9.1 The terms of this Agreement override any previous agreements between the Parties to the extent that there is any inconsistency.

10   Costs of the Mediation

Comment

The Mediation Agreement will (typically) require each Party to bear its own costs in relation to the Mediation. If this is to be altered as part of the final settlement, it should be expressly stated.

11   Governing law

Comment

This is very likely to be the laws of England, but it may be worth saying so for clarity.

12   Execution

Comment

Obviously all the Parties will have to sign the Agreement. If there is concern over whether any of the representatives has authority to bind the Party he represents, it may be possible to get his/her personal signature to the Agreement to give effect to clause 1.2 above. Failing that, Clause 1.2 can be amended to constitute a warranty given by the Parties, rather than the signatories.

APPENDIX A

Main Terms of Settlement.

APPENDIX B

Matters not resolved by Mediation.

E.2 HEADS OF AGREEMENT 2 (SHORT FORM)

THIS AGREEMENT is made between:

(1) [   ]

and

(2) [   ]

following mediation under the auspices of CENTRE FOR DISPUTE RESOLUTION of Princes House, 95 Gresham Street, London EC2V 7NA

and is made on:

(3) [date   ]

   at [   ]

(4) between the representatives of the Parties (both of whom have full authority to sign on behalf of the parties)

[   ]

[   ]

(5) in the presence of [   ] (the Mediator)

(6) in the matter of [   ]
referred to in the CEDR Mediation Agreement between the Parties, CEDR, and [the Mediator], and dated [   ]

1 AGREEMENT

1.1 The following Settlement is binding on both Parties upon signature. Initialling of each clause confirms that such clause accurately reflects the settlement terms.

1.2 This Settlement supersedes the terms of all previous agreements between the Parties in respect of the matters the subject of the mediation.

1.3 The details of this Settlement shall be confidential and not disclosed to a third party without the express written consent of the other Party.

1.4 The terms of this Settlement shall have immediate effect.

2 THE SETTLEMENT

2.1 [   ]

3 CONCLUSION

3.1 Fulfilment of this Agreement will be in full and final settlement of all claims by each Party upon the other.

[3.2 Failure by one party to fulfil [certain provisions of] this Agreement will release both parties from the terms of this Agreement.]

3.3 In the event of a dispute arising from the terms of this Agreement, the disputed matter shall immediately be referred to the [Centre for Dispute Resolution]. Such referral shall not prejudice this Agreement.

3.4 It is a condition of this Agreement that the Mediator will not be called by either Party as witness in any proceedings between the parties regarding the subject matter of this mediation.

DATED the [   ]

SIGNED . . . .
for and on behalf of

SIGNED . . . .
for and on behalf of

SIGNED . . . .
Mediator

E.3 HEADS OF AGREEMENT 3: SPECIMEN OF CLINICAL NEGLIGENCE CLAIM

(Note that this is a specimen agreement for existing court proceedings. The corresponding consent Tomlin Order is set out in Appendix F).

THIS AGREEMENT is made between:

(1) Ann Jones ('Party A')

and

(2) Barset NHS Trust ('Party B')

through the mediation of CENTRE FOR DISPUTE RESOLUTION (CEDR) of Princes House, 95 Gresham Street, London EC2V 7NA

THIS AGREEMENT is made on:

(3)   ; at

(4) the offices of Rook & Co, 1 The Strand, London WC1

in the presence of

(5)   (Mediators)

1 *THE AGREEMENT*

The Parties agree that:

All the rights of action claimed in proceedings brought by Party A against Party B No HQ0012345 are agreed to be settled on the following terms:

1.1 That Party B pays to Party A the sum of £ 74,245.86 payable as follows:

   (a) £50,000 within 14 days of this agreement;

   (b) £10,000 to be paid out of Court;

   (c) £14,245.86 notionally paid to Party A to be repaid to the Compensation Recovery Unit of the Department of Social Security

1.2 That in addition Party B pays Party A's costs of the action to be assessed if not agreed on the standard basis.

1.3 That Party B will express in writing their regret and apologies in relation to the subject-matter of Party A's claim, together (if he so wishes) with a similar expression of regret and apology by Mr Bernard Slicer.

1.4 The parties agree that an appointment will be made for Party A to attend at Barset NHS Trust's premises to view all relevant current documentation relating to Party B's cervical screening clinic patient information and advice leaflets and for Party B to take due note of Party A's comments on those.

1.5 Party B agrees to provide IVF treatment and cognitive therapy free of charge to Party A at the Barset Hospital Fertility Clinic on a priority basis for 12 months from the date of this agreement

1.6 Party A further agrees in consideration of this agreement not to refer any clinician involved in this dispute to their relevant professional body.

1.7 Each party agrees that they will keep the terms and the fact of this settlement agreement absolutely confidential and will not disclose any such details, in the case of the claimant, to anyone outside her immediate family, the Legal Services Commission and any partner in her General Practitioner practice, the East Barset Health Centre; and, in the case of Party B, to the NHSLA and any other insurer involved in the litigation and to the medical and administrative staff of the Barset NHS Trust; and in either party's case to CEDR and the court, unless all parties and their representatives and a Director of CEDR agree in writing to such disclosure.

1.8 That on payment of those sums and performance of the other obligations set out in this agreement, Party B and all clinicians involved in this dispute are discharged from any liability to Party A arising from the subject matter of the action.

1.9 That the solicitors for the parties will draft, sign and lodge a Consent Order in the proceedings recording these terms within seven days of this agreement.

1.10 Both parties agree that if any dispute arises out of this agreement, the parties will attempt to settle it by mediation before resorting to any other dispute resolution route. It will be initiated by notice to the mediator of the Mediation. If no binding settlement to such a dispute is reached within 28 days from the date of notice to the Mediator under this paragraph, either party may take any appropriate steps to enforce their alleged rights as they may be advised or think fit.

2   CONCLUSION

2.1 It is a condition of this Agreement that the mediator will not be called by any Party as a witness in litigation or any other process regarding any dispute between the Parties, whether as to what has occurred at the Mediation or otherwise.

2.2 Neither CEDR nor any Mediator appointed by CEDR shall be liable to the Parties for any act or omission whatsoever in connection with the services provided by them.

DATED

SIGNED

CONTENTS

Appendix F

Specimen Tomlin orders and consent arbitration award

F.1 GENERAL PRECEDENT OF A CONSENT TOMLIN ORDER

UPON hearing Counsel/Solicitors for the parties [and upon reading . . . .] AND BY CONSENT

1. IT IS ORDERED that all further proceedings in this action be stayed upon the terms of settlement agreed between the parties set out in the Schedule herein [and that there be no order as to costs]

2. IT IS FURTHER ORDERED that all further proceedings in this action be stayed except for the purpose of carrying this order and the said terms into effect and for this purpose the parties are at liberty to apply

THE SCHEDULE

Dated the   day of

F.2 SPECIMEN TOMLIN ORDER IN CLINICAL NEGLIGENCE CLAIM

(Note that this is the corresponding Tomlin Order to the specimen settlement agreement in Appendix E.3. This provides alternatively for having the terms of the agreement on the face of the Schedule, which may expose it to public access, or having them embodied in the settlement agreement referred to but not set out on the face of the Schedule to the Order).

IN THE HIGH COURT OF JUSTICE   No 1999.J.1234

QUEEN'S BENCH DIVISION

BETWEEN   ANN JONES   Claimant

and

BARSET NHS TRUST   Defendant

CONSENT ORDER

UPON THE PARTIES having agreed terms of settlement

BY CONSENT IT IS ORDERED that all further proceedings in this action be stayed upon the terms set out in [*the agreement identified in*] the Schedule to this Order except for the purpose of putting into effect those terms;

AND THAT either party may apply to the court to enforce the terms upon which this action has been stayed without the need to bring a new claim;

AND THAT the parties have agreed that any claim for breach of contract arising from an alleged breach of the terms set out in [*the above-mentioned agreement identified in*] the Schedule to this Order may, unless the court orders otherwise be dealt with by way of an application to the court without the need to start a new claim;

AND THAT the sum of £10,000.00 paid into court by the defendant is paid out to the claimant's solicitors without further order and all interest accrued on that sum be paid out to the defendant without further order;

AND THAT the defendant pays the claimant's costs of this action on the standard basis to be subject to detailed assessment if not agreed.

SCHEDULE

[The settlement agreement dated   and signed by the parties to these proceedings at the conclusion of a mediation held on that date, the original of which is held by [the claimant's solicitors] [the Centre for Dispute Resolution, Princes House, 95 Gresham Street, London EC2V 7NA] [the mediator named in the said agreement].

[1 The defendant will pay £50,000.00 to the claimant within 14 days of this order, being additional to the sum of £10,000.00 to be paid out of court as provided in the order above.

2 The defendant will in addition repay to the Compensation Recovery Unit the sum of £14,245.86 as required by the Certificate of Recoverable Benefit dated 12 December 1999.

3 The defendant undertakes to provide IVF treatment and cognitive counselling free of charge to the claimant at its Barset Hospital Fertility Clinic on a priority basis for 12 months from the date of this agreement.

4 Upon performance of its obligations under this agreement and the terms set out in the above order, the defendant is discharged from any further liability to the claimant in respect of the subject-matter of this action.]

DATED

WE CONSENT to an order in the above terms:

. . . .

Rook & Co   Cutter and Stitch

Claimant's solicitors   Defendant's solicitors

F.3 PRECEDENT CONSENT AWARD IN ARBITRATION

IN THE MATTER OF THE ARBITRATION ACT 1996

AND

IN THE MATTER OF THE INSTITUTION OF CIVIL ENGINEERS' ARBITRATION PROCEDURE (1997)/CONSTRUCTION INDUSTRY MODEL ARBITRATION RULES (1997)/THE CHARTERED INSTITUTE OF ARBITRATORS ARBITRATION RULES (1998)

AND

IN THE MATTER OF AN ARBITRATION

BETWEEN:

Claimant

and

Respondent

CONSENT AWARD

WHEREAS:

1. By a contract [under seal] dated   day of   the Claimant (Limited) undertook for the Respondent (Limited)
2. Clause   of the Contract provides for the settlement of disputes or differences by a Sole Arbitrator whose appointment is to be by mutual agreement of the Parties to the Contract or failing such agreement by appointment by the President of
3. Disputes and differences have arisen between the Parties.
4. By a letter dated   the Respondent invited me, ABC of . . . . to act as Sole Arbitrator in the dispute, the Claimant having previously agreed with the Respondent that I be invited to act.

or

4. On the   day of   The President of   appointed me ABC of . . . . as sole Arbitrator to determine the dispute between the parties.

5. I accepted the appointment in the disputes on   day
    of   and entered upon the reference.

6. Having heard the parties appearing by their Counsel/
    Solicitors AND BY CONSENT I HEREBY AWARD AND
    DIRECT as set out in the attached Schedule

IN WITNESS WHEREOF I have hereunto set my hand this   day
of

[THE SCHEDULE]

Signed . . . .

Witness . . . .

CONTENTS

Appendix G

CEDR model executive tribunal procedure

G.1 EXECUTIVE TRIBUNAL AGREEMENT

1. The parties ('the parties') to the dispute in question ('the Dispute'), the Neutral and The Centre for Dispute Resolution ('CEDR') will enter into an agreement ('the ET Agreement') in the form of the CEDR Model Executive Tribunal Agreement in relation to the conduct of the Executive Tribunal. This Model Procedure may be varied by the ET Agreement. All communications relating to, and at, the Executive Tribunal will be without prejudice (see para 17 below).

Neutral

2. An independent third party ('the Neutral') who will be nominated by CEDR, subject to the agreement of the Parties, will:

- attend any meetings with any or all of the Parties preceding the Executive Tribunal, if requested or if the Neutral decides this is appropriate;

- read before the Executive Tribunal each Summary and all the Documents sent to him/her (see para 7 below);

- chair, and (after consultation with the Parties) determine the procedure for, the Executive Tribunal (see para 10 below);

- assist the parties in drawing up any written settlement agreement;

- abide by the terms of the Model Procedure, the ET Agreement and CEDR's Code of Conduct.

3. The Neutral (and any member of the Neutral's firm or company) will not act for any of the Parties individually in connection with the Dispute in any capacity either during the currency of the ET Agreement or at any time thereafter. The Parties accept that in relation to the Dispute neither the Neutral nor CEDR is an agent of, or acting in any capacity for, any of the Parties. The Parties and the Neutral accept that the Neutral (unless an employee of CEDR) is acting as an independent contractor and not as agent or employee of CEDR.

CEDR

4. CEDR, in conjunction with the Neutral where appropriate, will make the necessary arrangements for the Executive Tribunal including, as necessary:

- nominating, and obtaining the agreement of the Parties to, the Neutral;

- drawing up the ET Agreement;

- organising a suitable venue and dates;

- organising exchange of the Summaries and Documents;

- meeting with any or all of the representatives of the Parties (and the Neutral if he/she has been appointed), either together or separately, to discuss any matters or concerns relating to the Executive Tribunal;

- general administration in relation to the Executive Tribunal.

5. If there is any point on the conduct of the Executive Tribunal (including as to the nomination of the Neutral) upon which the Parties cannot agree within a reasonable time from the date of the notice initiating the Executive Tribunal ('the ADR notice') CEDR will, at the request of any Party, decide the issue for the Parties, having consulted with them.

Participants

6. Each Party will state in the ET Agreement the names of:

- The executive that will be its Executive Tribunal panel member ('the Executive'). The Executive must have the necessary authority to settle the Dispute.

- Any other person(s) (such as professional advisers, expert witnesses) that it intends will be present on its behalf at, and/or participate in, the Executive Tribunal.

Each Party, in signing the ET Agreement, will be deemed to be agreeing on behalf of both itself and all such persons that they agree to the confidentiality provisions of the Model Procedure.

Exchange of information

7. Each Party will send to CEDR at least two weeks before the Executive Tribunal, or such other date as may be agreed between the Parties, sufficient copies of:

- a concise summary ('the Summary') stating its case in the Dispute; and

- all documents to which the Summary refers and any others to which the Party may want to refer in the Executive Tribunal ('the Documents'),

which CEDR will send on to the other Party(ies) and the Neutral.

In addition, each Party may send to the Neutral (through CEDR) and/or bring to the Executive Tribunal further documentation which it wishes to disclose in confidence to the Neutral but not to any other Party, clearly stating in writing that such documentation is confidential to the Neutral and CEDR.

8. The Parties should try, through CEDR and/or the Neutral, to agree:

- the maximum number of pages of each Summary and of their Documents;

- a joint set of documents from their respective Documents;

- the order and length of their submissions (and replies, if any) to the Executive Tribunal panel;

- the identity of witnesses and expert (if any) who will be participating in the presentation at the Executive Tribunal.

The Executive Tribunal

9. The Executive Tribunal will take place at the place and time stated in the ET Agreement.

10. The procedure at the Executive Tribunal will be determined by the Neutral, after consultation with the Executives. The usual procedure will be:

- Each of the Parties will make a presentation of its case to a panel consisting of the Executives and the Neutral. Each presentation will be in the order, and not exceed the length, set out in the ET Agreement.

- Each Party may reply to any of the points made in the other Party's presentation(s). The replies will be in the same order as the presentations and will not exceed the length set out in the ET Agreement.

- Presentations and replies may be made in any form and by any of the participants (see para 6 above) and may be supported by any of the Documents.

- The Neutral and the Executives may ask questions to clarify points raised in the presentation but otherwise the presentations and the replies will not be interrupted.

- As soon as possible after the conclusion of the presentations, the Executives will meet and attempt to negotiate a settlement of the Dispute. The Executives may, and usually will, invite the Neutral to be involved in, and facilitate, the negotiations.

- No person other than the Executives and the Neutral may attend the negotiations without the consent of all the Executives.

11. No formal record or transcript of the Executive Tribunal will be made.

12. If the Parties are unable to reach a settlement in the negotiations at the Executive Tribunal, and only if all the Executives so request and the Neutral agrees, the Neutral will produce for the Parties a non-binding written recommendation on terms of settlement. This will not attempt to anticipate what a court might order but will set out what the Neutral suggests are appropriate settlement terms in all of the circumstances.

Settlement agreement

13. Any settlement reached in the Executive Tribunal will not be legally binding until it has been reduced to writing and signed by, or on behalf of, the Parties.

Termination

14. Any of the Parties may withdraw from the Executive Tribunal at any time and shall immediately inform the Neutral and the other Parties in writing. The Executive Tribunal will terminate when:

- a Party withdraws from the Executive Tribunal; or
- a written settlement agreement is concluded; or
- the Neutral decides that continuing the Executive Tribunal is unlikely to result in a settlement; or
- the Neutral decides he should retire for any of the reasons in the Code of Conduct.

Stay of proceedings

15. Any litigation or arbitration in relation to the Dispute may be commenced or continued notwithstanding the Executive Tribunal unless the Parties agree otherwise.

Confidentiality etc

16. Every person involved in the Executive Tribunal will keep confidential and not use for any collateral or ulterior purpose:

- the fact that the Executive Tribunal is to take place or has taken place; and
- all information, (whether given orally, in writing or otherwise), produced for, or arising in relation to, the Executive Tribunal including the settlement agreement (if any) arising out of it,

except in so far as is necessary to implement and enforce any such settlement agreement.

17. All information (whether oral or in the form of documents, tapes, computer disks etc) produced for, during, or as a result of, the Executive Tribunal will be privileged and not be admissible as evidence or discoverable in any litigation or arbitration in relation to the Dispute. This does not apply to any information which would in any event have been admissible or discoverable in any such litigation or arbitration.

18. None of the parties to the ET Agreement will call the Neutral or CEDR (or any employee, consultant, officer or representative of CEDR) as a witness, consultant, arbitrator or expert in any litigation or arbitration in relation to the Dispute and the Neutral and CEDR will not voluntarily act in any such capacity without the written agreement of all the Parties.

Fees, expenses and costs

19. CEDR's fees (which include the Neutral's fees) and the other expenses of the Executive Tribunal will be borne equally by the Parties. Payment of these fees and expenses will be made to CEDR in accordance with its fee schedule and terms and conditions of business.

20. Each Party will bear it own costs and expenses of its participation in the Executive Tribunal.

Exclusion of liability

21. Neither the Neutral (including any Pupil Neutral and/or any Neutral's Adviser) nor CEDR (including any employee and/or agent of CEDR) shall be liable to any of the Parties for any act or omission in connection with their services provided by them in, or in relation to, the Executive Tribunal, unless the act or omission is shown to have been in bad faith.

G.2 GUIDANCE NOTES

The paragraph numbers and headings in these notes refer to the paragraphs and headings in the Model Procedure.

The same terms ('the Parties' etc) are used in the Model Procedure and the Model Agreement.

Introduction

The essence of the Executive Tribunal (and many other ADR procedures) is that:

- it involves a neutral third party to facilitate negotiation;
- it is quick, inexpensive and confidential;

- it enables the parties to reach results which are not possible in an adjudicative process such as litigation or arbitration and may be to the benefit of *both* parties, particularly if there is a continuing business relationship;

- it involves representatives of the Parties who have sufficient authority to settle. In some cases, there may be an advantage in the representatives being people who have not been directly involved in the events leading up to the dispute and in the subsequent dispute.

The procedure for the Executive Tribunal is flexible and this Model Procedure can be adapted (with or without the assistance of CEDR) to suit the parties.

An Executive Tribunal can be used:

- in both domestic and international disputes; and

- whether or not litigation or arbitration has been commenced; and

- in two-party and multi-party disputes.

Rules or rigid procedures in the context of a consensual and flexible process which is the essence of ADR are generally inappropriate. The Model Procedure (and these guidance notes) and the Model Agreement should be sufficient to enable parties to conduct an Executive Tribunal.

In some cases the agreement to conduct an Executive Tribunal will be as a result of an 'ADR clause' (such as one of the CEDR Model ADR clauses) in an underlying commercial agreement between the Parties. Where that is the case the Model Procedure and ET Agreement may need to be adapted to take account of the terms of the clause.

The Model Agreement, which has been kept as short and simple as possible, incorporates the Model Procedure. The ET Agreement can amend the Model Procedure either by setting out the amendments in the ET Agreement or by stating that amendments made in manuscript (or otherwise) on the Model Procedure are to be incorporated.

Executive Tribunal Agreement – para 1

If CEDR is asked to do so by a party wishing to initiate an Executive Tribunal, it will approach the other party(ies) to a dispute to seek to persuade it/them to participate.

Ideally representatives of the Parties (and the Neutral if he/she has been identified) and CEDR (or whatever other ADR body is involved, if any) should meet to discuss and finalise the terms of the ET Agreement.

Alternatively, the party who has taken the initiative in proposing the Executive Tribunal may wish to send a draft agreement based on the CEDR Model ET Agreement to the other party(ies).

Neutral – paras 2–3

The success of the Executive Tribunal will, to a large extent, depend on the skill of the Neutral. CEDR believes it is very important for the Neutral to have had specific training and experience. CEDR has its own body of trained and experienced Neutrals and can (and usually does) assist the Parties in identifying and appointing a suitable Neutral.

In some cases it may be useful to have more than one Neutral, or to have an independent expert who can advise the Neutral on technical issues 'the Neutral's Adviser'. All should sign the ET Agreement, which should be amended as appropriate.

It is CEDR's practice, as part of its Neutral training programme, to have a pupil Neutral ('the Pupil Neutral') attend most Executive Tribunals. The Pupil Neutral signs the ET Agreement and falls within the definition 'the Neutral' in the Model Procedure and the ET Agreement.

It is advisable, but not essential, to involve the Neutral in any preliminary meeting between the Parties.

CEDR – paras 4–5

CEDR's Code of Conduct covers such points as the Neutral's duty of confidentiality, impartiality and avoiding conflicts of interest.

The Model Procedure envisages the involvement of CEDR, because in most cases this is likely to benefit the Parties and generally to facilitate the setting up and conduct of the Executive Tribunal. Its involvement, however, is not essential and this Model Procedure can be amended if CEDR is not to be involved.

Participants – para 6

It is essential that the Executives are sufficiently senior and have the necessary authority from the respective Parties to settle the dispute without having to refer to anybody else.

Exchange of information – paras 7–8

Documentation which a Party wants the Neutral to keep confidential from the other Party(ies) (eg a counsel's opinion, an expert report not yet exchanged) must be clearly marked as such. It can be disclosed by the Party before or during the Executive Tribunal. It will not be disclosed by the Neutral or CEDR without the express consent of the Party.

One of the advantages of ADR is that it can avoid the often excessive discovery (including witness statements) of litigation and arbitration. The Documents should be kept to the minimum necessary to understand a Party's case and to give the Neutral a good grasp of the issues. The Summaries should be similarly brief.

The Executive Tribunal – paras 9–12

Professional advisers, particularly lawyers, can and usually do attend the Executive Tribunal. The lead role in the negotiations is usually taken by the Executives because the commercial interests of the Parties will normally take the negotiations beyond strict legal issues. The advisers, however, can play an important role in the exchange of information, in the presentation, in advising their clients on the legal implication of a settlement and in drawing up the settlement agreement.

The intention of paragraph 12 is that the Neutral will cease to play an entirely facilitative role only if the negotiations in the Executive Tribunal are deadlocked. Giving a settlement recommendation may be perceived by a Party as undermining the Neutral's neutrality and for this reason the Neutral may not agree to this course of action. Any recommendation will be without prejudice and will not be binding.

Settlement agreement – para 13

If no agreement is reached, it is nonetheless open to the Parties to adjourn the Executive Tribunal to another time and place. Experience shows that even where no agreement is reached during the Executive Tribunal itself, the Parties will often reach a settlement shortly after, as a result of the progress made during the Executive Tribunal.

Stay of proceedings – para 15

Although a stay may engender a better climate for settlement, it is not essential that any proceedings relating to the Dispute should be stayed. If they are stayed, the effect on limitation periods needs to be agreed. Although under English law the parties can agree to limitation periods not running, the position may differ in other jurisdictions and the position on this should be checked. Suggested wording for a stay, which can be incorporated in the ET Agreement, is:

No litigation or arbitration in relation to the Dispute is to be commenced [Any existing litigation or arbitration in relation to the Dispute is to be stayed] from the date of this agreement until the termination of the Executive Tribunal.

Confidentiality – paras 16–18

The CEDR Code of Conduct provides that the Neutral is not to disclose to any other Party any information given to him by a Party in confidence without the express consent of that Party.

In any related litigation in England and Wales any information (see para 17) should in any event be inadmissible and privileged as 'without prejudice' since it will have been produced in relation to negotiations to settle the Dispute. Documents which would in any event be discoverable will, however, not become privileged by reason of having been referred to in the Executive Tribunal and will therefore still be discoverable. The position may differ in other jurisdictions and should be checked.

Fees, expenses and costs – paras 19–20

The usual arrangement is for the Parties to share equally the fees and expenses of the procedure, but other arrangements are possible. A party to a dispute which is reluctant to participate in an Executive Tribunal my be persuaded to participate if the other party(ies) agree to bear that party's expenses.

International disputes – language, governing law and jurisdiction

The Model Agreement is designed for domestic disputes but can be easily adapted for international cross-border disputes by the addition of the following paragraphs in the ET Agreement:

Language

The language of the Executive Tribunal will be [English]. Any Party producing Documents or participating in the Executive Tribunal in any other language will provide the necessary translations and interpretation facilities.

Governing Law and Jurisdiction

This Agreement shall be governed by, construed and take effect in accordance with [English] law.

The courts of [England] shall have exclusive jurisdiction to settle any claim, dispute or matter of difference which may arise out of or in connection with the Executive Tribunal.

Where the law is not English or the jurisdiction not England, the ET Agreement may need to be amended to ensure the structure, rights and obligations necessary for an Executive Tribunal are applicable.

CONTENTS

Appendix H

CEDR rules for adjudication

H.1 PART 1

Appointment of an Adjudicator and reference to adjudication

A. Where parties to a contract have agreed to refer disputes to adjudication in accordance with these Rules, the following procedure shall apply if the parties are unable to agree on the appointment of an Adjudicator:

   (i) Either party may apply to CEDR to appoint the Adjudicator.

  (ii) The application shall be made in a form acceptable to CEDR containing brief details of the names and addresses of the parties, a copy of the relevant provisions of the contract providing for adjudication, brief details of the dispute, such other information as may be relevant and a brief statement of the redress sought. CEDR's standard application form is attached to these Rules at Annex A.

 (iii) The application shall be accompanied by CEDR's appointment fee due in accordance with CEDR's fee scale at the date of the application by the referring party.

  (iv) No later than seven days after being given notice of an application, CEDR shall (a) appoint the Adjudicator (who shall be provided with a copy of the application) and (b) send the parties the name, address and brief details of the person appointed.

B. The parties will promptly enter into a formal agreement with CEDR and the Adjudicator when requested to do so by CEDR, using

H.1 *CEDR rules for adjudication*

CEDR's standard form of agreement which is attached to these Rules at Annex B. Pending signature of an agreement they shall nonetheless be bound by these Rules as provided in para E below.

C. Where the Adjudicator is named in the contract or is appointed by agreement between the parties without the involvement of CEDR, a party wishing to refer a dispute to the Adjudicator shall give the Adjudicator written notice that a dispute has arisen. The notice shall contain brief details of the names and addresses of the parties, a copy of the relevant provisions of the contract providing for adjudication, brief details of the dispute, such other information as may be relevant and a brief statement of the redress sought. A copy of the notice shall be sent to the other party or parties when it is sent to the Adjudicator. The Adjudicator shall promptly upon receipt of the notice confirm in writing to the parties that the Adjudicator will adjudicate the dispute in accordance with these Rules.

D. Under these rules the date of referral of the dispute to adjudication shall be:

(i) Where para A above applies, the date on which the Adjudicator is appointed by CEDR, or

(ii) Where para C above applies, the date on which the parties, under these Rules, are treated as having been given notice of the Adjudicator's confirmation.

E. Parties who have agreed to submit to adjudication in accordance with these Rules shall be bound by these Rules (both Parts 1 and 2).

H.2 PART 2

Conduct of adjudication procedure

1. The Adjudicator shall be free to take the initiative in ascertaining the facts and the law and shall have complete discretion as to how to conduct the adjudication. The Adjudicator shall not be required to observe any rule, whether of evidence or procedure, of any court or tribunal. The Adjudicator shall have complete discretion as to whether or not to hold any meeting with the parties. However, the Adjudicator shall not take into consideration any statement (whether of a party or a witness) unless it has been made available to the parties for consideration.

2. The procedure in para 3 shall apply unless, within two days of the date of referral, the Adjudicator either establishes a procedure for the adjudication which does not require the written submissions mentioned below or fixes a preliminary meeting with the parties to be held within seven days of the date of referral.

3. The party that initiated the reference to adjudication shall, within four days of the date of referral, submit to the Adjudicator and to the other party or parties a concise statement of the issues in dispute and the relevant facts. The other party or parties may, not later than seven days following its receipt, submit a concise statement in response. Either statement may be accompanied by copies of essential documents directly relevant to the dispute.

4. The Adjudicator may at any time request such information and documents from the parties and/or access to any property as the Adjudicator considers appropriate. The parties will respond promptly to any such request.

5. If the Adjudicator at any time wishes to obtain legal or other specialist advice on any matter, he or she shall inform the parties with reasons. However, no adviser shall be appointed by the Adjudicator without the prior consent of both parties.

6. If a party fails to provide any information or documents or to attend any meeting requested by the Adjudicator, then the Adjudicator shall be at liberty to proceed with the adjudication and reach a decision.

7. The Adjudicator shall decide the matters referred to him/her as he/she may in his/her absolute discretion think fit, acting impartially and in good faith. The Adjudicator shall have the power to review and revise any decision made under the terms of the contract to which the dispute relates, except where the contract precludes this.

8. The Adjudicator may vary any of the periods specified in these Rules (except for the period for reaching a decision, which shall be dealt with as provided in para 9).

Decision of Adjudicator

9. The Adjudicator shall reach a decision as soon as practicable, the objective being to have a decision within 14 days of the date of referral. The Adjudicator may, but shall not be obliged to, give

reasons for the decision. The Adjudicator shall in any event reach a decision no later that 28 days from the date of referral. This period may be extended (a) by up to 14 days with the consent of the referring party, or (b) as agreed by the parties. If the Adjudicator requests an extension of the period for the decision but the agreement of the parties is not forthcoming, he or she shall within the time prescribed make such decision as he or she considers appropriate in the circumstances.

10. The parties shall be jointly and severally responsible for the fees and expenses of CEDR and the Adjudicator including the fees and expenses of any adviser appointed under para 5. The Adjudicator shall be entitled to withhold the issue of the decision until payment has been made in full. In the decision, the Adjudicator shall have discretion to apportion liability with regard to the fees and expenses referred to in this paragraph.

11. Every decision of the Adjudicator shall be binding on the parties and notwithstanding paras 12 and 13 shall be implemented without delay by the parties, who shall be entitled to such reliefs or remedies as are set out in the decision.

Notice of dissatisfaction

12. If a party is dissatisfied with the decision of the Adjudicator it may, within 60 days of being given notice of the decision (or within such other period as the parties may agree), give written notice of its dissatisfaction to the other party or parties and to the Adjudicator. If no notice of dissatisfaction is issued within this period the decision of the Adjudicator shall be final and binding upon the parties.

13. If a notice of dissatisfaction is given, the dispute will be finally determined by court proceedings or by reference to arbitration in accordance with the contract between the parties. Unless otherwise agreed by the parties, the court or the arbitrator(s) shall not be bound by, and shall have power to review and revise every decision of the Adjudicator.

Incapacity of Adjudicator

14. If at any time after the date of referral the Adjudicator becomes unable or unwilling to act, the parties shall endeavour to

agree the appointment of a replacement within seven days of being so notified. If they fail to do so, CEDR shall appoint a replacement Adjudicator within seven days of receipt of an application from either party and the provisions of Part 1 of these Rules shall be applicable to the new appointment.

Mediation option

15. At any time before the issue of the Adjudicator's decision the parties may agree to refer the dispute to mediation. In that case each party shall notify the Adjudicator and the adjudication shall be suspended. The mediation shall be non-binding until a settlement of the dispute is reached and confirmed in writing by the parties. The Adjudicator shall not act as the mediator. CEDR shall appoint the mediator on the application of either party if the mediator is not agreed between them within seven days from the date they agree to refer the dispute to mediation. If a settlement of the dispute is not reached within 28 days from the date upon which the parties agree to mediate (or if at any time either party abandons mediation) the adjudication shall recommence. If the dispute is settled by mediation, the adjudication shall be at an end and the parties shall promptly settle the fees and expenses of CEDR and the Adjudicator.

Liability

16. Neither CEDR nor the Adjudicator shall be liable for anything done or omitted in the discharge of their respective functions unless the act or omission was in bad faith. The same immunity shall extend to any employee or agent of CEDR or of the Adjudicator.

Notices

17. A copy of every notice and document submitted by a party to CEDR or the Adjudicator shall at the same time be sent to the other party/ies. A copy of every document issued by the Adjudicator shall be sent to the parties at the same time. Every notice or document shall be treated as being given two working days after it is posted or, in the case of fax or hand delivery, on the day it is delivered (or the next working day if delivery is made after normal working hours).

H.3   MODEL CLAUSE FOR APPOINTMENT OF ADJUDICATOR

Alternative A

Any dispute arising under this Agreement may be referred to the Adjudicator by either party. The adjudication shall be conducted in accordance with the CEDR Rules for Adjudication. The Adjudicator's decision shall be in writing and shall promptly be implemented by the parties. An Adjudicator's decision with which a party is dissatisfied shall be resolved by [arbitration/the court] in accordance with this Agreement provided that such party gives notice of dissatisfaction to the other party and to the Adjudicator within the period agreed by the parties or if none within 60 days of the date of the Adjudicator's decision. In the absence of notice, the Adjudicator's decision shall be final and binding on the parties without any right of counterclaim set-off or abatement and, if notice of dissatisfaction is given, the decision shall be binding on and implemented by the parties until the dispute is finally resolved as set out above.

* The parties agree that notwithstanding the issue of a notice of dissatisfaction, neither of them will serve a notice of arbitration or issue proceedings in relation to a dispute upon which the Adjudicator has issued a decision until after [practical completion] [or earlier termination] of this Agreement.]

If an Adjudicator is not named in this Agreement or if the Adjudicator, having been appointed, becomes unwilling or unable to act at any time, the Adjudicator shall be appointed by agreement between the parties or in default of agreement by CEDR.

* Optional extra wording.

Alternative B

Any dispute arising under this Agreement which cannot be resolved amicably between the parties shall, in the first instance, be referred to adjudication in accordance with the Rules for Adjudication of CEDR at present in force.

Note: Alternative A contains an optional provision which is intended to defer any legal proceedings over the Adjudicator's decision until after 'practical completion'. Both forms can be used whether or not an Adjudicator is named in the contract.

374

H.4   ADJUDICATION GUIDANCE NOTES

The numbers and headings in these notes refer to the Rules for Adjudication and accompanying documentation.

Text in square brackets may be inappropriate and therefore inapplicable in some cases.

The CEDR Adjudication Rules are presently designed for construction adjudications but may also be used for other adjudications.

Introduction

The essence of adjudication is that:

- it involves a neutral third party to decide the matter;
- it is quick, inexpensive and confidential;
- it provides for immediate practical implementation of the results – Rule 11 (subject to possible later confirmation or rectification, if sought – Rule 13);
- the Adjudication Rules are flexible and can be adapted (with or without the assistance of CEDR) to suit the parties.

An adjudication can be used:

- in both domestic and international disputes;
- whether or not litigation or arbitration has been commenced;
- in two-party and multi-party disputes.

Rules or rigid procedures in the context of a consensual and adaptable process which is the essence of ADR are generally inappropriate. The Adjudication Rules, the Adjudication Agreement and these Guidance notes should be sufficient to enable parties to conduct an adjudication.

In some cases the agreement to conduct an adjudication will be as a result of an 'ADR clause' (such as one of the CEDR Model ADR clauses) to that effect in an underlying commercial agreement between the Parties. Where that is the case the Adjudication Rules and the Adjudication Agreement may need to be adapted accordingly.

The Adjudication Agreement, which has been kept as short and simple as possible, incorporates the Adjudication Rules. The Adjudication Agreement can include amendments to the

Adjudication Rules; the amendments can be set out in the body of the Adjudication Agreement or the Adjudication Agreement can state the amendments made in the manuscript (or otherwise) to the Adjudication Rules and initialled by the Parties to be incorporated into the Adjudication Agreement.

CEDR adjudication procedure

The procedure is covered under Parts 1 and 2 of the CEDR Rules for Adjudication A to E (Appointment), 1 to 17 (Conduct) with the Model Clause (Appointment) and Application for Appointment (Annex A).

Adjudication Agreement

If CEDR is asked to do so by a party wishing to initiate an adjudication, it will approach the other party(ies) to a dispute to see if their consent can be obtained.

Ideally the representatives, the advisers (and the Adjudicator if he/she has been identified) and CEDR (or whatever other ADR body is involved, if any) should meet to discuss and finalise the terms of the Adjudication Agreement. Alternatively, the referring party may wish to send a draft agreement based on the CEDR Adjudication Agreement to the other party(ies). The CEDR Adjudication Agreement is set out at Annex B.

The adjudication

The success of the adjudication will, to a large extent, depend on the skill of the Adjudicator. CEDR believes it is very important for the adjudicator to have had specific training and experience. CEDR has its own body of trained and experienced adjudicators and can assist the Parties in identifying a suitable Adjudicator.

In some complex cases it may be useful to have more than one Adjudicator, or to have an independent expert who can advise the Adjudicator on technical issues ('the Adjudicator's Adviser'). All should sign the Adjudication Agreement, which should be amended as appropriate.

Rules 1 to 17 inclusive cover the actual conduct of the adjudication and the Adjudicator. The decision of the Adjudicator must be implemented immediately notwithstanding any appeal and final revision or review.

CEDR

The Adjudication Rules envisage the involvement of CEDR because in most cases this is likely to benefit the parties and generally to facilitate the setting up and conduct of the Adjudicator. Its involvement, however, is not essential and the Adjudication Rules can be amended if CEDR is not to be involved.

Documentation

Documentation should be kept as brief as possible and be circulated in accordance with Rule 17.

One of the advantages of adjudication is that it can cut down excessive discovery process (including witness statements) which often blights litigation and arbitration. The documents should be kept to the minimum necessary to give the Adjudicator a good grasp of the issues. The summaries should be similarly brief.

Stay of other proceedings

Although a stay may engender a better climate for adjudication, it is not, however, essential that any proceedings relating to the dispute should be stayed. If they are stayed, the effect on limitation periods needs to be agreed.

Although under English law the parties can agree to limitation periods not running, the position may differ in other jurisdictions and the position on this should be checked.

Confidentiality

The CEDR Adjudication Agreement provides that the totality of the adjudication be kept confidential, subject only to later legal proceedings (if any): clause 4 of the Adjudication Agreement.

Fees, expenses and costs

The usual arrangement is for the parties to share equally the fee and expenses of the adjudication, but other arrangements are possible. A party to a dispute which is reluctant to participate in an adjudication may be persuaded to participate if the other party(ies) agree to bear that party's share of the adjudication fees.

International disputes – language and governing law/jurisdiction

The Adjudication Agreement is designed for domestic disputes but can be easily adapted for international cross-border disputes by the addition of the following paragraphs:

Language

The language of the adjudicator will be [English]. Any party producing documents or participating in the adjudication in any other language will provide the necessary translations and interpretation facilities.

Governing Law and Jurisdiction

The Adjudication Agreement shall be governed by, construed and take effect in accordance with [English] law.

The courts of [England] shall have exclusive jurisdiction to settle any claim, dispute or matter of difference which may arise out of or in connection with the Adjudicator.

Where the law is not in English or the jurisdiction not England the Adjudication Agreement may need to be amended to ensure the structure, rights and obligations necessary for an Adjudication are applicable.

H.5   ANNEX A

Application for appointment of Adjudicator

To: CEDR

Name and Address of Referring Party:

_____

_____

_____ Date: _____

We, the undersigned, request CEDR to appoint an Adjudicator to deal with certain disputes arising under a contract between us and   of

Brief details of the contract, of the disputes to be adjudicated and of the redress which we seek are set out in the attached Schedule.

A copy of the [Adjudication Agreement/contract clause referring disputes to Adjudication in accordance with CEDR Rules for Adjudication] is attached.

We undertake to indemnify CEDR against any costs or liability which it may incur arising out of this application or any appointment and confirm that we are bound by the CEDR Rules for Adjudication.

We undertake to meet the reasonable fees and expenses of the Adjudicator should the adjudication not proceed for any reason.

We enclose our cheque for £ [   ] being the CEDR appointment fee payable in relation to this matter/We are members of CEDR and, therefore, understand that no appointment fee is payable.*

Yours faithfully,

For and on behalf of

(NB: Where a contract provides for adjudication in accordance with CEDR Rules, only one party's signature is necessary. In other cases all parties to the contract should sign an application.)

* (Delete whichever does not apply)

SCHEDULE

Details of contract and disputes referred to Adjudication:

1. Name and address of each party to the contract.
2. Date of contract.
3. Brief description of the subject matter of the contract.
4. Brief details of the dispute(s) to be referred to adjudication.
5. Brief description of the redress being sought.

H.6 ANNEX B

CEDR Adjudication Agreement

DATE _____

PARTIES

1. [   ] of [   ]
   ('Party A')

2. [   ] of [   ]
   ('Party B')

3. [   ] of [   ]
   ('the Adjudicator')

4. Centre for Dispute Resolution Limited trading as Centre for Dispute Resolution (CEDR) of Princes House, 95 Gresham Street, London EC2V 7NA.

Dispute

(the 'Dispute')

[Here set out details of the contract and brief details of the dispute(s) to be adjudicated.]

_____

_____

_____

_____

1. Appointment

The Adjudicator will adjudicate the Dispute between Party A and Party B (the 'Appointing Parties'). The Adjudicator's appointment shall take effect from [the date of this Agreement].

2. Conduct of adjudication

The adjudication shall be conducted in accordance with CEDR's Rules for Adjudication, a copy of which is annexed and which [as amended in Schedule 1] is incorporated in and forms part of this Agreement.

3. Costs

The Appointing Parties will be jointly and severally responsible to CEDR and the Adjudicator for their respective fees and expenses. Details of fees and of the initial payment obligations of the Appointing Parties can be obtained by emailing CEDR on: adjudicate@cedr.co.uk.

4. Confidentiality

The adjudication and all matters connected with it are and will be kept confidential by the parties except in so far as is necessary to enable a party to implement or enforce the decision of the Adjudicator or for the purpose of any proceedings subsequent to the adjudication.

5. Liability

The Appointing Parties expressly acknowledge that neither CEDR nor the Adjudicator (nor any employee or agent of either) shall have any liability for any act or omission, except as provided in CEDR's Rules for Adjudication.

6. Law & Jurisdiction

This Agreement shall be governed by English law and under the jurisdiction of the English Courts.

. . . .
Signed for and on behalf of Party A

. . . .
Signed for and on behalf of Party B

. . . .
Signed by the Adjudicator

Schedule 1

[Here incorporate any amendment to CEDR's Rules for Adjudication agreed between the parties.]

CONTENTS

Appendix I

CEDR model Expert Determination agreement

I.1 INTRODUCTION

Expert Determination –

- is quick, inexpensive and confidential;
- is informal;
- produces a binding result.

Expert Determination is used for a wide variety of commercial applications. The most commonly encountered are –

- rent review;
- valuation of shares in private companies;
- price adjustment in take-overs;
- transfers of pension rights;
- long-term commodity supply contracts;
- valuations of partners' interests in oil and gas field projects;
- construction contracts;
- IT contracts.

Expert Determination can be chosen as the method of dispute resolution either of –

- specific issues; or
- all disputes arising under a contract;

and it can be chosen –

- at the time of signing the contract; or

- later when a dispute arises.

Expert Determination differs from arbitration in its greater informality. Unless the parties agree that it should be, it is not subject to 'due process' and can therefore be more flexible. In particular, there is no need for a trial-type hearing. Unless the Parties agree otherwise, the Expert may conduct investigations independently of the Parties, and make the Decision based on those investigations without reference to the Parties. Parties should obtain legal advice when embarking on an Expert Determination, but do not strictly need to be legally represented during the procedure.

The expression 'Expert' is much more commonly used to refer to expert witnesses. In Expert Determination, the appointed Expert makes the Decision, and is not in any sense a witness.

I.2 MODEL EXPERT DETERMINATION AGREEMENT

Text in italics indicates where information has to be added.
Text in square brackets indicates where a choice has to be made.

Please refer to the guidance notes for commentary on and help with the completion of this Agreement.

DATE

PARTIES

1. . . . . ('Party A')

2. . . . . ('Party B')

3. . . . . ('Party C') etc
(jointly 'the Parties')   *Add full names and addresses*

4. . . . . ('the Expert')

5. . . . . ('the Pupil')

6. Centre for Dispute Resolution Limited trading as Centre for Dispute Resolution (CEDR) of Princes House, 95 Gresham Street, London EC2V 7NA.

DISPUTE
('the Dispute')

Here set out details of the contract(s) or other legal relationship(s) and brief details of the dispute(s) to be resolved by expert determination.

. . . .
. . . .
. . . .
. . . .
. . . .

1. Appointment of Expert

CEDR has appointed the Expert to resolve the Dispute. The Parties agree that the Expert will resolve the Dispute by Expert Determination. The Expert will act as an expert and not as an arbitrator.

2. Purpose of Expert Determination

Unless the Parties subsequently agree otherwise, this Expert Determination leads to a decision ('the Decision') being issued by the Expert. The Decision will be final and binding on the Parties.

3. Confidentiality

The Expert Determination process is private and confidential. The Parties, the Expert, the Pupil and CEDR will keep it confidential except to the extent that it is necessary in order to implement the Decision or is required by law.

4. Independence

The Expert, the Pupil and CEDR are independent of the Parties, neutral and impartial, and do not act as advisers to the Parties.

5. Conduct of Expert Determination

The Expert will conduct the Expert Determination in accordance with procedural directions which the Expert will seek to agree with the Parties. If they cannot be agreed, the Expert's directions will prevail.

6. Challenge to the procedure

The Parties agree that they [are/are not] permitted to challenge the Expert's rulings on issues arising during the procedure, including those on the Expert's own jurisdiction.

7. Mediation option

At any time before the issue of the Expert's decision the Parties may agree to refer the Dispute to mediation, in accordance with CEDR's Model Mediation Procedure. In that case each of the Parties notifies the Expert and CEDR, and the Expert Determination is suspended. The parties would be free to appoint the Expert and/or the Pupil as mediator(s). If the dispute is settled by mediation, the Expert Determination comes to an end and the Parties settle the fees and expenses of the Expert and of CEDR. If the dispute is not settled by mediation, the Expert Determination resumes, and if they have been acting as mediators the Expert and the Pupil may take up their previous roles.

8. Reasons in the Decision

The Decision of the Expert [shall/shall not] include reasons.

9. Interest

The Expert is empowered to award interest as part of the Decision.

10. Fees and expenses

Unless the Parties agree otherwise, the fees and expenses of the Expert Determination will be borne by the Parties in equal shares. The fees and expenses will be estimated by CEDR and paid to CEDR as a condition precedent for the Expert Determination to start. The Expert will be paid fees and expenses, and the Pupil will be paid expenses. Interim bills may be raised by CEDR to cover the Expert's fees at the Expert's option. A final account of the fees and expenses will be sent to the Parties by CEDR when the

Decision is ready for issue to the Parties, and the Decision will be released on payment by the Parties of any further amounts due. CEDR will reimburse the Expert. If the Parties agree not to proceed with Expert Determination, CEDR will refund a proportionate amount of the fees and expenses advanced, depending on the amount of work done by the Expert and CEDR.

11.   Implementation of the Decision

The Parties agree to implement the Decision within [eg seven] days of its being published to them.

12.   Challenge to the Decision

The Parties agree they [are/are not] permitted to challenge the Decision in any legal proceedings or otherwise.

13.   No liability

The Parties expressly acknowledge that neither the Expert, nor the Pupil, nor CEDR shall be liable to the Parties for any act or omission whatsoever in connection with this Expert Determination.

14.   Role of Pupil

The Pupil [observes/takes a full part in] the Expert Determination, but the Decision is the responsibility of the Expert.

15.   Role of CEDR

CEDR appoints the Expert and makes arrangements for the Pupil. The Expert is responsible for the procedure from then on. CEDR may be consulted by any of the Parties to this Agreement in case of difficulty. Should the Expert be unable to complete the task, CEDR will appoint a substitute Expert within a reasonable time.

16.   After the Decision

None of the Parties will call the Expert, pupil or CEDR (or any employee, consultant, officer or representative of CEDR) as a witness, consultant, arbitrator or expert in any litigation or arbitration in relation to the Dispute and the Expert and CEDR will not voluntarily act in any such capacity without the written agreement of all the Parties.

17. Law and jurisdiction

This Agreement shall be governed by English law and under the jurisdiction of the English courts. All the Parties to this Agreement agree to refer any dispute arising in connection with it to mediation first.

. . . .
Signed on behalf of Party A

. . . .
Signed on behalf of Party B

. . . .
Signed on behalf of Party C

. . . .
Signed by the Expert

. . . .
Signed by the Pupil

. . . .
Signed on behalf of CEDR

SCHEDULE

CEDR appointment fee	£	
Expert's fees	£	per hour
Payment to be made on account by each Party	£	by [date]

I.3   GUIDANCE NOTES

Essential information

The CEDR Model Expert Determination Agreement includes any Pupil and CEDR as well as the Parties to the Dispute and, of course, the Expert. The roles of the Pupil and of CEDR are defined in clauses 10 and 11 of the Agreement.

The section 'Dispute', when completed, sets out how the dispute arose with a brief description of the issue(s).

Clauses 1 and 2 establish the appointment of the Expert, that the process is Expert Determination, and that the result is a Decision which will be final and binding on the Parties. Clauses 3 and 4 establish the confidentiality of the process and the independence of the Expert, the Pupil and CEDR.

The procedure

Once appointed, the Expert will wish to establish the procedure. Clause 5 states that the Expert will seek to agree the procedure with the Parties, and that if agreement cannot be reached, the Expert's directions will prevail.

Procedural directions may deal with any or all of the following:

- a timetable for the submission of case summaries and supporting documents to the Expert with copies to each other;

- whether submissions are to be simultaneous or sequential;

- whether there should be one or two rounds of submissions;

- whether the Expert has the power to call for documents;

- whether the Expert has the power to award costs.

Challenge to the procedure

Clause 6 gives the Parties the choice whether they have the right to challenge the Expert Determination procedure before the Decision is issued. CEDR strongly encourages Parties to give up this right. This enhances the use of Expert Determination, is in the spirit of ADR and allows the Expert to do the work for the Parties as agreed without the time and expense of court applications.

Mediation option

Clause 7 provides that the Parties may agree to refer the dispute to mediation at any time before the Decision is made, provided the fees and expenses to date are paid, and that CEDR will organise the mediation. There is no reason in principle why the Expert and the Pupil should not act as mediators, but the parties may agree to appoint other mediators. There are obvious savings in time and cost in appointing the same people in the two different capacities. However, the Parties may have difficulty in being entirely frank with a mediator who may later act as Expert, and the Expert may have difficulty in dealing with confidential material disclosed during the mediation.

Reasons in the Decision

Clause 8 gives the Parties a choice as to whether to include reasons in the Decision. The inclusion of reasons increases the cost, but may make the resolution of the Dispute by this means more attractive and therefore worth the extra cost.

Interest

The Expert does not have the power to award interest unless the Parties agree, so clause 9 gives the Expert that power.

Fees and expenses

Clause 10 deals with fees and expenses, some of which are payable in advance.

Consequences of the Decision

Clauses 11 and 12 deal with the consequences of the Decision: the Parties agree to implement it within an agreed period (CEDR recommends seven days), and have a choice whether to challenge the Decision. A Decision can be challenged only on very limited grounds arising from its fundamental validity, and not from differences on issues of fact, law or professional opinion. The effect of excluding the right to challenge a Decision is uncertain.

No liability

Clause 13 gives immunity from liability to the Expert, the Pupil and CEDR.

Role of Pupil

The Pupil is a trainee who is gaining experience of the process and receiving guidance from the Expert. Clause 14 gives a choice as to the extent of the role that the Pupil plays, but makes the essential point that the appointed Expert is solely responsible for the Decision.

Role of CEDR

Clause 15 explains CEDR's role, in making the appointment and other arrangements, and collecting the fees and expenses.

After the Decision

Clause 16 ensures that those involved in the Expert Determination do not get involved in future proceedings without the consent of all the Parties.

Law and jurisdiction

Clause 17 establishes English law as the governing law of the Agreement, with disputes referred first to mediation and then to the English court. It may be necessary in international cases to provide that the language of the Expert Determination is to be English.

Index

Please note that references are to paragraph numbers. App stands for Appendix.

Index